TALKBACK

THE UNOFFICIAL AND UNAUTHORISED
DOCTOR WHO INTERVIEW BOOK

VOLUME THREE: THE EIGHTIES

Edited by Stephen James Walker

First published in England in 2007 by
Telos Publishing Ltd
61 Elgar Avenue, Tolworth, Surrey, KT5 9JP, England
www.telos.co.uk

Telos Publishing Ltd values feedback. Please e-mail us with any comments you may have about this book
to: feedback@telos.co.uk

ISBN: 978-1-84583-014-4 (paperback)
ISBN: 978-1-84583-015-1 (hardback)

Internal design, typesetting and layout by Arnold T Blumberg & ATB Publishing Inc
www.atbpublishing.com

Printed in India

1 2 3 4 5 6 7 8 9 10 11 12 13 14 15

British Library Cataloguing in Publication Data.
A catalogue record for this book is available from the British Library.

ACHNOWLEDGEMENTS

A big thank you to all the writers who kindly gave me their permission to include their original interviews in this book. Acknowledgements are due also to *Doctor Who Magazine*, in which one of the pieces presented here was first published.

TABLE OF CONTENTS

INTRODUCTION

Welcome to the third volume of *Talkback*. On the assumption that most readers of this book will already have sought out a copy of the first volume (and in the hope that, if they haven't, they will now be encouraged to do so!) I won't repeat everything I said there about the *raison d'etre* for the *Talkback* series. In a nutshell, its objective is to bring together, re-present and make accessible to a new readership, a collection of some of the finest and most informative interviews that have been conducted over the past 30 years with key individuals involved in the making of the 'classic' *Doctor Who* series that ran from 1963 to 1989 – some of whom are no longer with us and are thus unable to recount their stories in person.

As before, the pieces in this book appear in the same form as when originally published, barring minor editorial amendments and corrections; and where I have judged that additional comment is needed, I have added this in footnote form. Each piece is preceded by a short, newly-written introduction by me, explaining where it originally appeared and setting it in context; but, again, I have avoided reiterating what I said in previous volumes, in cases where this book presents the continuation of a multi-part interview.

I am very grateful to all those writers who have graciously allowed me to include their original interviews in this book. As always, though, thanks are due first and foremost to the interviewees themselves, all of whom gave freely and generously of their time and energy to share their memories of the contributions they made to what is, without doubt, my favourite TV series of all time!

Stephen James Walker

INTERVIEW: TOM BAKER—DOCTOR

Although generally thought of as one of the '1970s Doctors', Tom Baker remained in the role into the early 1980s, completing his tenure at the end of Season 18 in 1981. As a complement to the interview in the previous volume of Talkback, *which was conducted many years after the event, the following piece by Antony Howe, the then President of the Australasian Doctor Who Fan Club, is a contemporary account of an encounter that took place during a promotional visit that the actor made to Australia shortly before he started work on Season 17, which straddled 1979 and 1980 on transmission. It was originally published in Issue 10/11 of the fanzine* Zerinza.

I had not been too hopeful of being granted an interview with Tom Baker, because the very idea had seemed anathema to the ABC promotions people[1], but after several postponements, I finally got an appointment to meet up with the actor at the Wentworth Hotel on the last evening of his Sydney visit.

Tearing off from my office job, I panted into the resplendent foyer, bearing my tape recorder and briefcase with copious notes and lists of questions. An assortment of conflicting emotions fought within me. This encounter might be a total disaster. On the very first day of his visit, Baker had made some negative remarks to the press about 'adult fans' that had reduced me to a gloomy pessimism. We were 'irredeemable', he had said. University students were cultists and escapists, and anyone over the age of nine was merely 'on the bandwagon, pretending to understand what the kids like.' Tom's personality is aggressively direct, and he had already shown himself to be a devastating adversary in the many interviews given to journalists over the previous two weeks. My friends who had attended the two book-signing sessions at the Grace Bros stores in Chatswood and Roselands also had reservations about the current Doctor's attitude toward adult fans. 'He looked as if he was going to explode,' was the general consensus of opinion.

After 13 years of enjoying *Doctor Who*, and three years of 'alarums and excursions' with the ABC's policy-makers and programmers[2], I was determined to present *Zerinza* readers with an interview about the series, no matter how I might find the present leading actor as an individual. So it was a distinct relief to be met by Graham Bell, the ABC's Sydney rep coping with the visit, who had started by being discouraging about the likelihood of arranging the interview but who had at last managed to bring it about. He introduced me to Tom Baker, and I was immediately reassured by a welcoming grin, so familiar to *Doctor Who* fans. (He really has splendid teeth, and no, dear readers, they are *not* false!)

'Let's go and have a drink,' suggested Baker, with a longing glance towards the bar. In we went (I mentally counting the cash in my wallet – I'm not used to the pub scene of 'shouts', and couldn't tell you the difference between a middy and a schooner if you paid me). The bar was a horrible confusion of noise and voices. Mr Baker's expletives were unprintable. We had only an hour before an interstate phone-call would put an end to the interview, so we took the lift to his room, where the fridge dispensed cooling beers and quiet descended. We would never have managed to talk in the bar, and my concentration would have dissipated in the

---

1 ABC was the channel that broadcast *Doctor Who* in Australia.

2 This is a reference to the sometimes rocky relationship between Australian *Doctor Who* fans and the ABC. The fans had mounted a campaign to keep the series on the air at one point, when the channel threatened to drop it.

fumes and smoke haze.

Tom Baker hurled his large frame into a chair and stared at me as I fiddled nervously with the tape-recorder levels and levers. 'Is that working?'

I nodded, shuffled the sheaf of papers on my clipboard, swallowed the twitching frog in my throat and asked the first question that came into my head. 'You must have come across a lot of people from the series?'

Tom Baker's eyes looked concerned. 'Yes, I met Patrick Troughton. Did you know that Pat had a heart attack? A couple of weeks ago, just as I was leaving, I met him in Birmingham, where he was doing, for the second time, *The Old Curiosity Shop*[3], and he did tell me he was finding it fiendishly trying, which was an odd thing. It's not that he's a great age, but Quilp is a bounding-around, physically very "sudden" part – all right when you're 42, but he's 52 now!'

He gazed abstractedly into his glass, and to change the depressing subject I remarked: 'It's been difficult to form a really cohesive fan club in Australia, because even Sydney is sprawled all over the place, and it's too hard to hold meetings.'

Tom Baker nodded understandingly and answered, 'I don't think they meet very often in the United Kingdom. I was very impressed by the organising of the annual meeting.'

'Was that the PanoptiCon?'

'I think that was the second one. The first was held in a Methodist Church Hall, and they rented it out and had a lovely event. The next one I went to a few months ago. They held it at Imperial College, and it was extremely impressive. They can only meet once a year, coming from all over the country. Most of it is done by correspondence; the fans break down into little friendly groups and, apart from contact with the secretary at headquarters, they develop, sharing critical views, depending on what their sympathies or aversions are. It's very difficult for me to cope with the disappointment of some fans, because by definition, they are zealots, and they often get protective about some aspect of the programme. They get very strong views and take out that sense of betrayal by writing protesting letters to me.'

I commiserated. 'That's not fair.'

'It's not good, because there is very little I can do about it. Often they are preoccupied with tiny details, as opposed to the overall picture. I would not do anything to subvert the character. I think the British Appreciation Society understands that, but from time to time some people might be disappointed.'

He ran a hand through his woolly mop and sighed, looking defensive. I thought, let's not introduce the subject of adult fans! I asked, 'Were you not well on the flight, or just before you left London?'

'I was ill on the flight coming out, which was very distressing on an aeroplane, especially on the last leg from Singapore.'

I remembered the welcome at the airport, and how exhausted he'd been, and abruptly switched the subject again. 'Could I just ask about the proposed *Scratchman* feature film? I've heard this is a possibility still. Is there anything in that?'

Those enormous eyes gleamed with interest. '*Doctor Who Meets Scratchman*, which was the provisional title – I thought a very good title – is now to be called *Doctor Who and the Big Game*. I suppose the details are known out here? Yes? Well, Ian Marter and I wrote it, and then James Hill, who has done some good films, wrote the screenplay, and at long last the options

---

3 This was a BBC serialisation of the Charles Dickens novel. Troughton had previously played Quilp in 1963 in another BBC adapation.

in the end are James Hill and me. There are two problems. One is raising finance, which I don't know will be all that difficult now; and I think the discussion of production money to shoot the exteriors in Australia is an optimistic thought. In *Scratchman*, or *Big Game*, there are a lot of big exterior sequences. We wanted to shoot in Lanzarote, because it has that lively, black, shiny moonscape there, but I think it would be better to come to Australia if we could. The second problem is, what time would I have to do it? If it happens at all – because I can't go on and on doing this part; the audience should be allowed a change – it would have to be done in the Spring of 1980, starting in January. But before I consider giving someone else a go, I would like to get the film in first! I've written the film. People take awful risks when they adapt television things for a film; they inflate a television script, and what is acceptable on a 24-inch set at home, won't stand the big screen. So it's got to be conceived filmically. There's a big, epic villain in it now, a sort of galactic mischief-maker, to be called Scratchman.'

'Something to do with the Devil?'

'"Scratchman" actually is an old word for the Devil, rather like "Old Nick", or "Beelzebub". This is why I liked it. He thrives on chaos and we frustrate him. At one time, the ideal casting people were interested. I know Vincent Price was interested in playing Scratchman. Then we wanted Twiggy to play the girl. Twiggy has a zany quality, a bit of an "off the ground" quality that would be very good. Now she's had a baby and I don't know if we could get her, but I don't think it would be difficult to get a good girl in it'.

He sat back pensively, and I had a quick vision of Twiggy tagging along behind the Doctor, plaintively plucking at his scarf as she tiptoed over the Nullarbor stones[4]. I asked, 'You wanted to exploit the interior of the TARDIS, I believe?'

'I've always though it a terrible pity that I'm often engaged in galactic uproar, when if the TARDIS is larger on the inside, logically it can be immensely large, can't it?'

'Like in the "The Invasion of Time"?'

'That's right. You can do anything you want. You can have a garden as big as Queensland, and in the garden is where some of the uproar takes place. In other words, a domestic crisis within the TARDIS, inside the Doctor's head, on a personal level. What are his views? What flowers does he like? Has he got a photograph album? Has he got a Black Museum? Has he a VTR[5] of the past adventures? Does he keep records of what he's done? All this would interest writers.'

'When Patrick Troughton started, I believe his Doctor had a 500 year diary.'

Tom Baker smiled. 'Patrick played his Doctor very quaintly.'

'The Cosmic Hobo.'

'It was a good phrase, that! We appear to have moved on. The fans want it more rapid and decisive, and funnier. There's a general consensus that it should be laced with some humour. You are a year behind, here. You've got Leela, played by Louise Jameson. We have a Time Lady called Romana. We did that back-to-back, as we work very fast. So you've got a whole story still to come, with the girl played by Mary Tamm. She was the juvenile lead in *The Odessa File*. Mary has just completed the one season; the shortest time in the series. On 15 March I start filming with Lalla Ward, a very enigmatic-looking blonde, very pretty in a strange way. She has done some very good work. She was in *Rosebud* for Otto Preminger. Last year she did *The Prince and the Pauper* with George C Scott and Oliver Reed. She played the child in *The*

---

4 Nullarbor is an arid region of Australia.

5 Video-tape recording.

Duchess of Duke Street; Gemma Jones's daughter. She's got a strange quality that will be a help to the series. So you've got that to look forward to. I shall look forward to it, to begin with. We've got a brand-new script editor, Douglas Adams, a very young man not long down from Cambridge, who worked with the Monty Python crowd on the scripts, and won an award for a marvellous series on the radio called *Diary of a Galactic Hitchhiker*.[6] He's very lively and dynamic and innovative, in the sense that he will approach it, and very brave: he even asked Tom Stoppard if he would write a script, which was a nice thing to do. Tom said he was rather busy. You've got to try: Tom just *might* have said, "Well, all right!"'

Returning to the subject of *Doctor Who* on the big screen, I asked, 'What do you think was wrong with the two 1960s films about the Daleks? Was it that they were taken from the television plays?'

'Yes,' replied Tom Baker. 'They were adaptations. The first terrible mistake was to miscast it. They didn't give it to Billy Hartnell, they gave it to Peter Cushing, who was largely associated with horror films; and under the pressure of making the film in about six weeks, Cushing had to give an impression of Billy Hartnell in order to get an impact in the United Kingdom. So he was playing a benevolent, doddery old gent who could not even sort out a fuse, let alone the Daleks! Again showing the problems of television adaptation, they split the narrative. The script's dilemma, which the Doctor had to solve, was not complex enough to carry through 95 minutes of a film, so they had a second string, with some travellers, I think – two things going on. They also managed to have about 50 Daleks in one of the scenes, but it was not at all threatening. Roy Castle and Bernard Cribbins, the actors, could not make a contribution, because they were giving their version of someone else. It's like a young fan giving an impression of me; they might be briefly amusing or arresting, but it won't endure. On film, and television, you need to widen the thing when something is well established. You can't struggle for it; the camera will blow your cover. You can't do sleight-of-hand stuff. You have to grip it, in your head. You can paper over the narrative by sheer expertise, but not when you're starting.'

'In every season,' I noted, 'you get one or two stories in which "This time the universe will be destroyed", or there's the worst baddie imaginable and you've got to defeat him. Do you feel there is a tendency on the writers' part to over-dramatise your crises?'

'This is really a script editor's problem. Writers are not in cahoots, so each is writing separately. One interesting fact is that although the Doctor occasionally makes references to his past – the scripts indicate that he's a great age, with great experience – he very rarely uses this expertise. Each story begins as if the Doctor has no fear of anything – at least I try to insist that they start like that, very low-key – and then something occurs. For example, the Doctor is not frightened of a big monster that comes over to the TARDIS, 19 feet tall. I might go up and say "Hello!" and then he clubs me to the ground, and it's only when I recover consciousness that I say to the girl, "You've got to look out for him!" That is the first thing, and then his innocence is broken, there is some kind of threat, and I suppose this is why writers often fall into the trap of each one being the worst yet.'

I pushed on with the argument: 'Yes, but for years and years, the Daleks were the most evil power in the universe, and then there was Sutekh, and Omega, and various other beings.'

He chuckled. 'That's right. It could be much more intense and more localised. I think that

---

6 Baker was misremembering the title of Adams's *The Hitchhiker's Guide to the Galaxy*, which at this point had yet to acquire its legendary reputation.

is a very valid point.

'The Daleks are coming back this year,' he added, rather glumly.

'I gather you are not too keen on the Daleks?' I asked.

'To make it work, you need a lot of ingenuity. We often laugh, because if the Doctor ran upstairs, how could the Daleks get after him, or indeed, anyone? The easy way to deal with a Dalek invasion would be to put three treads around the entire country, and they couldn't do anything! They couldn't travel. Their predictability is tiresome. I can't understand why they are so potent, unless it is for historical reasons, as so many fans got used to them, and also I suppose small children find Daleks very easy to imitate.' He frowned. 'They don't say anything complicated, just "Exterminate".'

'No real character,' I added. 'You couldn't expect a Dalek to feel pity.'

He nodded. 'I must admit that the character of Davros was good, and Mike Wisher, the actor who did that, did it well. It's possible to conceive of a situation where the Doctor might align himself with the Daleks for some strong reason, to save the balance of power. He might line up with the Daleks as political groups make alliances in real life.'

I suggested another idea. 'If the Doctor was caught between the Cybermen and the Daleks, well …'

Baker grinned at me. 'That would be interesting!' He gestured expressively. 'The Cybermen trying to expand, or take over the universe or some section of it, would cause a big shift in an entire galaxy! And you could have the complexity of some kind of power-play or compromise, for the greater good in the end.'

He paused and asked, 'The dog, K-9, you haven't seen yet? It's a huge success in the United Kingdom.'

Graham Bell, who was watching our animated conversation, sat forward and announced, '"The Invisible Enemy" begins on 26 February.'

I had to have a jibe at ABC policy; now was the chance. Looking at Tom Baker, I said, '"The Brain of Morbius" has the Doctor nearly dying, mind-wrestling with Morbius and pushing you back through your incarnations. That story has been A rated. Are the ABC going to show it?'

Tom Baker's expectant smile brought a hasty answer, which was more of an apology, from the ABC rep: 'We tried to schedule it, but took it out again for an evening timeslot.'

I tried to convey my disapproval by flinging another bone of contention at Tom Baker. 'You have conflicts with Mary Whitehouse, but we have conflicts with the censor. Maybe they're in cahoots. They chopped little bits out of some stories – "Robots of Death" they chopped, and "The Talons of Weng-Chiang", where the rat grabs Leela by the leg! They rate some of the stories A, and quite a few – four of five – Jon Pertwee ones have not been shown. In "The Brain of Morbius", the Doctor is seen to be very vulnerable; not a superman or an aloof super-being.'

Tom Baker screwed his face into a thoughtful grimace. 'Alfred Hitchcock demonstrated, in his life's work, that the concern and tension are in proportion to the characters' vulnerability, usually by allowing the audience to know more than the characters. Therefore if I was too omniscient or altogether too grand, there would be no tension. That's the technique used to encourage the audience to suspend disbelief.'

'How much of the character can be given away, though,' I asked, 'while still allowing him to remain an enigma as an alien Time Lord?'

'One of the hardest things is to keep the alien quality. I can't be so alien that I need redefining. I've got a body, and a scarf and hat, so it's very difficult to suggest that I come from somewhere else. How is it that, no matter where I turn up in the galaxy, no-one is surprised at the way I'm dressed? No-one says, "Isn't he dressed in a very strange way, General?"'

'You were dressed appropriately in "The Talons of Weng-Chiang", but in "The Masque of Mandragora", set in an era where everybody is dressed according to a code of conduct, along you come, quite out of place, and nobody bats an eyelid.'

He grinned again. 'In melodrama, there's some kind of sweetness about that; like the early Buster Keaton comedy two-reelers, all founded on sweet, innocent stories. In *Doctor Who*, there's a kind of sweetness about it. No dirty fighting, or ghastly recognisable violence. No heartbreak. The Doctor would never get involved with a girl and then hurt her, or allow himself to be hurt. Obviously, it doesn't grate on the fans, but occasionally it would be nice to actually have someone amazed at the way I'm dressed, or be so impressed by me helping them that *they* all dress up like me! I could have an army – in *Doctor Who*, armies are only 16 men strong – all dressed up like me, and I could be drilling them, all tripping over their scarves ...'

It was a hilarious picture. Even Graham Bell managed a nervous smile. I looked at the list of questions – time for another angle. 'Would you like the Doctor to have a background, with a family? The first Doctor had Susan as his granddaughter. Some people explain that away by saying it was only a term of endearment.'

He thought for a moment, then agreed with a shrug. 'That's probably the best way of explaining it. They were feeling their way at the beginning, then suddenly had to make a story around the character – a myth – rather quickly. I don't think it would stand the involvement with a family now. The modern audience would prefer him to be strange and not have too many cosy, recognisable contexts – like kitchens ...'

What an idea: the Doctor operating the controls on a Whirlpool accompanied by Dame Edna! I hastily explained: 'That's not what I had in mind! What about if the Doctor *had* had a family, and had left them behind?'

'You'd need rather delicate writing to go back. It might be solved by the device of a photograph album, and some insights to go back with the pictures, to make veiled references ...'

'Hartnell's Doctor kept referring to being an exile. Possibly he could have been thrown out?'

'Yes,' Tom Baker reflected, 'he did go on about being an exile. It would be interesting to use Gallifrey and the Time Lords' Panopticon to make them quite quickly and effectively share some of the plot load. In melodrama, the hero is set up for a big job, and the dreary stuff of beating out the situation, as in James Bond, is done by someone else. M calls Bond in and says, "Now listen, James, this is the situation," and then James says, "I see," and they go down to the quartermaster and draw the gear. And off you go to Singapore! I have the problem of carrying all that myself, and in such small units – you have to get to the crisis fast. Someone says, "What's happening, Doctor?" and I say "Now, look, this is the way it goes." We should try involving some character from Gallifrey.'

'That could be a job for the Celestial Intervention Agency – the CIA,' I murmured. '"The Deadly Assassin" has not been shown here either, for the same reason; it's been A rated.'

Tom Baker frowned, and glared at the squirming Mr Bell. 'I thought it one of the best ones!' he thundered. 'It was violent, but *surreally* violent!'

Hastily Graham Bell intervened. 'These programmes have not been lost. They will eventually go to air.'

Time to defuse the overcharged atmosphere. I examined my notes again. 'Events in one story will flatly contradict another one – you get lack of continuity. Some fans get worked up about details, but do you feel there's an advantage in not being bound by previous stories?'

Tom Baker liked this. 'You see, if you get into an area of dogma, it's limiting. If you can bend time and space, then attitudes can change! They are not fundamental changes, so people have to be flexible about this, as it would limit us. There are ferocious limitations on the character of the Doctor, which requires great ingenuity on the part of the director, and the actor, to make it bearable. How can you define the Doctor to someone who has never seen the series? It's practically beyond me to explain, but he does remain dramatic and he engages the audience's imagination, and I suppose it's because one gets ingenious within those limitations. You don't "flatly contradict" them. I don't suppose any fan would have noticed, but when a girl is hurt and I have to handle her, I do it very clumsily, as if to suggest that I'm not very good at handling girls. And I always affect surprise if anyone is interested in power – I get out my jelly babies or yo-yo to cut across it. In any moral dilemma, the hero is predictable; he will always come down on the side of good.' He paused. 'There are varieties of pace. If an actor is coming through a door, there's a way of doing it that can be very surprising, when it's an ordinary thing to do. It's the responsibility of the actor to be surprising or sometimes touching, or funny – or a bit angry.' He went on to speak of the role as being much sought-after, and to comment on how he was scathing of writers who were slack in their thinking and included things like the Doctor using a knife, which he refuses to do.

I consulted my notes again. 'The last season you did had the overall theme of the Key to Time. I gather there was a good Guardian and a bad Guardian. How do you feel that worked?'

'That was a policy decision from the production office. I thought that having an overall theme created an additional difficulty, because in a small unit of half-an-hour, and getting to a crisis point about every minute or two, it was very difficult to keep two things in the foreground. I hope we did keep them in the audience's mind, but I think that an umbrella theme could be an obstacle.'

'The Time Lords, I gather, foisted the Lady Romana character on you in the story?'

He waved a hand. 'I suppose we will make the transference from Mary Tamm to Lalla by the usual reincarnation.'

'Is Lalla a Time Lady?' I asked, and he lifted his eyebrows with a wry expression.

'It's very difficult to dispose of the Time Lady! Although some fans would jib at that, because one time I explicitly said to Elisabeth Sladen's character that she couldn't come to Gallifrey because women were not allowed. But you can get a bit Jesuitical about that and say, "Well, the Doctor meant aliens; that is, Earth people," because on Gallifrey there *are* females!'

'Leela went to Gallifrey; that cuts across the continuity,' I objected.

'That's right,' he laughed. 'I was very sad about the disposal of Leela. The "traditional" thing about her falling in love with someone was pitiful, awful. We could have done better than that.'

'What liberties can you take with the script if you feel it's a bit dreary or contradictory?'

He shook his head. 'I don't get to pre-production meetings – I'm too busy – but I spend a lot of time in the evenings working on scripts. Often I get them just before the read-through, and obviously I'm allowed a certain amount of influence, because I'm not unskilled at writing dialogue, especially for Doctor Who – the litmus test for our scripts. I don't look out only for my own scenes, because I want everybody to be as good as possible. If there's a scene with four or five characters and we read it through, I think I have a good ear for any potential tensions in it. We go through it once or twice and they say, "What are you moaning about, Tom?" and I say, "Let's change the names and just juggle them round and listen again, and if it makes no difference, the scene is slack." Then, if the director concedes it's slack, we rip it out and re-write it.'

15

'What stories have you been most displeased with?'

He chuckled quietly. 'I think it would be very smug of me to say I've been delighted with only some, but some *have* pleased me more than others. I liked "The Ark in Space" a lot. I liked "The Brain of Morbius"' – and at this he threw a challenging stare at Mr Bell – 'and it had possibilities, considering it was really a pastiche *Frankenstein*. And then "The Deadly Assassin"' – and again his large eyes surveyed us with an air of defiance. 'I don't want you to think I can stand up and say "We are not doing this scene!" Here he flung back his head, as if about to turn on a temperamental act. 'I can't. If I did a confrontation like that, somebody could turn on me very cruelly, but very correctly, and say, "You are just paid to say the lines."' He shrugged. 'In modern ways of working between actors and directors, no-one does that, because you have to contribute, and sometimes the contributions don't come from me; the assistant floor-manager (who is about 19) may suddenly make a remark and illuminate a whole scene. So you look for that group effort. That doesn't mean letting every Tom, Dick or Harry come in with his pennyworth – you would get bogged down with that – but informed comment you take from anywhere you like.'

I looked quickly at my watch. Our time was rapidly diminishing and still there were many questions left to ask. The local press reports had covered such angles as the Renegade Monk, the Lad from Liverpool, the Actor's Ego. But I hadn't seen anything about where his interests lay, or what type of fiction he liked, so I asked, 'Do you prefer science fiction, fantasy or historical stories?'

'I prefer the fantasy world. I read a lot of science fiction, but not as an addict; I'm a science-*fantasy* devotee. One of my favourite writers is Kurt Vonnegut, who is very easy and freewheeling, and always informed, with a wonderful sense of compassion. He's never really recovered from Dresden.[7] But currently a favourite writer of fantasy is Stanislaw Lem, who is simply wonderful; so freewheeling and brilliantly translated into English. *The Star Diaries* and *The Futurological Congress* are great.'

'And *The Cyberiad*?'

He nodded enthusiastic agreement. 'Marvellous! If you stay in fantasy, you are not then pushed. In a series such as ours, it's vitally important to think in terms of short units. You might look at a story, and someone says, "This is a good read!" But you come back quickly and say, "Yes, good over an hour, but how do you break it down into 25 minute units? Is it a good read then? Is it going to hold visually, over the 25 minutes?" With science fiction, you have to spend a lot of time re-defining things, because if you get very futuristic, what can you recognise? What will cars look like in the year 4,000? How will people travel? What will medical care be like? What will weapons be like? My guess is that they'll be so refined as to be utterly dreary! One can only record the consequences, rather than be interested in the weapons. But in the fantastic, one can use the artefacts, methods of travel, clothes, humanoids and so on, then freewheel in and out.'

I thought of the stories involving Earth history, and asked, 'Any particular time period you would like the Doctor to be involved in?'

'I'd like to go back to the Wild West sometimes, but I'd dearly like to go back to meet *real* people and have arguments and discussions. These are very nice points and very difficult to decide on. I can make suggestions, but I don't have to take the responsibility. It would be very

7 This is a reference to the Allied bombing of the German city of Dresden in the Second World War, in which Vonnegut was caught up as a prisoner of war.

interesting for the Doctor to meet Izaak Walton and talk about fishing, or Isaac Newton and talk about gravity, and say, "Look, kid, you've got it all wrong," and demonstrate that he's wrong, and find that this is so far beyond Newton's experience that he has me thrown out by the servants! We are stymied by the cost of everything. These ideas that people throw around are very difficult to realise visually. So we settle for more traditional stuff.'

Thinking about some of his earlier roles, I asked, 'Do you see any relationship between Koura the Magician, Rasputin the Mystic and the Doctor as an "alien wizard"?'

He considered the question in silence for a moment. 'Yes. It's a bit glib, but as an actor, filtering an emotion under the pressure of fictional time as opposed to real time – for an hour in the movies – they are compressed, the unities are not held on to. Yes, there would be *one* thing that would link them. The tremendous gusto of these characters; their acts of sheer energy and their convictions. There is a kind of life-force, when you come across perfectly outrageous people, who are totally convinced about what they do. I'm not now talking about criminals, in the area of psychosis. But Rasputin had such conviction that he was irresistible, he was a breath of fresh air, and people said, "At last we've met someone who is totally relaxed about his relationship with God, or his attitude to sex or money – and totally simplistic in his politics." The fact that he was finally wrong doesn't alter his influence at that time. There was something mesmeric or Messianic about him, as there is about people such as, in politics, Mr Enoch Powell, who can really hold an audience with that amazing rhetoric, and simplify things, so that people can understand them. Koura, the wicked magician, he got his comeuppance at the end, but it's his energy that makes it interesting.'

Pursuing the thought about the Doctor's 'wizardry', I asked, 'Are you particularly interested in magic or mysticism?'

'I don't think so. I'm interested from moment to moment in anything, like UFOs or mysticism. I just respond when things are happening to me.'

'Do you see *Doctor Who* stories as fulfilling the role of fairy-tales, now superseded by television?'

'Well, yes, I suppose they are fairy-tales, in the sense that they are morality tales, broadly. I've said this a thousand times about *Doctor Who*: it doesn't admit a comparison to anything, and that is a huge advantage. For example, it would be an advantage in a city the size of Sydney to be the only afternoon newspaper, which had hooked all the potential readers – since then there would be no competition. To be nearly unique, as *Doctor Who* is unique, is a wonderful advantage. It's a wonderful mixture of the heroic and the humorous. It's a great deal in my opinion. In a science fantasy like *Star Wars* – which was very funny, and had interesting machinery, which was what really made it – one of the young pilots had a slick, American sense of humour. In *Doctor Who*, all the emphasis is on the characters, and certainly my character is successful. On television, you cannot go into special effects; they have a diminishing return. You've got to found the interest of the audience on the characters.' He paused and flapped a hand at me imperiously. 'When someone interesting is talking on the television – as when you go to a dinner party – you *listen* to him, because people are interesting. If someone is saying something compelling, you listen. It's no good making a cowardly retreat all the time into special effects, because audiences everywhere have seen the real thing, the inside of Cape Canaveral! Not the inside of a ship with some poxy little console with a few lights flashing! They've seen two thousand receivers with two thousand technicians biting their nails with real anxiety about two men in a capsule in outer space.' He gave a sharp laugh and said, 'I'll be very interested to see what *Battlestar Galactica* is like.'

17

'Terrible!' was my instant reaction.

'I'm so glad you said that, because one of the notices I've got back from America said: "I've been watching *Battlestar Galactica*. That cost $10 million for the first two episodes, and I was quite unimpressed. But the BBC put on a programme called *Doctor Who*, with a sort of thyroid Harpo Marx tearing through it, and they did it for about fourpence – and it leaves the other for dead!"'

'What do you feel about Doctor Who being likened to Harpo Marx or Charlie Chaplin?'

He laughed. 'I think that's an accident, because no-one has any idea how large I am, and Harpo Marx was actually bald and wore a fright wig! But suddenly some child said, "He's like Harpo Marx", and once that goes into your head, it's irresistible, you can't get it out. But the real, flash trimmings of acting, like eating sandwiches while drinking and smoking a cigarette as well, which is supposed to be naturalistic, I find insufferably tedious. Not because I don't like people talking with their mouths full, but because it's a device. And there are ways of phrasing lines in which you affect a spontaneity by perhaps struggling to remember the lines – those are the externals of acting. If the character and his motivation are in your head and you play that character from *his* point of view, as long as you are true to his point of view, you can do anything, because there's an unswerving logic in it. If you are playing the Fool in *King Lear*, it's no use trying to sound very moving; what you actually do is grip the Fool in your head – the Fool doesn't play the King. That's when you get confusion, when you have resonant, competent acting. It's an axiom of acting that people forget: you've got to stick with the point of view of the character – what would he do here? – and then you do it, and if your conviction lines up with the text, it will work and the audience will find it acceptable.'

'What do you feel about the sonic screwdriver and K-9 providing technological wizardry to solve the Doctor's problems?'

'The dog is a big asset, because it amuses the audience. The sonic screwdriver is a terrible device, a kind of crutch the writers use. I get through the door with the sonic screwdriver, and on the other side the door closes, and when I turn round, the sonic screwdriver won't open it! That's when I turn to the camera with a Tom Baker line, "Even the sonic screwdriver won't open this one ..."'

The phone rang, and Graham Bell noted us looking at him with obvious displeasure. It was not quite the full hour; still five minutes to go. Quickly he asked the caller to phone back, and Tom Baker gave me a conspiratorial wink. Hastily I handed him some biographical notes to check, with a couple of books to sign and an excellent portrait of him made for me by Andrew Szabo – which he admired before he scrawled on the margin: 'For Tony, from Tom Baker. 1st fan club interview in Sydney, 1979.'

Then he looked enquiringly at me and I asked, 'Did you co-write the script for *The Sorcerers*?'

He shook his head firmly. 'No. That's a mistake in Halliwell's book.'[8]

So much for reference works, I thought. 'What movies do you like?'

'I've got a very catholic taste in movies. I go to nearly all the popular movies, because I need to know what's going on.'

'What sort of music?' He looked up in surprise, so I added, 'No-one ever seems to ask you that.'

---

8 The Boris Karloff-starring movie *The Sorcerers* (1967) was co-scripted by a writer named Tom Baker – but not *this* Tom Baker, as implied in an edition of the *Halliwell's Film Guide* reference book.

'No, they don't! Terribly traditional: mostly I listen to Beethoven, and Mozart string quartets'.

'How much of the Doctor's costume, and the jelly babies, the yo-yo, scarf and hat, was your choice?'

He was busily reading through the list of notes, making alterations, and replied vaguely, 'The scarf was an accident, as you know, but all these things grew by accident. The jelly babies and yo-yo are often just desperation, we just put them in ...'

As he spoke, the phone rang again, and Graham Bell muttered, 'Time to wrap it up, now.'

I said, 'Thank you very much,' and got a cheerful grin from Tom Baker. 'There's piles of stuff I haven't asked yet, but still ...'

Mr Baker handed back my notes saying: 'Thanks, Tony. So sorry we're out of time, but there you are. You're welcome to another hour or half-hour some time, if we can fit it in. If you keep in touch – I know I'm flat out ...'

Graham Bell interjected apologetically, 'Tomorrow is the last day in Sydney, and you're booked right through.'

The tall actor gave me a firm handshake. 'Let's shake your hand then, Tony. Goodbye!' He turned to take the phone from Graham Bell.

I grabbed books and papers and filled my briefcase, took the recorder from the table and went over to the door, whispering my goodbyes to Graham Bell. Tom Baker's gaze followed me, and he waved as I left the temporary TARDIS and headed for the rush-hour streets outside.

Antony Howe

INTERVIEW: MATTHEW WATERHOUSE—COMPANION ACTOR

While most of the Doctor's travelling companions have been young women, one exception was Adric, played by Matthew Waterhouse, who made his debut in the Season 18 story 'Full Circle' (1980). Matthew was born in 1962, the son of a company solicitor. He joined the BBC as a clerk, working in the news and information department, while he also pursued an acting career. His first TV part was as a public schoolboy in the BBC's dramatisation of To Serve Them All My Days *(1980), but he had not even started work on that production when he auditioned for and won the role of Adric. He remained in* Doctor Who *for just over a year before being memorably killed off in the Cyberman story 'Earthshock' (1982). Subsequently he worked mainly in the theatre, his stage roles including Puck in* A Midsummer Night's Dream, Peter Pan *in* Peter Pan *and Edmund in* The Lion, the Witch and the Wardrobe. *He also starred in a one-man show,* The Adventures of Huckleberry Finn, *adapted by him from Mark Twain's novel. He has lived in Connecticut, USA, since July 1998, and self-published his debut novel,* Fates, Flowers, *in 2006.*

The following interview by Paul Mount was conducted right at the start of Matthew's time in Doctor Who, *when Season 18 was still in production and had yet to begin transmission. It originally appeared in Issue Six of* The Doctor Who Review, *dated June-July 1980.*

Recently, the national press introduced 18 year-old Matthew Waterhouse, a *Doctor Who* fan himself, who will be portraying Adric, a character who will be introduced into the series at about midpoint in the forthcoming eighteenth season.

Matthew's interest in science fiction does not begin and end with *Doctor Who* – far from it. Occasionally he reads sci-fi – 'My favourite author is Harlan Ellison', he says – and his favourite genre films include *2001: A Space Odyssey, Forbidden Planet,* the *Planet of the Apes* series, numerous Hammer horrors, *Star Wars* and the two *Doctor Who* spin-off movies of the '60s. Of *Doctor Who*'s biggest TV 'rival', *Star Trek,* Matthew feels: 'It was just a collection of clichés *dressed up* to be revolutionary, and is left far behind by *Doctor Who.*' His musical tastes include Kate Bush, Peter Gabriel and Lene Lovich.

I first asked Matthew just how familiar he is with *Doctor Who,* and what his earliest memory of the series is.

'I have fairly substantial knowledge of the series – its history, the stars, the monsters. I've been a fan of it since way back, and by "fan" I mean more than just a regular viewer. I'm a "sleeper" in fandom. I have read quite a few fanzines, though I've never contributed in any way. I think I'm unique in that I can appreciate the show both from the fan's viewpoint and from the professional's viewpoint. But I'm digressing. My earliest memory of the series is of William Hartnell's Doctor. I've been a keen viewer ever since – and I'll continue to be!'

Which is his favourite Doctor, and why?

'Tom got it right when he said that *Doctor Who,* and the lead role in particular, is "actor proof". No-one has screwed the part up. They have all experienced phenomenal success in the series, both commercially and as actors. I don't have a favourite Doctor – I like each Doctor and his interpretation for different reasons. That said, though, Patrick Troughton is the man I would most like to emulate, because he is quite simply one of the best character actors in the world.'

Has Matthew any favourite monsters from the series?

'Loads! I love them all! They're so … cute! I think the most terrifying creatures were the Autons, mindless slaves of the Nestenes. The fact that they were grotesque, featureless parodies of human beings made the horror more immediate. I would very much like to see them revived. I also admire the Cybermen, and for similar reasons: the Cybermen were once themselves humans. I think that Cybermen and the Autons stand out in my mind because their resemblance to humans makes them "closer to home", more terrifying. A reflection of us, and what we could become.'

To what does Matthew attribute the series' tremendous popularity?

'That's a difficult question. I think it has something to do with its ability to change with the times. Apart from certain continuing elements like the TARDIS and the Daleks, *Doctor Who* 1980 bears little resemblance to *Doctor Who* 1963. The style of stories has changed a great deal, and even the title character has changed – not only is it a different actor in the role, but a whole new persona, a completely new set of traits; in fact, a different person.'

Regarding now his own role as Adric, which story does Matthew actually debut in, and when is it likely to be transmitted?

'I join the series in a truly superb story called "The Planet That Slept".[9] How's that for an obscure title! It's written by an incredible person of 19, who is phenomenally talented. It will be broadcast in November and it's the third of the season.'

In how many stories will the character of Adric be appearing alongside Lalla Ward's Romana? Or will she exit in his introductory story?

'No, she won't be leaving just as I join. That would be terribly neat and contrived – one person coming as the other goes. Lalla will, in fact, be leaving quite near the end of the season – and not necessarily in the normal way.'

How does he view the character of Adric, and does he see any areas in which he may be able to develop the role in future serials?

'Right now, I honestly don't know what will happen to Adric's personality. I don't think one worries too much about such things. The *Doctor Who* universe is basically cardboard, with whiter-than-white nice guys and black-hearted villains. Any characterisation that *does* occur tends to be contrived. That said, though, Adric is less whiter-than-white than most!'

Previous male companions in the series have tended to be overshadowed by the more dominant personality of the Doctor. Does Matthew foresee this happening to Adric?

'It's inevitable that this will happen, and I wouldn't want it any other way. The Doctor is the star of the programme and Adric is a secondary character – though I like to think that he's a good secondary character. It's better like this than the other way around. In *Blake's 7*, the star, Blake, was overshadowed by a secondary character, Avon, which was not really a terribly good idea. It would not be a good idea if Adric became as forceful a personality as the Doctor. Adric is much more than just the Doctor's sidekick, though. He is not his assistant at all; rather a "travelling companion" with a mind of his own. In fact, his presence aboard the TARDIS is not entirely wanted. These aspects might be fun to play around with for the sake of a trivial sort of characterisation. In fact, Adric does some rather clumsy things as a "freshman" aboard the TARDIS, but relations improve as time passes, so one could say that Adric is not "dominated" by the Doctor.'

This role in *Doctor Who* will undoubtedly thrust him into the public eye overnight. How does he think he will cope with this sudden stardom?

'"Star" is a horrible word. I'm not a star at all. For every one person who watches *Doctor Who*, there are five who don't. Over half the population of Britain haven't even heard of Tom!

9 Retitled 'Full Circle' before transmission.

They most certainly won't have heard of me! I'll know I've made it when I can tell the BBC how much they'll have to pay me and when I don't have to audition for parts. Adric's a bigger part than my previous one[10], but a lot more people will see me in the latter.'

What audience does he think that *Doctor Who* should be aimed at?

'*Doctor Who* is something of an unknown quantity. I suspect that even people who have worked on the series for a long time are not quite sure what it is. It's most certainly not a children's programme, but nor is it an adults' programme, in that it does not go out at a supposedly adult hour. It's for everybody, really. When doing the show, we are conscious of the fact that our audience ranges from under five to over 80, so while there may be some concession for the children, perhaps by slightly diluting the horror, we never do anything that would insult the intelligence of an adult.'

Is Matthew called upon to do many stunts for *Doctor Who*?

'Not really, no. Occasionally I've done things that might be called stunts, but I have not yet been in any scene that requires much physical work. I have been told, however, that the next story we do will require Adric to do some action-orientated scenes, and there certainly won't be anyone standing in for me.'

Does Matthew think that there should be more horror in *Doctor Who*, and was he ever scared by the series as a child?

'Yes, it scared the hell out of me! That, in fact, was part of that old *Doctor Who* magic – the horror had you on the edge of your seat, but it was a "safe" horror; terrifying, but pure fantasy. I don't really think that the programme needs more horror than it already has. It is basically a science fiction adventure, and we never lose sight of that. Sometimes there is horror, sometimes humour, sometimes satire, but excitement is the name of the game.'

What is his opinion of *Doctor Who* fandom?

'Fandom is a great idea. People of like mind gathering together, be it in person or in the pages of an esoteric 'zine like *The Doctor Who Review*, is wonderful. However, some aspects of *Doctor Who* fandom are not so healthy. While *Doctor Who* is a programme that one should take seriously, it can be overdone. Dissecting each minute of the programme, analysing every aspect, takes away the enjoyment of the whole. Torn to bits, *Doctor Who* isn't such a big deal, but the whole is greater than the sum of the parts. Recently, something in *Celestial Toyroom*[11] annoyed me; the article *Decay in Studio*, a snippet about a new season story, gave away one of the major twists in the plot. I promise you that people who have read that article will not enjoy the story "State of Decay" as much as those who have not. A shocking, surprising revelation unfolded slowly in episode two – all blown because somebody went and let the cat out of the bag.[12] How can one be shocked about an occurrence one already knows about? "State of Decay" is, I think, going to be a classic, but the very people who supposedly love the show – the fans – are not going to get full pleasure out of it, if you follow my meaning. What I'm trying to say is this: fandom is fine when it sticks to covering the history of the series, but it detracts from, rather than enhances, your enjoyment of *Doctor Who* if you know the stories in advance. Despite this, fandom is an important aspect in the *Doctor Who* world, and indeed in science fiction in general. And it *can* be fun!'

How much is Matthew allowed to influence the scripts, and can he make changes in his own dialogue for the series?

10 His role in *To Serve Them All My Days*, transmitted in October 1980.

11 The monthly newsletter of the Doctor Who Appreciation Society (DWAS).

12 The revelation in question was that the story featured vampires.

'On *Doctor Who* we are a team. Our aim and our hope is to create the absolutely best programme we possibly can. Sometimes Tom or the director might make a small change to the script where they feel that the original line is not satisfactory, or not in the spirit of the programme, but any changes made by anyone are discussed in depth at the producer's run, where the producer watches a run-through of the scenes to be recorded and makes suggestions. So any changes that *are* made are very carefully considered.'

Does he find it difficult to take recording seriously when he is confronted by an actor in an outlandish costume?

'It really depends on what you mean by "seriously". The whole atmosphere on the show is one of hard work, but in an enjoyable way. We laugh a lot, do some silly things and have a great deal of fun, but at the end of the day, it's serious, tough work, and extremely long hours. So yes, I may make a joke if somebody turns up dressed as a gorilla, but only on the short term.'

What sort of costume will he be wearing in his debut serial? Will his clothes change in each serial?

'My costume is very much out of the ordinary, somewhat futuristic and practical rather than attractive. It is, however, very impressive, and Amy, the costume designer, has done a wonderful job! I will be retaining this costume for several stories, but it is unlikely that it will be permanent.'[13]

What is Matthew's opinion of K-9? Does he think the robot dog is an asset to the show, or does he feel that it tends to slow the action down?

'Like everyone else, I love him! When I first met him, I was totally overawed! Bob Baker and Dave Martin were very clever when they created him, because they ensured that his presence was a positive contribution to the show while preventing him from being all-powerful and omnipresent. It is true, however, that his use as an instrument in stories is rather limited. Companions in *Doctor Who* have never stayed more than three years because, with very few exceptions, they are limited and begin to prevent the series from moving forward. Virtually every possibility for K-9 has been used, which is why John, the new producer, will be resting him from some stories.'

Has he yet done any location filming for the series?

'I'm due to do quite a lot of location filming soon, but I don't yet know where.'

What does Matthew think of the current science fiction boom?

'I think it's wonderful that at last more people are realising that science fiction is an exciting genre. Films like *Alien*, *Close Encounters Of The Third Kind* and *Star Trek: The Motion Picture* are proving that SF need not be synonymous with *Flash Gordon*, while more family-orientated films such as *Star Wars* are preparing young children for more sophisticated science fiction. In fact, for many, I would think that going to see *Star Wars* was the first time they had been in a cinema. Many SF fans who have been around for a long time feel that the boom has opened the genre up to crass commercialism. To those I would say, perhaps so, but the same boom has been responsible for such excellent publications as *Starburst* and the Marvel SF comics, including *Doctor Who Weekly*!'

Finally, does he intend to continue acting when he finally leaves the role of Adric?

'As the Doctor himself would say – who knows?'

Paul Mount

13 In the event, Adric's initial costume, designed by Amy Roberts, was retained throughout his time in the series.

INTERVIEW: SID SUTTON—GRAPHIC DESIGNER

In the previous volumes of Talkback, *I presented a two-part interview with Bernard Lodge, the graphic designer responsible for all of* Doctor Who's *groundbreaking title sequences of the 1960s and 1970s. Now the spotlight falls on Sid Sutton, the creator of the first three title sequences of the 1980s, which broke from the past with a new 'star field' look. This interview, in Question and Answer (Q&A) format, was conducted and written by Philip Newman and first appeared in Issue 21/22 of* The Frame, *dated Spring/Summer 1992. Subsequently Sid continued his career as a graphic designer and, with his associate Terry Handley, established the facilities house Damson Studios, which has been responsible for titles and opticals on productions including the movies* The Believers *(1987),* A Fish Called Wanda *(1988),* High Spirits *(1988),* The Mighty Quinn *(1989),* Jacknife *(1989) and* Metroland *(1997), and the TV series* Keeping Up Appearances *(1990).*

Q: How did you first become involved in the world of television graphics?

A: Well, I did the usual sort of art school training in graphic design, and came to the point where I wasn't quite sure what I wanted to do. I didn't particularly want to go into advertising, which is where a lot of people went from art school. So I spent a summer sort of mulling it over and thought that I'd go back and do a teaching degree, which would give me another couple of years to make up my mind. Anyway, it was getting towards the end of the summer holidays when Dick Bailey, a friend of mine, who had actually left college with me and gone to work at Thames Television, rang me up and said, 'Do you fancy a job working with us down at Thames?' I said, 'That sounds interesting. What do I have to do?' It transpired that what he wanted me to do was to come in, set up the type for the captions on the old 'Tide washes whiter than white' commercials, print them on the photo-slide and put it in front of the camera. I didn't think it sounded very exciting, particularly as it was only going to be about 1½ days' work, so I asked what I'd be doing the rest of the time, and was told, 'You'll be working on programmes.' 'Ooh!' I replied. '*That* sounds exciting … How much do they pay?' 'About £17 a week.' 'Great!' So, he organised an interview and they took me on.

Q: How then did you come to 'change sides' and start working for the BBC?

A: Well, I was only a holiday relief at Thames, though they did want me to stay on. However, they had a tie-up with Ulster Television and they wanted to bring over a designer from Ulster for six months to catch up on all the development in London, and send me over there to replace him. I didn't fancy going to Ulster very much, and I'd just heard about the possibility of a vacancy at the BBC, so I rang them up and went along and had an interview. In fact, they didn't have a vacancy, but they said they'd keep my details on file for when they did. About two weeks later, they phoned me up and asked me when I could start!

Q: What did your first position with the BBC entail?

A: I went in as an assistant to a guy called Tom Taylor in the Presentation Department doing trailer captions and helping to make programme trailers. I stayed in that Department for quite a long time, because Tom was basically a painter who did illustrations – he wasn't a designer, as such – so anything that smacked of 'design' he used to hand over to me. It was a smashing place to start working, because instead of being like an assistant who just made the tea and did bits of LetraSet, I was there designing from day one – which was great!

In those days, the majority of the captions were black and white and just put in front of the camera. We used to produce anything from 20 to 60 a week; some of them were just a photograph with a bit of type, but a lot of them we actually 'designed' and did drawings for. Then gradually we broke into doing simple animated sequences with rostrum cameras and it all progressed from there. At that time it was a long, slow process for designers to get their hands on 'moving' equipment – that is, machines that could make things 'move' – but it was actually a very exciting time to be in television, because it was really the first time that designers got involved in that aspect of production. And, of course, the advent of colour TV was another great boon that we had to survive!

Q: Can you recall the earliest programmes you worked on?

A: I think I started with the original *Points of View* titles – I can't be sure. Working in what we called the Presentation Department, we were doing trailers mostly – although, unusually for that type of department, we did put out some programmes as well, especially when BBC2 started. We did things like *Late Night Line-Up*, the two film programmes *Film 73* on BBC1 and *Film Night* on BBC2 – and the weather forecasts. Two or three years after I arrived, Tom Taylor left and I took over the running of the Department, which by then had been expanded due to the heavy workload involved in supplying trailers for two channels. I ended up with ten people working for me, including designers and photographers. Then, about five or six years before I left the BBC, I changed from the Presentation Department to General Programmes.

Q: So, what was the first fully-fledged graphics sequence to bear your name in the credits?

A: Apart from one or two light entertainment shows, I think probably one of the earliest to be taken note of was *Target*, the Patrick Mower series, which, because Mary Whitehouse was very big at the time, was taken off by the BBC for being 'too violent.' That was replaced by *Shoestring*, for which I also did the titles. I enjoyed doing both of those.

Q: How then did your involvement with *Doctor Who* come about?

A: Well, it was just one of those things! Bernard Lodge had done it for several years, and his titles were always considered to be – and they were – very innovative. They were held up as a sort of milestone, you know. Well, the Assistant Head of Department, John Aston, just walked in one day and said, 'We need a new set of *Doctor Who* titles – do you fancy doing it?' It was a rather unenviable decision, because it really was a case of 'follow that!'

Q: Did John Nathan-Turner lay down any particular guidelines as to what he wanted?

A: No, not at all. I mean, he was the new producer and he wanted something different, something new, that was all. When the news got around that I was going to do the titles, everyone was saying, 'Poor old Sid! Dear, dear. Fancy having to try to do something after

Bernard's. Rather you than me!' So it was with a bit of trepidation that I actually tackled it.

Q: Did you have a tape of the new theme music to work to, or was that composed after your sequence had been completed?

A: Well, Peter Howell was working on the music and I was working on my ideas. I can't remember the exact sequence of events, but at some stage we got together and discussed various things. Then there came a point while we were both finalising our work when we met up again and he added some extra bits into the music to emphasise bits of the film, so that the two married together.

Q: How and why did you come up with the idea of using 'space' as the basis for the titles, rather than 'time'?

A: Well, I thought Bernard's titles were smashing – the way he developed them over the years from the original idea – but the one thing about them that kind of bugged me was that the tunnelling effect they had gave me a sort of 'enclosed' feeling. I'm not saying that in a disparaging way – it's just how it felt to me. What I wanted to do was to open them up. The idea really was that Doctor Who is a mysterious figure who came from the galaxy somewhere, and that was the kind of image I wanted to portray. So originally, with the first Tom Baker sequence I did, there was a galaxy that we were travelling through, with stars rushing past. Then some of the stars stopped, then a few more stopped, until eventually they made up the face of the Doctor, like a being literally coming from outer space. That basically was the idea – a very simple idea, really. Later on, in the Peter Davison and Colin Baker sequences, we made that aspect slightly more subtle and played up a bit more on the effects side, giving it more colour and so on.

Q: How was the 'star field' effect actually realised?

A: Every bit of the sequence was done on a rostrum camera as a series of overlapping tracks. We had something like 40 overlapping tracks on one piece of film, so each frame had about half a dozen exposures on it, to produce a multi-image effect.

Q: Was the new 'neon tube' logo entirely your idea too?

A: Yes. I think the previous logo was very 'Edwardian-ish' in appearance, and I think I'm right in saying that John wanted it slightly more modern-looking. Well, I didn't want to use chrome, because everyone was starting to use chrome at that time, so I tried to make it look like glass. Later on, again, I re-did that by shooting the original artwork through a prism, which created the coloured dilations around it. That was for the Colin Baker sequence.

Q: Your Tom Baker sequence was used for only one season, to be replaced by a very similar one for Peter Davison ...

A: Yes, well it was similar for that very reason; we didn't particularly want to change the titles very much at that stage. The reason why there were fewer stars and things was that Peter

Davison's head was less interesting in shape. Tom had this rather large face and lots of hair, so it gave us a nice, interesting shape to work with, while Peter's was a lot smoother with less hair and so on, so the sequence seemed less 'full up' on screen. Then, when Colin Baker came along, and he was going to play the character with that very colourful outfit, we – that is, my associate Terry Handley and I – decided with John to give the whole thing a lot more colour and life. So in addition to the star build-up, which was now getting a bit lost in the effects field, we had these big stars whooshing out, shooting bits of coloured light around to build the figure up. So that was quite fun, giving it a new lease of life.

Q: Bearing in mind what you said earlier about wanting to 'open up' the titles and move away from the 'tunnelling' effect of the Bernard Lodge ones, how did the multi-coloured tunnel-like image come to appear in the Colin Baker graphics?

A: Well, there had been quite a lot of letters from people asking, 'Where's the TARDIS?', 'What happened to the tunnel?', that sort of thing. So I thought we'd try to re-introduce a bit of the feel of the tunnel whilst still retaining the space field. So I invented a different type of tunnel, in fact. It was basically just black and white artwork with one or two coloured gels, but I think we got away with it, and it did give a tunnel-like feel to it. The other thing we introduced then was the Doctor smiling, which was John's idea. He wanted him to be put across as a slightly more friendly kind of character. We talked about putting live action into the head, but that would have been reasonably difficult to do and would have added quite a bit to the cost. So we did a photo session with Colin, getting him to do a few smiles, and then mixed the transparencies for the finished sequence.

Q: Apart from the three title sequences, you have another connection with *Doctor Who*: your work on some of the early BBC Video covers. How did that come about?

A: Well, it all came about when I was toying with the idea of leaving the Beeb and setting up my own design practice. I put together a showreel of various bits and pieces, and within the space of a couple of days I received two phone calls. One was from a Swedish television company asking if I could design a whole new corporate identity for its two channels, and the other was from the man behind the setting-up of the BBC's Home Video division, who wanted me to come up with a logo design, letterheads, catalogues and covers – a complete business package. So, armed with those two jobs, I resigned from the BBC.

Philip Newman

INTERVIEW: TERENCE DUDLEY—DIRECTOR, WRITER

Terence Dudley had a distinguished and extensive career in British television, unusually working in three different capacities – producer, director and writer – throughout, and almost exclusively for the BBC. His first credits as a producer and a director were gained in 1961 on the crime drama series The Men from Room 13, while his scriptwriting debut came in 1962 on the adventure serial The River Flows East. Many further assignments followed. In the telefantasy field, the most notable of these were as producer of the highly successful 1970s series Doomwatch and Survivors[14] – for which, again, he also occasionally directed and wrote. He effectively retired in the mid-1980s, his last directorial credit coming on the 1983 Christmas special of the popular All Creatures Great and Small.

Terence turned down an opportunity to write the very first story for Doctor Who when it was launched in 1963 (just as, in the late 1970s, he declined an offer to produce another cult favourite, Blake's 7), and then did not get to work on the series until some 17 years later, when he directed the story 'Meglos' in Tom Baker's final season. He went on to script three stories for Peter Davison's Doctor – 'Four to Doomsday', 'Black Orchid' and 'The King's Demons' – plus the pilot episode 'A Girl's Best Friend' for the subsequently-abandoned spin-off K-9 and Company.

I met Terence on only a couple of occasions, the last of which was in the summer of 1988 at a TellyCon convention in Birmingham, where we had a brief conversation and he agreed that I could get in touch with him at a later date to set up a full interview. Sadly, before I had an opportunity to do that, the news came in that he had died, on Christmas Day 1988, from cancer.

Having always greatly regretted that missed opportunity, I was delighted to learn when I started putting together this book that Antony Howe, one-time President of the Australasian Doctor Who Fan Club, was able to make available to me a fascinating, previously-unpublished interview with Terence, originally intended for inclusion in the Club's fanzine, Zerinza. The Club's initial contact with Terence had been made in September 1987 by its then Secretary, Patricia French, who had sent him a copy of a recent Zerinza issue containing, amongst other things, positive reviews of 'Black Orchid' and 'A Girl's Best Friend' – and a scathing critique by Antony of producer John Nathan-Turner – known to his friends and colleagues as JN-T. This had prompted Terence to send the following reply, dated 6 October 1987:

Very many thanks for your irresistible letter enclosing a copy of Zerinza Issue 33/34/35, received today! What a great joy it is to have one's work praised for all the right reasons!!! Thank you.

To say that I was fascinated by the copy of Zerinza would be a vast understatement. I was gripped from first to last by its intensity and its scope. I've long since ceased to be amazed at fans' enthusiasm and acumen at the conventions I've attended, but Zerinza represents something little short of omniscience! Antony Howe's scholarship is prodigious and his perception exciting. Please tell him that I agree wholeheartedly with his review of the Doctor Who situation and that behind that agreement is 30 years' experience …

I can't pretend that I wasn't delighted with the virtual disembowelling of JN-T. I know

---

14 For further details of Dudley's involvement in Survivors, which is not covered in this intereview, see The End of the World?: The Unofficial and Unauthorised Guide to Survivors by Rich Cross and Andy Priestner (Telos Publishing, 2006).

John very well; knew him before he began on *Doctor Who*, when he was production [unit] manager on *All Creatures Great and Small*. He's a first class administrator but entirely without editorial judgment; and, I fear, what power he has, has turned his head. Antony Howe is exactly right. John couldn't have done a better job of demolishing *Doctor Who* if he were employed by the competitor. That's a thought!!!

If only I'd had sight of *Zerinza* when it was published – well over a year ago! – I might have been able to put all its intelligence to productive use. I little knew you had such access to the programme's preparation background: that and the archival research presented could well have saved the programme if pushed at Michael Grade with back up. As it is, what's on the screen at the moment has to be seen to be believed![15] It's an all-time low, and the programme will never survive it save through divine intervention. …

Give my regards to Antony Howe – my regards and admiration for his perception.

Encouraged by this praise of his work, Antony proceeded to arrange the interview. As interviewer and interviewee were on different continents, it was conducted partly through correspondence – Terence wrote four further letters, dated 2 February 1988, 21 February 1988, 22 March 1988 and 22 November 1988 respectively – and partly by the unusual method of Terence recording on tape, in August 1988, the answers to a list of questions sent to him by Antony, along with some clarifications of and expansions on points made in the earlier letters. The text below has been compiled together by me from the contents of the letters, transcribed and annotated for my benefit by Antony, and from the aforementioned tape recording, a copy of which Antony kindly supplied to me for this purpose.

Q: How did you get started in the business?

A: I began many years ago as an actor, but decided I would rather direct. I directed in weekly rep[16] for ten years, at one time having my own company – the Swansea Theatre Company in South Wales. Among those I worked with were Tom Bell, Dinsdale Landen and Mollie Sugden. It was after directing a play with music called *Meet Me By Moonlight* at the Aldwych that I joined the BBC TV Drama Department to direct a number of plays of my own.

Before *Doctor Who* began, the original producer, Verity Lambert, asked me to write the very first story; but I was heavily engaged elsewhere and it finished up with Tony Coburn. In those days, Verity knew nothing of TV and had a very experienced associate producer called Mervyn Pinfield to help her with the technicalities.

Actually, it's not quite true to say that Verity knew nothing of TV. She was with a firm called ABC in the old days, before she came to the BBC. ABC became, in due course, Thames Television, as it is now. When I first met her, she was at ABC, working as a production secretary, I think over a number of programmes, not necessarily drama. When Sydney Newman, who also was with ABC, as Head of Drama, came over to the BBC, he brought a number of people with him, and Verity was one of them. I imagine probably quite a lot of work was done on *Doctor Who*, in the setting up stages, between the two of them, although quite obviously it would have been started, initiated, by Sydney.

15 Dudley was referring here to Season 24, the first starring Sylvester McCoy as the Doctor.

16 This is a reference to plays performed in the network of regional repertory theatres that existed in the UK for many years.

Q: I believe Anthony Coburn's story had been commissioned by Donald Wilson, acting on Sydney Newman's ideas, before Verity Lambert joined the BBC. Did she want to drop Coburn's story and get you to write a replacement?

A: Although I remember Verity Lambert's invitation vividly, I can't remember her saying anything about other contributors or others' involvement. She gave me a copy of the format document (on blue paper) signed by Sydney Newman. From what you say, it would seem that she was approaching a number of writers. The series needed several contributors, and she was probably hedging her bets. It's possible Tony Coburn wrote that one before I was approached, and it's possible that it was done at the instigation of Donald Wilson. Donald was head of the Script Department, which comprised quite a large establishment of writers; David Whitaker, for instance. But, as far as I know, *Doctor Who* was Sydney Newman's baby. And there was never any love lost between Donald Wilson and Sydney Newman.

At that time, you see, the Script Department was separate from the Drama Department, although they worked together. There were two different empires. I don't think Sydney liked this, and what he did eventually was to disband the Script Department. He very much favoured having script editors – whom he insisted on calling 'story editors' – working on individual programmes; and that is how it developed; that is one of the changes he made when he came to the BBC.

Donald Wilson was a tall, pipe-smoking, agreeable Scotsman, who was quite clever. He came from films. I think quite a number of the people with him in the Script Department came from films. The one with whom I had most contact was John Hopkins, who I think is a near-genius and still has the record – in my view anyway – of writing the definitive television drama. It was a quartet of plays called *Talking to a Stranger*[17] and told a story about a family four times, from the different points of view of four members of the family.

Tony Coburn was an agreeable, rough, blunt, tubby Australian. We worked together for a while – he was in the Script Department – with another writer quite well known in those days: Berkely Mather, who wrote crime fiction with a quirky idiom. His real name was Colonel Jasper Davies. He, too, was Australian, and an Indian Army man. He began writing while on service in India. He told me that while he was there, he saw the names of two shops, one was Berkely and one was Mather, and thought they'd make rather a good pen name, so that was the origin of that. He had an idea for an espionage series called *Downward Blow*, and Tony and I worked on it with him, but it never got off the ground. I liked Tony very much, but lost touch with him when I produced programmes in which he was not involved. He was responsible for developing a number of good ideas: *The Regiment* and *The Onedin Line*, for example. He died not long after; something that was unexpected and saddened us all.

Q: Did you watch *Doctor Who* in the early years?

A: Yes, I took an enormous interest in *Doctor Who*, having been asked right up front to contribute to it. Pat Troughton was my favourite Doctor, I think because I like him enormously as an actor, but also because he had something about his personality that was essentially sensitive, childlike, and yet authoritative at the same time; and if one thinks of the Doctor as being vaguely eccentric, the eccentricity that Pat brought to the role was most

17 First transmitted on BBC Two in 1966.

attractive. He was undoubtedly the Doctor I enjoyed the most.

Q: What are your recollections of your involvement with *Doomwatch*, created by Kit Pedler and Gerry Davis, which I believe was the first science fiction series you worked on?

A: I was invited to produce *Doomwatch* after producing series like *Dr Finlay's Casebook*, *The First Lady*, *Cluff*, *The Mask of Janus* etc. I also wrote and directed a number of the episodes.

Gerry Davis I knew as an editor before I met Kit Pedler. He and I had worked together on *The First Lady*. That was a late-1960s series starring Thora Hird as a woman town councillor, who was a bit of an interfering body; certainly a troubleshooter, in a way, and a fixer. It was quite a good programme, because it allowed a certain amount of rather serious social comment. It's quite possible, although I don't remember ever speaking to Gerry about it directly, that the idea of *Doomwatch* might have had seeds in the soil that had been tilled by both him and Kit for *Doctor Who*.[18] It was never mentioned; but Gerry came to me with the format for *Doomwatch* – through Andrew Osborne, who was Head of Series at that time – and it captivated me, as did Kit.

It went to three series, although I quarrelled with Kit and Gerry after the first. Dr Pedler was, in my view, a great man with a gut mission in life, which I admired and respected. Unfortunately he was so obsessive about the 'message' of the series that he was convinced all the villains should be depicted as fools or rogues, and I felt that to fall in with this view would depreciate the format: Aunt Sallies don't make for much opposition, and drama is conflict; conflict of ideas, conflict of opinions, conflict of emotions; conflict of interests. The best example I can think of, off the top of my head, is Ibsen's *The Enemy of the People*. Here, the doctor concerned is drawing the attention of the town council to the insalubrious state of the drainage system of the town, saying it must be attended to because it is likely to cause epidemics, particularly in summer seasons. The point is that the town is a tourist attraction, and the political and economic interests of the community appear here to be threatened by the doctor. The doctor, of course, digs his heels firmly in the ground and won't move. That is the sort of thing I mean by dramatic conflict. Many plays can actually begin and develop from conflict within one character.

We quarrelled about the over-simplification that Kit particularly wanted in the characterisation of Doomwatch's opposition. I felt that it was too tendentious – and too like propaganda, actually, to be dramatically viable – and so Kit and Gerry withdrew after the first series. I stayed on for the second and third series, without a script editor – I didn't want any more script editors. In fact, I produced a number of programmes in my time without benefit of a script editor; sometimes they make for very heavy weather, and if the producer is also a writer, it is probably unnecessary.

Usually what happens when a new series starts is that a net is thrown out by the script editor, who will be familiar with the format and know what is wanted and will distribute this information among writers that he thinks might be interested, or that he knows are good and will give him what he wants. Then, by and large, what happens is that when a script comes to the script editor, he passes it to the producer, who reads it. Then there's a conference between the script editor and the producer, where they try to find solidly unanimous ground on the

---

18 Gerry Davis had been script editor of *Doctor Who*, and Kit Pedler a writer and unofficial scientific adviser to the series. Together they had created the Cybermen for the 1966 story 'The Tenth Planet'.

script. They iron out what needs to be ironed out, clear up what needs to be cleared up, and so on, and bring it generally into line with what the series is about and how it should develop. Then, when the agreement between the script editor and the producer is achieved, it is passed on to the writer, who goes about rewriting or reshaping as the case may be: whatever he is asked to do. The second draft is probably more what the script editor and the producer want together – if not, it goes back for more treatment. That is generally what happens on a series. All work on a series gets a bit heavy from time to time, and help from a script editor can be very valuable; but I found quite often I didn't need it.

I didn't enjoy the schism with Kit and Gerry, but *Doomwatch* was a great success. I didn't see Kit again before he died, which was a great tragedy in my view, but I did meet Gerry quite often after that, and we remained firm friends – mates, as he would call it.

Many years before *Doomwatch*, I had actually produced and directed a science fiction serial entitled *The Big Pull* by Robert Gould. It was concerned with an attack on Earth from space through the Van Allen belts. Don't ask more! It's a hundred years ago!

Q: How did you come to be involved with *All Creatures Great and Small*?

A: Bill Sellars, the producer of *All Creatures …*, asked me to direct and write for the series; something that gave me great joy. I first met JN-T while working on that. He was production unit manager; a role limited to budget, logistics etc. He was never concerned with any creativity. He was, without doubt, a first rate administrator, and a very agreeable fellow.

The three original series were based on three of James Herriot's books. The books are anecdotal; they tell little stories of his experiences as a vet in the Yorkshire Dales, and these are not necessarily linked together in any way. What we attempted to do in *All Creatures …* was to give each episode of 50 minutes a narrative order, so that certain of the incidents were taken from the books and then expanded upon and put together with a beginning, a middle and an end; in other words, made into a dramatic whole. It was largely haphazard, because the writers who were invited aboard that particular programme were offered the remainder of the anecdotes that other, earlier writers had not already used, and sometimes this was getting near the bottom of the barrel, so to speak. By the time I got to the third series, in which I wrote episodes one, two and 14, there wasn't a great deal left. Episode one, which in a sense was a reintroduction to the series, was practically all me; very little of it was Herriot. That sort of invention was necessary; his material had almost run out by then. I greatly enjoyed inventing situations to fit his characters. If you love the characters, you can't go wrong. Certainly episode 14, when Siegfried and Tristan went off to war, was all me. I introduced a Polish vet in order to point up the war and the difficulties that enterprises like veterinary surgeries faced, being put in a terrible muddle by the war, and the fact that certain professions were excluded from military service. Both Siegfried and Tristan, in real life, joined up; they didn't wait for conscription.

I most enjoyed directing episodes I'd written, particularly that last one.

Q: Tristan Farnon was of course played by Peter Davison, who went on to become the fifth Doctor in *Doctor Who*. How well did you know him from *All Creatures Great and Small*?

A: Peter Davison was an awfully nice fellow, but I didn't really know him all that well. One thing about directing or producing a series is that although you get to know some aspects of the people you work with, it doesn't go very deep; the social contact is very minimal anyway, because the working relationship takes up most of the time. Usually I've found that the director and actors would like to be apart for a certain amount of the time, and go their own ways, since they're in each other's pockets, on and off, all the way through a considerable length of time.

Q: Your first work on *Doctor Who* was directing 'Meglos', JN-T's second story as producer. Did he invite you to do that; and, if so, was it because he was familiar with your previous work?

A: Yes, JN-T knew my work well, and it was he who invited me to direct 'Meglos'; not a happy experience, Tom Baker being a spoiled and undisciplined actor and impossible to work with. I think JN-T was hell-bent on making significant changes, to make a name for himself; an understandable trait. I think he tried to engage people whose work he respected and people he knew. Let me say immediately that (forgive the immodesty) I enjoy something of a reputation as a director and a writer, and JN-T, new to his job, relied on such reputations. This wasn't very different from the norm in general terms: a producer hires the best talent available.

But, as I say, directing 'Meglos' was a very unhappy experience, and I would never have directed another story. Apart from Tom Baker and his incessant time-wasting, which I think was due to a grave sense of insecurity, there was insufficient rehearsal time, particularly camera rehearsal time. It has to be remembered that where a story has film inserts – which can sometimes constitute up to half the total running time of a programme – this leaves longer to rehearse the remaining scenes and record them in the electronic camera studio. A week's rehearsal can be of great benefit to a programme lasting 25 minutes if, say, 13 minutes is already in the can. But 'Meglos' had no film inserts, and the designer and I created a planetary landscape using an electronic device called scene-sync.[19] Because of pressure of time, I had very little contact with JN-T.

I don't think the shortage of rehearsal time was due to cost-cutting on JN-T's part. I think it was probably due to the availability of one actor or another. Sometimes an actor is very heavily involved in one show and needs a bit of a breather, a bit of a respite, in preceding or subsequent shows. This can be an important factor in the scheduling of rehearsal time. Another possible factor is that an artist may be in a play in London, or already doing a film or some other work to which he has previously committed.

Q: Did you find the special effects work on 'Meglos' very challenging? Did the effects obscure elements that take precedence in other shows?

A: I don't think so. In fact, it was rather fun using the scene-sync. It was just a little time-consuming, because it was a new thing and still being developed in its use – which was a problem when time was also being consumed elsewhere, to whit with Tom Baker.

---

19 Scene-sync is a sophisticated version of colour separation overlay (CSO), also known as chromakey or green- or blue-screen, an electronic effect by way of which certain areas of a video image that are in a key colour – typically blue at this point in *Doctor Who*'s history, although yellow and green were also used – can be replaced with the equivalent areas of a different image. Scene-sync allows for tracking, panning and zooming of the composite CSO image by computer-controlling the movements of the different cameras involved, so that they remain in synchronisation.

Q: Could you elaborate on the difficulties you encountered working with Tom Baker?

A: 'Poor, tortured Tom' I think is a phrase that would sum him up. He was so very complex a person; basically terribly insecure, and very immature. And the trouble was keeping him on the ball; keeping his mind on what was in hand. He used to digress an awful lot, and insist on doing an awful lot of unnecessary chat, which he would term 'delving into the character' – or indeed someone else's character – when either there was no need of this, or the characterisation was so two-dimensional that it didn't allow for it to be done. It was, in fact, conscious time-wasting, in order to show, in a sense, what an intellectual person he was. There's no doubt that he had quite a good mind, but it was the particular neurosis that we got, not the benefit of clear or deep thinking.

Q: How was he handled by the production team?

A: Indulgently, I think; although I can remember him being screamed at once by the production assistant, the late and much lamented Goldie – Marilyn Gold – who said quite distinctly and firmly, 'Shut up, Tom, and get on with it!'

Q: What was the working relationship like between Tom Baker and Lalla Ward?

A: Lalla Ward would not exactly back Tom Baker up, but really I suppose supply him with a useful echo: 'I'm on his side.' It was astonishing news to me that, shortly after I worked with them both, they got married. It was like a union between two boxers on either side of a ring!
  I remember that, because I was pushed for time, I became very impatient with Lalla Ward on the studio floor on this production.

Q: Did you direct from the studio floor or from the gallery upstairs?

A: Most of the time, I directed 'Meglos' from the floor, because it meant intimate and direct contact with the scaled-down models that were used in the scene-sync operation, and I was of more direct use on the floor than I was relaying my instructions through Goldie, although she was doing a wonderful job anyway. So that one I directed mainly from the floor; usually I don't.

Q: Why was Jacqueline Hill cast as the High Priestess in 'Meglos'? Was it because JN-T wanted her, due to her past role in *Doctor Who* as the first Doctor's companion Barbara?

A: I don't remember being approached by John Nathan-Turner about casting her. I'd liked her for a very long time. I realised that she had done something in the series in the past, but I think she had said, in response to me, that she'd like to appear again, that it would be fun; something of that order. And therefore she did.

Q: What did you think of the script ideas, for example having a cactus as the villain?

A: I think a cactus makes as good a villain as any! Think of the Triffids, for instance.

Q: Did JN-T attend all the taping of the story?

A: Yes, he did. All producers do. What they do normally is attend a rehearsal or a read-through at the beginning of any one episode and then stay away from it until a thing called the producer's run. That's at outside rehearsal, and it enables the producer to see what has taken shape, what is ready, or very nearly ready, to go into the studio, to be rehearsed in the studio and then recorded. He comes to that, and makes observations and notes, if he wishes to, about how it's going. He then sees a bit of what goes on in the studio subsequently, which is basically the camera rehearsal – familiarising cameramen, sound men and everyone else with what is happening in the sets – otherwise called a technical rehearsal. Usually the producer is in and out of that, and probably attending to other things simultaneously if he's doing more than one job. But he always is there when the thing is taped. He sees it therefore made literally frame by frame, and John was punctilious with this, as any other television producer would be.

Q: How important is the final editing of a story, after the taping has been completed?

A: The editing is very important. In films, the director has no right of a final edit. In television, it's not quite the same. If, in fact, a director couldn't have the final edit built into his contract, he wouldn't work again for that producer. I think it's as simple as that.

Q: Going back to what you said about JN-T wanting to make radical changes, do you think it is really a good idea, on a series like *Doctor Who* with established traditions and styles, for all the old personnel to be ditched at once?

A: I don't think a question of personnel being 'ditched' would really come into the lining-up of people to work on a new series, or of one already in train or being revived. I think that is the prerogative of the producer, and only the producer. He expects overall responsibility, and is expected by others to be responsible. He is the focus, if you like.

   In my view, a good producer is one who recognises story material for what it is, and talent in writing and acting for what it is, and attracts all this, drawing together threads of individual contributions to make a cohesive whole. He isn't some sort of dictator, isn't some sort of charge-hand, isn't a one-man band. He is using a fusion of different but integrated talents. It is a very poor producer indeed who tells a director how to direct. What he does in the first instance is employ the director because he knows what sort of style the man will direct in – or that the man is amenable to a suggestion that a particular style should be brought to the telling of the story, or the making of the programme. Then he stands back and looks at it. He is the person to whom people come when things go wrong. He is the person who, because he is responsible, is expected to put those things right. And this is the mark of a good producer. He will not stir up trouble. He will not be disliked. He will be – because he is content to stay in the background – someone who can be judged fair and balanced and equitable.

Q: How would you describe your working relationship with JN-T at that time?

A: When I first met John Nathan-Turner, I liked him enormously. I think I still do, although I haven't seen him for a very, very long time indeed. But people do change with different roles, and I think that possibly he might have been a little young to be given so much responsibility.

The other thing is that although I met him quite often, and we were chums and drinking companions apart from anything else, one is never really in anyone's mind enough to know what they intend to do, or what they want to do, unless in fact they tell you. I was actually told by John Nathan-Turner that I was the first person to be told about the casting of Peter Davison as the Doctor, and was asked by him if I would please keep it under wraps, which of course I did. It seemed to me at the time to be a good choice, because I think the Doctor is best depicted as a sort of Edwardian gentleman, and Peter Davison with the cricketing image did live up to that as a metaphor.

It should be said that a producer and a director work apart from each other most of the time. When a director is directing a rehearsal he is not conscious of the producer, and the producer is not conscious of the director – he's usually working elsewhere on other aspects of the production, or another production for which he might be responsible. John might have treated me a little differently from other directors; younger directors. I'm considerably older than he is. He knew a great deal about my earlier work. I'd like to think that I enjoyed his respect in this sense; he certainly enjoyed mine.

Q: Very shortly after 'Meglos', K-9 was written out of the series. Did you get a sense that JN-T saw K-9 as problematic?

A: I don't quite know what was in John's mind about K-9. I think it's pretty fair to assume that there were no difficulties with it. It was very popular. I always thought it was a bit of a giggle; and the late Bill Fraser, who was in 'Meglos' if you remember[20], said with his tongue in his cheek that he would only accept the part if he got to kick K-9, which we accommodated by giving him a token little kick of K-9, which he didn't really mean, in the course of the programme. I don't think John was unhappy with K-9 at all, particularly since there was the idea of a spin-off in *K-9 and Company*.

Q: Do you know how *K-9 and Company* came about?

A: Again, I don't know the background to that. At that particular time, I was pretty heavily involved with a series called *Flesh and Blood*. That was quite a lengthy series – it was in 20 episodes of 50 minutes each – and I directed all of it. The stars were Bill Fraser, Thora Hird, Anne Firbank and the late Nigel Stock. It was written by John Finch and was about a family firm in the north of England, in Yorkshire. It was quite a family saga; like *The Forsyte Saga*, only brought up to date. I know that a spin-off as far as K-9 was concerned was very firmly in John's mind. Whether it originated with him or elsewhere I don't know; I suspect it originated with him. It would have gone along in parallel with *Doctor Who*, or as a between-seasons replacement for *Doctor Who*. If you can imagine *Doctor Who* being transmitted while *K-9 and Company* was being recorded, and vice versa, there would be no gaps; there would in fact be a *Doctor Who*-type programme that would give continuity to that particular slot, which I think was probably popular with the programme controllers at the time. It might be that they handed some sort of idea down to John, though I doubt it; ideas of this sort don't usually originate with controllers, unless they have been in the Drama Department previously, and that situation is very rare – although it exists at the moment with the Controller of BBC One,

20 Fraser played the part of General Grugger.

Jonathan Powell, who was once Head of Series and Serials.

Q: After 'Meglos', you continued your involvement with *Doctor Who*, but as a writer rather than a director. You said before that you wouldn't have been prepared to direct for the series again, but what if you had been invited to direct one of your own stories?

A: I certainly would have directed one of my own scripts. You couldn't issue such an invitation to a director who is also a writer and have him turn it down! It would be impossible; it's too much of a gift.
    Barry Letts once asked me, many, many years ago when he was producing, if I would do a *Doctor Who* story, and again, though I wanted to, as when Verity Lambert had asked me, I was far too involved elsewhere, so I didn't.

Q: Barry Letts of course returned to *Doctor Who* as executive producer when JN-T was first appointed as producer. Do you know what the thinking was behind that?

A: Barry, as a past producer, 'oversaw' JN-T, who was untried in that capacity. I've no doubt Barry was of help to JN-T, but to what extent and in what kind I know not.

Q: Was it when you came to work as a writer on the series that you started to have differences with JN-T?

A: JN-T didn't interfere with my directing or my editing on 'Meglos'. In fact, I was never conscious of him obtruding: he wouldn't – with me. But it was when writing for the series that I became conscious that, although a great administrator, he had no editorial judgment and was, patently, no judge of a script editor. He and Eric Saward – one or the other, but JN-T was responsible – would rewrite my scripts *without* consulting me, leaving me to discover the rewriting when the script was printed and distributed. I objected vigorously. The rewriting was without reason; derived from subjective attitudes and seeking to put a handprint on creative work.

Q: Was it a question of there being a particular 'house style'?

A: I think what has emerged demonstrates that there was no deliberate style, nor was there ever any firm control. What's come out is the worst aspect of the amateur; a dabbling with no clear vision or intention; a rudderless tyro on a choppy sea.
    Including *K-9 and Company*, I wrote four stories in all, and all were rewritten without my being consulted – which is illegal. The writer must be *asked* for rewrites. Only when he's unavailable is rewriting permitted. I always found out too late. My script would be accepted, paid for, rewritten and then printed for rehearsal. I would find the appalling stuff added at the readthrough. I had a volcanic row with Eric Saward over *K-9 and Company*, and flatly refused to have my dialogue monkeyed with, so my original dialogue was restored to the script.
    As I'm sure you will know, there was later some sort of division between Eric Saward and John Nathan-Turner. Eric Saward wrote to me, saying that he was bringing an accusation of abuse of copyright against John and asking if I would support him. Frankly I found the whole thing incomprehensible – he's not a very coherent fellow anyway – and I rather ignored it. I

37

did toy with the idea of warning John that someone was about to stab him in the back, but I thought it was all too petty to bother about.

Q: Were you approached in the first instance to write for *Doctor Who*, or did you contact the production office with an idea?

A: I was approached to write for *Doctor Who*. This is usual. As I remember, I was first invited to write by John himself at an exhibition at Madame Tussauds.[21] I then liaised with the script editor, Chris Bidmead, although I don't remember having an enormous amount of contact with him, actually. His successor, Tony Root, I remember quite distinctly, because he was a most agreeable young man and had enormous tact. He also had resilience, and he had a great deal of strength, and his observation about written material was good; it was always, as I remember, on the ball, particularly with 'Four to Doomsday'. I thought it was a great pity to lose Tony for Eric Saward, whom I didn't like at all; he was tactless, clodhopping, argumentative, a bit patronising and altogether a different person from Tony.

Q: Were you given a detailed brief as to what was required?

A: I was given no brief for 'Four To Doomsday'. JN-T asked me if I'd write a script, and I came up with that. Tony Root subsequently helped me with some sound advice when I'd delivered the draft. The brief for 'Black Orchid' was 'a story set in the '20s and with a twin for Nyssa.' That's all! For the next, I was asked for a medieval story in England with a castle and a metal robot. 'The King's Demons' was the result.

Q: The *K-9 and Company* pilot, 'A Girl's Best Friend', was the first of your stories to be transmitted. What was your opinion of the finished production?

A: *K-9 and Company* was a total disaster! What I wrote was that three members of the coven – Tracey, Tobias and Wilson – should be made memorable at the opening ceremony, so that we would recognise them instantly when they came face to face with Sarah Jane – Tracey when she arrived on the scene and Tobias and Wilson in turn when she was seeking help from them in her investigations. All ignored – resulting in total dissipation of the plot. There was no pacing, no timing, and the denouement was so rushed and perfunctory that we failed to recognise the identity of the High Priest and High Priestess. Oh well!

Q: Do you think the production team decided to conceal the coven-members' identities to make it all more of a mystery?

A: No, I don't think there was any conspiracy to make *K-9 and Company* a mystery; certainly not a mystery to the audience. A mystery to an audience is usually cleared up; that is the whole point. But here, in the final shots, we did not recognise the High Priest and the High Priestess, which was all-important. The thing about our not seeing the coven closely enough at the beginning to be able to identify the three characters – Tracey, Tobias and Wilson – was simply that it lost the dramatic irony of when Sarah Jane comes face to face with a villain, we know it

---

21 The Madame Tussauds waxwork attraction in London mounted a *Doctor Who* exhibition in 1980.

but she doesn't. That's why it was important: dramatic irony.

Q: How did you research the background to the story, such as Sarah's character and the other *Doctor Who* links – for instance her Aunt Lavinia? Did you get advice from fans such as Ian Levine, who is said to have worked as an unofficial script consultant on *Doctor Who* at that time?

A: No, I knew nothing about Ian Levine. He apparently was involved with the title music.[22] I simply saw most of the episodes in which Elisabeth Sladen had appeared. I relied on memory for the background details of K-9. The only other thing is that I went quite a lot into the deeper kinds of witchcraft of which details are available in libraries, and also market gardening.

Where Eric Saward and I disagreed over this story, basically, was that he didn't believe in the witchcraft angle; he thought it didn't exist; he thought it was all fairy-stories; he pooh-poohed it. He needed to be convinced. It was simply a question of youth and ignorance on his part. He didn't really know that the 'black art' was still, in fact, very much alive in this day and age.

Q: Was there any written format document for *K-9 and Company* as a series, or did you approach it as just a one-off project?

A: As far as I know, there was no written format for *K-9 and Company*. All I was charged with, or briefed with, was to write Sarah Jane Smith, and the lead-in to her, Aunt Lavinia, and K-9 and Brendan. The rest was me: there was no real format. I don't think a great deal of thought had been put into it. I knew it was intended to go on as a series – a spin off – but the dreadful direction and the lamentable title sequence put paid to that. I've always loved Elisabeth Sladen – she was in one of the early *Doomwatch* episodes that I did[23], and I've known her for a long time – and I think she is an intelligent woman with an enormously attractive, direct personality that shines through in any role she plays. She was, in my view, the very best of the Doctor's companions. I went for a Sarah Jane who was an echo of the Doctor, since she shared his manners and mores. I think K-9, as an idea, works very well. Robots are, after all, our past, present and future, and a mobile dog is as diverting as any other device.

Q: I think that a series centred around K-9 might work better if it was set in the future, in outer space. Having the action confined to present-day Earth poses a lot of credibility problems. For instance, how would Sarah get K-9 through customs if she went to another country? And wouldn't the CIA or the KGB attempt to steal K-9 to make use of the advanced technology?

A: I think Sarah would simply present K-9 as a toy, even though we, as an audience, would know it wasn't a toy. And the CIA and the KGB, yes, sure, they'd want to steal it; that makes very good story material, doesn't it?

Q: Turning to 'Four to Doomsday', what did you think of how that one turned out?

22 The title music for *K-9 and Company* was composed by Ian Levine and Fiachra Trench.
23 One of Sladen's earliest TV roles was as a terrorist in the 1972 *Doomwatch* episode 'Say Knife, Fat Man', which is currently missing from the BBC archives.

A: 'Four to Doomsday' was a travesty. Monarch, Persuasion and Enlightenment were written as three large South American tree frogs, two of which later take human form. What I got were three made-up actors, allowing Stratford Johns to be recognisable in a leading role. The whole point – the representation of an age-old giant intelligence from space as frogs – was lost.

Q: Do you think this was because JN-T wanted to capitalise on Stratford Johns' popularity as Barlow from *Z Cars*? Was he cast essentially for PR purposes as a 'name'?

A: Yes, I think John was enlisting the aid of 'stars' – people very well known on television or elsewhere – and Stratford Johns was indeed very well known.

Q: Why had you particularly wanted the aliens to be represented as frogs?

A: Simply because when monsters appear we tend, even in *Doctor Who*, to anthropomorphise them, and this is what I didn't want; I didn't want something that was recognisably humanoid, but a frog; a highly intelligent frog. It seemed to me quite a frightening concept.

Q: Peter Davison once commented that he thought 'Four to Doomsday' had originally been written for Tom Baker's Doctor. Was that the case? If so, was Nyssa added as an 'afterthought', given that she was not originally intended to be a companion?

A: 'Four to Doomsday' was written with Peter Davison in mind. The cricket ball was an essential property that rescued the Doctor from suspension in space. I don't remember Nyssa being an afterthought.

Q: How did the production team make their wishes known regarding the proposed characterisation of Davison's Doctor? Did they send you notes, discuss it, or just leave it up to you?

A: When invited to write for *Doctor Who*, I knew the Doctor was to be Peter Davison, but there was no mention of characterisation or style beyond that he was to be cricket orientated. There's no doubt in my mind that the cricket idea originated with a charity match, brilliantly organised by JN-T, that had taken place in Yorkshire between two teams captained respectively by me – directing *Flesh and Blood* in Weardale – and Peter Davison – representing *All Creatures Great and Small* in Wensleydale. I don't know how keen Peter Davison really was on cricket. He wasn't, in fact, a very good cricketer. He used a cross-bat as a batsman, and his action as a fast bowler was more bash than any art; but that's something entirely on one side.

I think the casting of someone in the role of Doctor Who is largely a question of personality; what personality will come to the part to achieve a difference, given that basically the Doctor is a gentleman, and non-violent; that he is clever, in the sense of having intelligence, and quick-witted; and that he is profoundly experienced. I think if these things are taken into consideration, then the performance after that is purely personal personality performance.

In my experience, many producers, when casting a personality, will rely on the performer's natural characteristics and mannerisms to replace 'characterisation', of which in fact none exists. I think this is what happened with Davison.

Q: Were you any happier with how your next story, 'Black Orchid', turned out?

A: 'Black Orchid' was done very much on the cheap and lacked any tension or menace – it was without atmosphere.

Q: This story did, though, allow for the Doctor's interest in cricket to be used to good effect, with the cricket match in the first episode.

A: Right from the beginning, Doctor Who has been, for me, what Sydney Newman asked for; an Edwardian gentleman. Cricket is a metaphor for this. I used, when younger, to play well. I captained the First XI at school. I love it and all the game implies, and I'm very, very sad to see the way the game's going ... and gentlemen are on their way out, too.

Q: Were you also dissatisfied with the finished product on 'The King's Demons'?

A: 'The King's Demons' was, again, entirely without atmosphere or invention, with the scripts' nuances and subtleties overridden. The duel between the Doctor and the Master was deplorably comic.

Q: You mentioned earlier that you were asked to incorporate Kamelion before you actually started writing 'The King's Demons'. What did you think of the concept of such a shape-changing robot becoming a companion?

A: I gave the robot its name. I was taken to see the thing being worked on in a workshop near Oxford, and I advised at the time that such a robot could be time-consuming while working, and very limited in scope if it was to retain its original shape and composition for any length of time. Its movement was controlled by two computers. I remember saying that it would be better to paint up an actor.

Q: In your later novelisation of 'The King's Demons', you make clear a link between the Plantagenets and the Devil, hence the story title. Was this something that was cut from your scripts in the televised version?

A: I put back into the novel a lot that was cut from the TV scripts. Cutting in TV happens on even the best-regulated productions: overrunning is the cardinal sin in scheduling terms. But there was nothing cut out about the Plantagenets. Information, if it's given as information, in any piece of drama is just bad writing. It has to be incidental. It has to support something that is being said directly. If, indirectly, the background comes out, that is good writing. When I came to do the novel, I thought more background – more history – would be of interest.

Q: How did you come to write the novelisations of *K-9 and Company*, 'Black Orchid' and 'The King's Demons'; and why did you not also do 'Four to Doomsday'?

A: The publishers, W H Allen, asked me to novelise the stories. I just hadn't time to do 'Four to Doomsday'. Please don't ask why and where the novels differ from the TV stories! Most of the differences are explained by having to write 50,000 words. A lot of the differences in the novel version of *K-9 and Company* were expansions.

Q: On a more general note, what would you say are the essential elements of the Doctor's character? Would you agree that he's a Pied Piper-like figure, leading viewers into his adventures?

A: It's very clear to me, as aforesaid, that he's an Edwardian gentleman. I think his penchant for jelly babies is totally believable, as in Damon Runyon's *The Lemon Drop Kid*[24], and I don't think he would – or should – say goodbye to anyone; no Edwardian gent would. If there is a hint that he may turn nasty, it points up his humanity. As a gentleman – a man of honour – he controls the temptation. That's the reassurance. I think the Doctor's intelligence, his learning and his experience (age) make him a formidable hero. The representation of these values carries the moral significance that right is might – that good must always overcome evil. I don't think the Pied Piper is a good analogy. He was a magical pest disposer: of both ratus sapiens and homo sapiens.

Q: What are your views on the inclusion of horrific material in *Doctor Who*? It's often said that children watch 'from behind the sofa'; that they like to be frightened by the stories.

A: Children don't like to be frightened – nobody does. 'Tell me a story' pre-dates literature. We enter a fantasy world voluntarily: that's the difference. We're not frightened, we're excited. We take stock of characters and situations and assess them. We take sides. We identify. We have faith in a satisfactory ending to a tale – even if it may be unhappy. I think the 'sofa' is mythical. I'm pretty sure it emanated from a patronising reviewer. Children don't like to be frightened, but they like to be thrilled; it's a sensation that carries with it a built-in protection, which they recognise. Consider a rollercoaster, for instance. If a notice on a rollercoaster said 'People who travel on this contraption do so at their own risk', no-one would go on it. It's because these things are regularly monitored and declared safe that parents allow their kids on them, or that kids themselves, if they have any autonomy, are attracted to them. It's a thrill that they go for, not to be frightened.

I think a great deal of nonsense is talked about the influence of television on children, or indeed on anyone, and the need for it to be regulated. The parents regulate what is seen in the household with a television set, not in fact the makers of the programmes. I think the programme-makers' responsibility is to be honest; programmes should be made honestly and not as propaganda. I don't think we need that sort of thing. Once television and radio programmes become propaganda, we are in a fascist state; and we've got all the makings of that in Britain at the moment.

Children do not imitate television in the sense that is meant by the general public, and in the sense that is meant by people like Mary Whitehouse, who are interferers, and who in fact are a little caught up in their manipulation of power. You will get imitative behaviour from someone who is subnormal – one would expect that – but not the general norm. Not that I think senseless violence, gratuitous violence, should ever be shown, as it sometimes is actually in factual programmes, in news programmes. If people are killing each other – not exactly on our own doorsteps, but a couple of hundred miles away – one should know of it, but should one see it? I don't know. I think honesty, in this case, is the best policy, and let people judge for themselves.

Q: Do you see *Doctor Who* more as an adventure-odyssey, wherein viewers explore new

24 This Runyon-scripted film, starring Bob Hope, was released in 1934.

worlds etc, or an action-orientated series, with the emphasis on chases, fights etc? How important is it for there to be mystery in the show?

A: This is interesting. As an entertainer, so to speak, from way back – as an actor, a writer, a producer and so on – I have a tendency to moralise in things I write. I'm more interested in reading things that have something to say about the world we live in. I do think *Doctor Who* is basically an adventure-odyssey, but it's less a question of experiencing and exploring new worlds than mirroring or reflecting our own, so that the same standard of values, in a moral or a philosophical sense, is shown to be in action, whether in new vistas or in old. The new somehow should illuminate and inform the old. I think the basic tenet of drama, originating from the Greeks, is self-revelation, or illumination of the human condition. I think this is very important. It can be done in a fun way just as in a deadly serious way, though I think because a deadly serious way is not entertaining it is less likely to be of interest. Peter Ustinov is awfully good at writing plays that are in fact fables, and highly moral, but they are all terribly funny; and I think if a moral point can be made in a fun sort of way, it not only sticks, it somehow makes something that is abstract, concrete.

Q: A couple of years ago, *Doctor Who* was 'rested' by Michael Grade. Did you have any dealings with him?

A: I met Michael Grade once and liked him very much. I asked for the meeting in an attempt to interest him in a series about the German opposition to Hitler; a subject little known, for a variety of significant reasons. He liked the idea but thought the public needed to be reeducated for such a project to succeed. I think what he meant was that people, and particularly Jewish people, are understandably going to think that, at the time of the Second World War, all Germans were Nazis. They weren't. In fact a minority, to begin with, were Nazis. Most of the German opposition to Hitler began long before he actually came to power in 1933, and from then on, concentration camp populations went up in their hundreds, so that they were crammed with dissenters, crammed with people actively against Hitler. There was in fact, in 1938, before Hitler went into Czechoslovakia, a great deal of movement between Germany and England, where the German underground were willing to go ahead and form a pro-tem government if Hitler could be deposed.

Subsequently I wrote to Michael offering to produce *Doctor Who*; a letter he answered politely and dismissively.

Q: How could *Doctor Who*'s fortunes be revived? What would you do?

A: That's a really leading question, isn't it! What I'd do is to go back to basic good storytelling. I think that I'd start with a sort of a traditional Doctor Who, in that I would cast an agreeable personality, of the kind I meant when discussing Pat Troughton and Elisabeth Sladen. I would go for Peter Egan, and certainly do a season with him, to bring back the old image of the Edwardian gent. Then I'd go on from there. I'm not sure, but I might even think of Les Dawson as possibly another Doctor Who in the future. He is not just a North Country comic; he is in fact a very good actor, and splendid in Shakespeare.

Antony Howe and Stephen James Walker

Interview conducted by Antony Howe

INTERVIEW: MALCOLM THORNTON—DESIGNER

Malcolm Thornton was production designer on four Doctor Who *stories, all during the 1980s: 'Logopolis', 'Kinda', 'The Five Doctors' and 'Planet of Fire'. The following interview was conducted by Philip Newman in Malcolm's office at the BBC on 21 August 1995, but was not published back then. It sees print here for the very first time, and has been transcribed and written up by me from the original recording of the interview, which Philip has kindly supplied for this purpose.*

Since the mid-1990s, Malcolm has continued a very successful career in TV design, initially still on staff at the BBC and later as a freelancer. His many credits include Cold Comfort Farm *(BBC 1995), episodes of* Hetty Wainthropp Investigates *(BBC, 1996-1997),* Our Mutual Friend *(BBC, 1998),* Vanity Fair *(BBC, 1998),* Oliver Twist *(ITV, 1999),* Dirty Tricks *(ITV, 2000),* Othello *(BBC, 2001),* Tipping the Velvet *(BBC, 2002),* William and Mary *(ITV, 2003),* The Long Firm *(BBC, 2004),* Fingersmith *(BBC, 2005),* The Family Man *(BBC, 2006),* Viva Blackpool *(BBC, 2006) and* Mrs Ratcliffe's Revolution *(BBC, 2007).*

Q: How did you get started in design? Had you always wanted to be a designer?

A: I lived in Southampton, so I did a foundation course at Southampton Design College, which was a general grounding in design. At that stage, I thought I'd be ending up working in interior design and architecture. I applied to architectural college, got a place at Kingston to study architecture, but failed one part of my maths paper, and as they didn't consider engineering drawing an academic subject, although I'd got an A Level in it, I couldn't take up the place. That rather disillusioned me, so I spent a year doing nothing, really, but sort of just kept on the fringes of design while deciding what to do. I'd always enjoyed watching television – including *Doctor Who*, when I was a lad – and fancied the notion of working in television design, but didn't know where you went to study it, or how you studied it, or who taught it. In my foundation year, I had done a little bit of research and visited a few studios – LWT ran a design department then; in fact, most of the television companies had their own design departments – and had quite liked and been quite intrigued by what I saw of that television design role. It seemed to be a mixture of theatre, exhibition design, interior design, some graphics: it seemed like every facet of design was involved in television design; which is exactly what it's all about, really.

I decided in the end to try for a place at Hornsey College of Art to do what was then a DipAD – it would be a Bachelor of Arts degree now, I suppose – in exhibition design, interior design, which I got. I chose Hornsey because I felt that the way they taught, and the structure of the course, was the most suitable background, as far as I could see, to training in television design. It wasn't a television design course, but it seemed quite closely aligned to it. So I did three years at Hornsey and got my degree. Then at that stage I met a designer called Jim Clay, who is now a film designer but was an assistant here at the BBC up until 1973. I met him just by chance, and he passed my name on to Stephen Money, who was Head of Design here then, and I got an interview for a short contract. I went for the interview, and the BBC offered me the contract. This was three months before my diploma show, but the college released me, because the chance of a job was just too much to pass up, really. The college released me from my last three months, and the BBC released me to do my diploma show, so between the two of them, I was able to finish my course but also to take up the contract.

For the first year at the BBC I was on three- and six-monthly temporary contracts until a staff job as an assistant came up in 1974 or 1975. I got that job, and it felt almost like doing an apprenticeship, because, as I say, there was nowhere else to train in television design. Coming here and learning on the job was the only way to get the background, really. I was an assistant until 1978 or 1979, until I got a permanency as a designer. I don't know that I assisted on any *Doctor Who*s, but certainly I assisted on mainstream drama; mostly naturalistic and some stylised drama. I then moved for a couple of years more into current affairs and light entertainment. That mixture of experience – the variety of periods and styles – gave me a good background for when the *Doctor Who*s came along.

Q: 'Logopolis' was the first one that you did, wasn't it? That was Tom Baker's final story, transmitted at the beginning of 1981.

A: That's right. The action involved a radio telescope, which I think was originally supposed to be Jodrell Bank. We used BBC Radio Caversham as the main location for the receiving station. We built one of the sort of cabins at the end of the pivot point of the telescope and had model shots, with a model that matched the Jodrell Bank telescope.

Q: Did you actually ask to work on *Doctor Who*, or were you simply assigned to it?

A: At that stage, we used to have fairly regular interviews with our bosses and the people who were allocating us, and there was very much a structured career progression. We had managers and senior designers in our group who would watch our progress and then would recommend us for things according to whatever stage they saw our career development as being at. They would say, 'Well, this young designer is right for a *Doctor Who*,' or 'He should be doing some light entertainment,' or whatever. Producers back then were all staff producers, and they would communicate with the departmental managers very carefully, and would have an interest in career progression as well. So 'Logopolis' would have come to me by me being allocated to it, on the recommendation of my management, and then by me being sold to John Nathan-Turner as a new, young designer who'd had training and earlier BBC experience in the sort of work that suited me to being a designer on *Doctor Who*. So it would have been a straight allocation. Once I'd done one, and it seemed to go down quite well, on the subsequent ones that I did, I was asked for by John or by the directors involved; but getting the first one was part of this career development.

Doctor Who was always seen as a highly challenging production for designers, because of the low budget and the high expectation of creative input, the high standards that had been set. The biggest challenge was to try to maintain the 'look' of *Doctor Who* but to push it onwards a bit, really, to get the best value for money out of the budget; to try to be as inventive as possible on the minimal budget. I think the potential was seen in those days for bringing on new designers and using *Doctor Who* as a testing ground. Without it now, there are very few opportunities for young designers to cut their teeth on shows like that, where you could make the odd mistake: you could try out using different materials, or different lighting techniques, and if it didn't quite work, it wasn't the end of the world. If the sets wobbled a bit, it didn't matter that much, really. I mean, one didn't like to see the sets wobble – I think that's a bit of a cliché anyway, although we know what people mean when they say it – but if you couldn't try things out and experiment on *Doctor Who*, where else could you? So getting your first *Doctor Who* was always like a big breakthrough. You might have got a *Z Cars* or a *Dixon of*

45

Dock Green to do, but they were very naturalistic drama; not that challenging. You'd do what you could with them, but it wasn't exactly the most creatively challenging work. But in the 1970s and 1980s, doing a *Doctor Who*, or maybe a redesign of the *Top of the Pops* set, or even the *Tomorrow's World* stock set – these were seen as the plum jobs for new designers, because they expected a high degree of design input.

In those days, it felt like television design led the way rather than reflected things that other people were doing, which sadly tends to be the case now because of what's happened in television in terms of politics and just the type and quantity of programmes that viewers want to watch.

Q: Presumably one of the biggest challenges on 'Logopolis' was to create the 'brain-like' architecture of Logopolis itself, with all the little alcoves and so on. Was that something that came from the script, or something that you thought up from scratch?

A: I think the idea of this planet that resembled a brain was always there, but the biggest problem from my point of view was creating that on the sort of budget that we had. We had to get a sort of amorphous feeling to the streets, and I seem to remember we had a model shot of the surface of the planet, which showed this idea of the brain canals and channels. Just to recreate sections of that in the studio with non-linear, amorphous flattage – in the way that *Doctor Who* did, with a sort of T-form corridor, so you could shoot from every which way – with the sort of budget we had was pretty difficult, really. We had rock falls as the planet was gradually deteriorating and eroding, so we had the problem of having the form of the set being initially intact and then fairly obvious bits of it crumbling away. It was very difficult to reset and do more than one take on those scenes; we had an opportunity to reset little bits, but there were some quite strategic points on the set that would collapse, and there were quite big chunks of flattage that would come down, and certainly resetting those was never an option. But the budget was the biggest problem. I remember originally drawing up a larger ground-plan for that set, and it seemed to me that I was forever having to cut another three feet off, or cut an outcrop back by another two feet. Everything was costed down to almost the last penny in those days.

Although the planet surface is the major set that I remember, there were other sets to do, and they had to have equal attention. I remember we tried a shot looking through a doorway using a photograph to show rows of these monks or whatever sitting at their computer screens, but the perspective wasn't quite right, so the door was shut a bit quicker than you might want! I mean, the shot was there, but in those days, a photographic or painted backing showing some sort of repeated image like that was about the best you could do. The shot wasn't worth the time in post-production to replicate using electronic techniques. The technology we take for granted now existed only in some quite crude form then. If we'd had more time to work out the geometry of that basic sort of theatrical technique, we could have got it working better than it did, but you had to put it in the context of everything else you had to do, and the time just wasn't there.

So in that one story we had model shots, and perspective backings, and collapsing buildings and so on; all the elements of a sort of typical *Doctor Who*!

Q: There was quite a complicated set-up for the sequence of the Doctor falling off the telescope, wasn't there?

A: Yes, that's right. I talked to Tom Baker about this a couple of times. I enjoy making actors work quite hard, really, and Tom was quite responsive to being asked to do certain things. This was his last one, so he was less than enthusiastic generally about putting himself out too much, but we worked out the whole thing of him climbing up the telescope and getting out onto the dish to rearrange the aerial, or whatever the story was, and the Master starting to rotate it to try to throw him off. We built the gantry leading out to the back of the dish from one of the control cabins at the end of the axis – the sort of metallic structure and platform that Tom had to climb out onto from the cabin – and it was a reasonable sort of journey for him, really; he had to work a little bit at it, and we shot it against a green CSO screen so that we could insert the appropriate image behind the set. Again it was a case of using the electronic techniques we had back then and the limited budget and trying to make something of it. We really didn't have much chance to do a lot. I'm sure if I looked back at these episodes now, I would wince at the crude results, but at the time it seemed that we were getting the best that we could; and often we were.

Q: Was there an 'end of an era' feeling in the studio?

A: Yeah, I think there was, really, because Tom was very popular – he was my favourite Doctor, I think, and I enjoyed working on it because of that. As I said, I used to watch *Doctor Who* as a lad, before I went to art college, and to find myself working on it, and working on it with Tom, was great. So, yes, it was quite a poignant moment to see Tom doing his last scene.

Q: Did the director, Peter Grimwade, have much input? Because you also worked with him on your next story, 'Kinda', didn't you?

A: He did, but on *Doctor Who*, and other programmes with science fiction and abstract-type design concepts, the designer does lead an awful lot. The director can't really respond to much until the designer presents some ideas, unless he has a very strong view from the word go of how he wants something to look. There were the stage directions on the page but, certainly the way I work, Peter really couldn't have done much, in terms of thinking about the overall piece from a visual point of view, until I'd reacted to those. When I read a script, I might just visualise one movement of an actor through space. He might be climbing up some stairs, or up a ladder, or whatever, and that one movement will quite often dictate the whole set – as with that scene of Tom Baker on the gantry. I tend to work in a spacially-orientated way, where other designers might work in a different way. So a lot of my sets are dictated by a move, and I have to sell that to the director first; it might not be a move that he has seen, but it's something that he responds to, really. That happened again on 'Planet of Fire', jumping ahead a bit. There was one shot in that of Peter Davison surrounded by flames, with great jets all around him, and that – the angle of him with the flames, and how he got to that position – was an image that came to me very quickly, and sort of dictated the rest of that set, and how he moved from another area into that little cavern space. As I said, I quite enjoy giving actors something to do, and if it works, it makes for good pictures.

Q: 'Kinda' must have been quite a challenge to design, with its planetary setting?

A: Well, it just seemed like the whole thing was set in a jungle, and this had to be done all in the studio. Greenery is about the most difficult type of dressing to control and afford, and yet we wanted to achieve this feeling of a verdant paradise, with jungle clearings and so on. There's a park out the back here with rock pools and waterfalls and things, and we actually went round there and used parts of that as a style for some of the landscape on the planet. We just thought, 'What can we use?' and remembered this ornate little park; not ornamental as such, but with quite an interesting landscape. So we took that as a sort of theme, and I said that it would be nice to have a rock pool and a waterfall of some sort, although it was quite tricky to achieve. We had a glade with strange wind-chimes, which were just vacuum-formed, clear plastic prisms; we wanted them to look almost like glass, but that was all we could afford. We also had to have a base where the explorers lived. I came up with the idea of having a geodesic dome within a tubular steel structure, as if the explorers had been dropped there and built the thing themselves and then lived within this controlled environment. There was also that strange machine that Richard Todd drove around in![25]

Again, from a design point of view, the effect of the jungle, the clearings and the whole pastoral background was hard to achieve on the available budget. Trying to control greenery is difficult, and we needed to have a clear studio floor for the cameras to move across, and for this machine in the story to trundle around on, so the best we could do was to have a few leaves and suchlike on the floor. We had to be constantly going behind or in front of cameras, sprinkling stuff on the floor as they tracked along, and the trailing cables would sweep it all away as they moved. We were forever ordering up more bags of leaves and so on, and that did severely stretch the budget. You can never have enough, really; the sets always look less full on camera than they do to the naked eye. We were in the studio for about three days on one of the recording blocks, and even after the first night we just knew that we didn't have enough greenery by any means, so we had to get more shipped in first thing in the morning and dressed in. It all had to be damped down, because the firemen are very hot on the safety aspect of having flammable material in the studio, so we had to send some of the prop boys in to spray it all down with sprinklers connected to water-bottle backpacks. One of these guys, Bert Havish, was very good at doing bird noises, and he would go off into the jungle and start doing exotic bird calls. It was quite jolly in the mornings to feel that you really were in a tropical jungle! To get the required depth and layers we just had to keep throwing greenery at it, really, and that was very expensive.

I quite enjoy doing greenery sets in some ways, although they're quite difficult, with the landscaping and the trees. We had to have Tegan sitting in a tree in 'Kinda': that tree was reused from a production of A Midsummer Night's Dream, which had been done in a studio next door the previous week. It had some scaffolding inside, so she could sit on the branch and it wouldn't collapse. So that was a bit of Doctor Who scrounging!

Q: Was the studio lighting a factor? I think the jungle might have looked more effective if it had been less brightly-lit.

A: Yes, it's always a problem in video studios. This can almost sound like a cliché, because there's always this argument about video studio lighting compared with film lighting. I think up until fairly recently most video studio lighting was prone to being over-bright. That wasn't necessarily the lighting director's fault; between him and the viewer there were engineers

---

25 Richard Todd played Sanders in the story. The machine in question was the TSS (Total Survival Suit); a device to enable the explorers to traverse the planet's surface while remaining in a safe and sterile environment.

racking the levels up and down, checking their little dials or whatever to determine what was acceptable and what was not from a technical point of view, and of course the sensitivity of the cameras then was not what it is now, and they needed more light to give good pictures. But it was always a battle. I remember we were hanging up camouflage nets, painted gauzes and things; trying anything just to make it darker, and also to lose the voluminous look of the huge studio. You try to storyboard the camera angles as well as you can, but working three or four weeks in advance of the studio on the storyboards and then shooting for real after an outside rehearsal period, it's very difficult to control things. From a design point of view, it can turn into a nightmare, really, if you haven't got all the things you need to do the shots justice.

Q: Did any particular issues arise on the dome set?

A: I was intrigued by the question of what sort of doors people would use in the year 3050, or whenever it was. I wanted to have sound-effect doors, so that you would have an opening or a portal but there would be nothing there to represent the door. People would walk towards it, you would just hear a noise to signify the door opening, and then they would make a deliberate stepping motion through it, but there would be no physical door there. This was an idea that I tried to sell to Peter Grimwade, but he didn't quite grasp the concept of doors that didn't actually exist! In the end, we came to a compromise and had some pairs of concertina-like folding doors. I designed a mechanism so that you only opened one, and the other one opened with it automatically; they were racked on pulleys. We also had a sort of a pastiche on a medieval drawbridge; a ramp thing that dropped down for the travel machine to descend when they wanted to go out into the jungle. The structure of the geodesic dome itself was hired in from a playground equipment manufacturer, and we stretched gauze all over it to make the main living area. There were lots of flexi-pipes inside, as I remember, and boxes.

Q: Were you pleased to be asked to work on the twentieth anniversary story, 'The Five Doctors'?

A: Yes, I was pleased to be asked to work on it, because it was a major milestone for *Doctor Who*. The progression of having watched the series as a boy, then having found myself working on it, and then being asked to contribute on this major anniversary was really very exciting. I seem to remember that I first thought about the budget rather than anything else, because it was a 90-minute special and obviously a very demanding script in terms of the amount of locations and sets and the potential scale of those sets. I think, looking back, it was an opportunity to take techniques we had tried before, on previous stories, and 'recycle' them, to cope with the length and scale of the thing. I seem to remember that we had various crude matte shots and model shots; we were using scenery hoists in vision in the studio; and I had to design some of the sets so that they could be taken out easily at the end of one studio session and then revamped and used again for different things in the next studio session, because we couldn't afford to have new sets completely. There were some continuity resets that we had to do, because certain interiors had been established in earlier stories that I hadn't worked on. The old Time Lord costumes were got out of the stores as well and revamped slightly. The continuity went down even to the level of the typography; I remember talking to John Nathan-Turner about the Time Lord writing or hieroglyphics that we needed to have on the side of the harp, and he said 'Oh, well, if you go and look at such-and-such an episode …' Things like that were different from the requirements of other episodes. This was really the only time that

I had to go back into the design archives to see what other people had done. But I think the major challenge was really just the scale of it, which entailed a lot more project management on my part than a standard story, and again trying to be as economical as we could with the resources. The budget was bigger than for a standard story, but it still wasn't huge for what was being expected of us, and there was still just the two of us – me and my assistant – working on it as an art department.

One thing we had to do on 'The Five Doctors' was to redesign the TARDIS interior, and update it a little bit. So we added sort of chevron shapes to it, and a fourth wall, and redesigned the console – Mike Kelt, the visual effects designer, did the console, and there were elements of decoration around that that were a reflection of the set, really.[26]

Q: Your last story was 'Planet of Fire', directed by Fiona Cumming. Did you go out with the team to the Lanzarote location for that one?

A: Yes, I did. I think that when Fiona talked to John about doing it, it was with Lanzarote in mind, to represent a volcanic planet. We had two recce trips out there – John, Eric Saward, Fiona and I – because although we were always going to use the island, we had to find the specific locations. Fiona knew the island – she'd been there on holiday – and had ideas for where certain scenes could be shot, so we visited those, and they were fine. There was a wonderful high outcrop look-out point that looked across to an adjacent island, and we used that for one of the interiors for Peter Wyngarde's character.[27] Then we just spent a long time out in the lava fields looking for very specific locations, although the authorities would only let us go to certain places; you can't just drive out or walk out wherever you like across the lava fields, they have very strict regulations on access to the place. So we would find somewhere and then see how close to that we could arrange to get, or if there were alternative areas that they could recommend. We tried to use as many aspects of the island as we could that were off the tourist track. Most of the really spectacular bits are tourist spots anyhow. We tried to schedule it and select locations that gave us the best of the island without having to interrupt the whole tourist aspect of it with our filming.

The biggest problem for me then was to create studio interiors that felt consistent with the island locations. We had to design a mould for an underground area, an inner part of the planet, so all the walls had to have a sort of lava finish and be coloured to match the lava flows that we were seeing on location. So we brought back bits of lava and stuff and used those as reference to make vacuum-formed panels that we could then cover the walls with, to suggest that they were of carved lava rock. I mentioned earlier the scene with Peter Davison being thrust into a chamber and threatened by flames. That was an interesting set to do in terms of the colouring and textures. The lava on location was very hard and sharp – you could rip your shoes to pieces walking across it – so to try to create a similar feel in a studio set, with the fire element as well, was quite a different challenge from the ones I'd faced on the previous *Doctor Whos* I'd done.

Another challenge from the design point of view was just working out the logistics of shooting overseas. We took a lightweight replica of the TARDIS with us and set it up on a

26 For further details of Thornton's work on 'The Five Doctors', see the 'Script to Screen' chapter on that story in 'The Handbook: The Unofficial and Unauthorised Guide to the Production of *Doctor Who*' by David J Howe, Stephen James Walker and Mark Stammers (Telos Publishing, 2005).
27 Wyngarde played Timanov in the story.

beach – which just happened to be a naturist beach, so the crowd control aspect was quite interesting! But the funniest thing was that when we came back to Gatwick Airport, this TARDIS for some reason wasn't treated as a piece of freight but came out, separated into its component panels, on the luggage carousel. The reaction of people at Gatwick Airport at 10 o'clock at night or whatever, seeing the bits of this police box coming out on the luggage carousel, was very amusing. Another funny story is that when we were on location shooting the scene where Peri gets into trouble in the water and yells for help, at one stage a nude German swimmer appeared around the headland and obviously thought that she was really in trouble – he hadn't realised that we were filming, because he was too far away – and we had to stop shooting while somebody explained to him in German that this was actually not a real-life rescue! It was quite fun to see his embarrassment when he realised what was happening.

Q: What sort of work did you go on to after that last *Doctor Who*?

A: I moved more into mainstream one-off drama and film, which I do now quite a lot. I've done a few other drama series since. I did one called *Star Cops* not long after *Doctor Who*. It was a ten-part science fiction series; I designed five and Dick Coles designed the other five.[28] It was quite challenging from a design point of view. There was also a bit of a design concept conflict between Dick and me. I had originally been going to start the series off, but the producer felt I think that I wasn't experienced enough at that stage to set the style of the series and do the stock sets, although he was happy for me to follow on once things had been established. The director of the episodes I designed was Graeme Harper, who also did some *Doctor Whos*. He was a terrific director to work for from a design point of view, and we got on very well and would bounce ideas off each other. We both felt that we should have been starting it off, and although we weren't, we were both very committed to what we felt was the right look for the series; and that was quite a realistic look, because it was set only a few years into the future.[29] We felt that, although the premise was that this was an era when there was a need for some sort of space police force, the technology ought still to be quite recognisable from the viewer's perspective, rather than too futuristic. I also wanted my interiors to have layers of moon dust lying around – dust that had got into the ventilation systems – and that sort of thing. I felt that if people were living in space or on the moon in 50 years' time, their tunics wouldn't all be neatly pressed and so on. But Dick and the other director[30] felt that it ought to be moved on further and be more pristine. So when I saw the final thing – and I suppose you could almost expect this – it felt visually a mixture of styles.

Stephen James Walker

Interview conducted by Philip Newman

---

28 One episode of this series was ultimately abandoned due to industrial action at the BBC, so only nine were transmitted; Thornton was the designer on the fourth, fifth, sixth and ninth of the transmitted episodes, as well on the abandoned tenth.
29 The series was set in the year 2027.
30 Christopher Baker.

INTERVIEW: PETER DAVISON-DOCTOR

Peter Davison has had a long and successful acting career, mainly in television, beginning with supporting parts in series such as The Tomorrow People *(1975) and* Love for Lydia *(1977) and coming right up to date with starring roles in shows including* The Last Detective *(2003-) and* The Complete Guide to Parenting *(2006), with many other notable credits in between. To many members of the general viewing public, he will probably be best remembered as vet Tristan Farnon in* All Creatures Great and Small *(1978-1990), but to Doctor Who fans, he will forever be known as the man who portrayed the fifth incarnation of their favourite Time Lord – a role he continues to play, in audio CD dramas for Big Finish.*

In 1983, shortly after completing work on the twentieth anniversary special 'The Five Doctors' and prior to recording his final TV season as the Doctor, Peter visited Australia with his then wife, American-born actress Sandra Dickinson, on a promotional book-signing tour arranged by the Myer department store chain. As will be apparent from the opening paragraph of the interview below, which was conducted by Stephen Collins on the Brisbane stop of the tour, many Australian fans were horrified by the way Peter and his wife were treated by their Myer hosts, as they were subjected to an extremely hectic and demanding schedule with very little time allowed for rest and relaxation in between engagements. Peter remained characteristically good-humoured throughout, however, and left those fans who met him with a very favourable impression indeed. Although this interview naturally does not cover Peter's last few stories as the Doctor, it remains one of the most interesting, detailed and candid he has ever given about his time in Doctor Who. *It originally appeared in Issue 30/31 of* Zerinza, *the fanzine of the Australasian Doctor Who Fan Club, and is reproduced here with thanks both to Stephen Collins and to Antony Howe, the Club's then President and publisher.*

Peter Davison is one of those rare people who really deserves the description charismatic. Indefatigable and utterly charming, he endured his poorly organised and inhumanly demanding tour of Australia with gentle smiles, cheery humour and a kindly interest in the needs of his audiences. He was joined in this Herculean effort by his delightful wife, actress Sandra Dickinson, a gentle and beautiful woman who displayed the same virtues just as effortlessly.

Arriving in Sydney at 6.00 am on 7 April 1983, Peter was not only weary from the arduous journey, but also from the gruelling experience of the BBC's *Doctor Who* twentieth anniversary celebration event at Longleat – an event that had been attended by some 70,000 devoted fans replete with books, photos and magazines all ready for autographing. And yet, he was neither irritable nor resentful of the demands that were being placed upon him. Having spent a scant hour recuperating at Sydney airport, Peter was whisked to Brisbane, where he was shunted from one radio station to another until three interviews had been recorded, and then bundled off to his hotel where the Myer organisers 'graciously' allowed him an entire hour of rest before he was thrown into a large press conference attended by almost every working journalist in Brisbane – along with a Dalek, provided by local fan James Collins.

A mass press conference like this is something that has to be seen to be believed. Mobs of journalists – apparently starving, if the way these ones shovelled away the free food laid on by Myer is any indication! – crowd around the hapless celebrity and then proceed to fight to see who gets the first interview. What is the most amazing thing is that the poor celebrity is required to answer the same mindless set of questions over and over again as each media representative thrusts his or her microphone or camera forward. There is no joint asking of questions, no communal inquiry, as is common with political press conferences. Each reporter delivers his or her barrage of questions, checks the recording, whether audio or video (or both), and then retires to allow another story-hungry newshound the chance to demand answers to virtually the same set of dreary questions.

Throughout it all, our fifth Doctor remained calm and refreshingly charming, despite the fact that he was visibly wilting. The heat, the pressure and the after-effects of the long journey were all taking their toll. Yet the smiles were genuine, the manner sincere and the attitude friendly and relaxed. He seemed quite pleased to meet me and my companion, possibly because neither of us was attempting to stick any kind of recording apparatus anywhere near him, but probably because he is the sort of man who likes meeting and talking with people, whether they are his fans or not. An unnecessarily long photo session followed the press conference. One very 'intelligent' specimen repeatedly attempted to make Peter pose with an especially unattractive made-in-Korea stuffed koala, and could not understand why Peter's expression was wry instead of soulful.

The meet-the-press session finished, the meet-the-fans programme commenced, and Peter was whisked away from his hotel, having been granted the boon of ten minutes to effect a change of costume, to the clamour and throng of his first autographing. During the rest of that day and the next, he coped with six book-signing sessions, one radio and two television interviews and a long cocktail party! On the Friday night, he still smiled and radiated goodwill. A cancelled television programme ensured the frazzled man an early night, but the next morning it was all systems go once again as Peter's limousine zipped off in search of Myer stores nestling on the border between New South Wales and Queensland. Two more autograph queues were faced, and though the Tweed Heads[31] store turned out to be a bit of a wash-out, another couple of hundred attentive fans were treated to the Davison touch of class. The mass of signings finally complete, Peter's chauffeur began a helter-skelter dash to the Brisbane airport, where Peter was scheduled to catch a flight to Sydney. And there the entire ghastly process was due to be repeated ...

During his brief but hectic stay in Brisbane, a small group of dedicated fans provided the visiting Doctor with a costumed entourage. Of his own volition, Peter developed a bond; he remembered names, chatted openly, spilled secrets and, most importantly, was in no way condescending. He treated us as equals. He was the quintessence of sincerity. And this was so even though those responsible for his presence in our country insisted on treating him like a commodity, a parcel of expensive goods, a piece of meat. He rose above all that to display the qualities that made him a perfect Doctor Who.

Consequently I was only partly daunted when the prospect of interviewing Peter and his actress-wife Sandra Dickenson finally became reality. The Myer warders had granted me two hours of their stars' 'free' time. Thankfully, Peter did not begrudge the time. In fact, he seemed quite happy to chat, free from the rigours of autographing, at least temporarily anyway. Perhaps the most admirable trait Peter Davison displayed while on tour was his easy ability to speak with candour and clarity on a wide range of subjects. Our talk together was made all the more worthwhile because of this ability.

He described his entry into the entertainment industry with a twinkle in his eye that

31 A town in New South Wales.

betrayed his passion for his work. 'I became involved in acting at school in nothing more than school plays. Then I joined an amateur dramatics society and from there took a chance of applying to a drama school, simply because I didn't do very well with exams – I like to think that was because I didn't try, but I don't know ... At any rate, because I got the equivalent of only one pass, I was able to do what I wanted to do rather than be directed towards a certain profession. So, I applied to drama school and, very fortunately, got into the Central School of Speech and Drama, where I was for three years. After that, I worked for three years in different repertory companies around the country, and then I had a year and a half out of work.' He paused for a moment, and then, with a new edge of wistfulness in his voice, continued, 'Every actor has to have a year and a half out of work. It teaches him humility – I think. After that I was very, very lucky in that I got two very big television parts following each other.

'The first was a thing called *Love for Lydia*, which I'm not sure has come out here yet.' I indicated that it hadn't been screened in Australia to my knowledge, and he grunted annoyance, saying that he had been quite pleased with it. He then explained that the part of Tristan Farnon in *All Creatures Great and Small* had been his second big break. 'Playing Tristan was a very interesting time for me. I know it's been said to me, so it's obviously appeared in print somewhere, that I think Tristan was the nearest I've ever played to myself; but when I first got the part, I thought I was totally unsuitable for it. But there again, I can't think of a part that I've ever been offered or accepted that I haven't thought I've been really totally unsuitable for – including Doctor Who! It's just that I was really very shy and I couldn't string two words together in a social situation. So, in a way, I grew like Tristan, I suppose. Not that I went around playing practical jokes on everyone; I just think that it brought me out of myself a bit.'

I asked Peter what it was like working with Robert Hardy and Christopher Timothy on *All Creatures Great and Small*. 'Well, Robert Hardy particularly was a marvellous help to me, because he took me under his wing. I was what the BBC calls a "newcomer", even though I had done a television series before that. I was still a BBC newcomer! You can be a BBC newcomer at any age up to about 85, really. But anyway, that's what I was, and Robert Hardy – who was, of course, vastly experienced – took me under his wing, and he really almost insisted that the parts of Tristan and Siegfried were written up together, because he felt it was a good relationship. It also helped – it sounds a terrible thing to say – but it helped my role that Christopher Timothy walked in front of a car one Christmas and broke his leg. Because of that, he couldn't move around on the set at all for a time. I don't know how many people knew that over here, but there were whole scenes where he did nothing other than stand and then limp out of shot while someone else spoke. He couldn't do anything. He couldn't move anywhere for about three months, and that meant that a lot of scenes that should have been Christopher Timothy and Robert Hardy became Robert Hardy and me. So that built the character of Tristan up and did me a lot of good. Poor old Chris.'

Earlier in our discussions, Peter had told me that almost as soon as he returned to England, he would begin work on *All Things Bright and Beautiful*, a 90-minute Christmas special featuring the entire *All Creatures Great and Small* team. This, he explained, was the reason why his hair was parted on the opposite side to the way he wore it in *Doctor Who*. 'I have to part it this way so that when it is cut short for Tristan it will sit right.' He went on to speak of the content of the special. 'It's set just after the war. The last episode we recorded, three years ago now, was us all going off to war, and this is just about when we come back and how we all then go our own different ways.'

Sandra Dickinson, Peter's wife, is well known for her association with Douglas Adams's *The Hitchhiker's Guide to the Galaxy*, but most people are unaware that she was actually the *second* member of their family to be approached to take a role in the television version of the successful radio series.[32] As Sandra put it, 'Peter was phoned up by his agent for an availability check for *Hitchhikers*. Peter wasn't free, because he was doing *All Creatures*, and then the next thing we knew, I had an availability check! So I guess that they thought if they couldn't get him, they'd get me ... And he would've looked so cute in that red outfit!'

Ignoring Sandra's joke, Peter continued the tale. 'I was disappointed not to have been in it, because I would have loved to have done it. At the same time, I think it would have been a mistake to replace Simon Jones – because that was the role the availability check was for, Arthur Dent. It's the rather foolish idea that when you do a television version of something from the radio, if you have a leading man who is perfectly good but who hasn't been seen much on television, then you replace him with someone who is well known. It would have been a mistake to get another actor to do it, especially as Douglas Adams wanted Simon Jones. But, even so, I was disappointed, because I would have liked to have been in it.'

I mentioned that I had enjoyed Peter's cameo in the series as the Dish of the Day. Immediately, Sandra became animated. 'What happened was that we were in rehearsal one day, and the producer said, "Oh, who can we get to play Dish of the Day?" And I said "What about Peter?" Because he'd just been in the vet thing, and I thought, anything to get him into *Hitchhikers* and keep him happy! Anyway, the producer thought it was a wonderful idea, and Peter thought it was a wonderful idea – I sort of talked it up and said it was a really great vignette! – and it worked out very well. I think it's Douglas's favourite scene in the whole series.'

I asked Peter if the costume had been difficult for him, and the twinge he gave said it all. 'What it involved was going down to the Visual Effects Department and having a bucket of dental plaster poured over my head. They let me have a straw in my mouth so that I could breathe! This plaster gives them an actual "face" to work with, so they went away and made the model around it. When it came to the actual day of recording, it took forever, hours and hours to get the thing on me – they filled in round the eyes, and round the mouth. After I got into it, the scene took two minutes to do ... Didn't seem really worth it, somehow. And the worst thing is that people either don't believe it's my voice but believe it's me in the costume, or they don't believe it's me but think it's my voice! It's the strangest feeling ...'

I remarked that it was not hard to believe that people had doubted it was Peter's voice, because it was so convincingly unlike how he usually speaks. Smiling generously, he told me: 'I didn't know what voice to use initially, but we had an actor, David Prowse, who speaks with a wonderful West Country accent – he was in the same episode, playing Hot Black Desiato's bodyguard – and suddenly I latched onto this wonderful sound.' With a raising of his eyebrows, Peter effortlessly went into his Dish of the Day voice and reprised a few lines of dialogue. The effect was made all the more disconcerting for me because he was doing this dressed as the Doctor! Visions of a West Country Time Lord have troubled me fleetingly ever since ...

Peter spoke only briefly about his other major television appearances. He was fairly lukewarm in his comments about *Holding the Fort*, and I got the impression he considered it to have been not the best possible vehicle he could have chosen for continued TV exposure,

---

32 Dickinson played the part of Trillian in the TV series.

55

although he was heartened to hear that the series had done fairly well on Brisbane's Channel Seven. By contrast, he was obviously enthusiastic about his other comedy, *Sink or Swim*, and explained that that was probably because the role he played, the bespectacled not-so-nice elder brother, was such a change for him that it had been a joy to do.

Sandra reminded me that Peter was one of the youngest celebrities ever to be honoured on *This is Your Life*, and I asked Peter how he had been 'set up' for this programme. 'It was really quite devious and took me completely by surprise,' he admitted. 'I had completed my first season of *Doctor Who*, and they told me they needed to do a bit of extra filming for a promotion for the show, in Australia no less. So I went along, and I must admit that I did think it was a bit strange that Sandra was so keen to get me out of the door, as she was not normally so worried about my being on time. Little did I know! I turned up for the filming, and never twigged. And they had me come out of the TARDIS, followed by Sarah Sutton and Janet Fielding, and then Matthew Waterhouse came out, and even then I didn't realise. Finally, Anthony Ainley came out too, and I was just about to say "What's going on?" when up came Eamonn Andrews, and that was that.'

Peter went on to recall that most of the cast of *All Creatures Great and Small* had come along to share memories, and Beryl Reid, who had guested in 'Earthshock', had also been there. Producer John Nathan-Turner and other members of the *Doctor Who* team had also been there.

Mention of John Nathan-Turner in the context of *This is Your Life* reminded me that Peter had first met his *Doctor Who* producer behind the scenes of *All Creatures Great and Small*. 'Yes, that's right. He was what is called a PUM – a production unit manager – on *All Creatures*, which basically meant that he held the purse strings. He told people what they could and couldn't do with the money available. And then he left to be PUM on *Doctor Who*, so he wasn't on the last season of *All Creatures*. He became producer of *Doctor Who* some months later. And I would say I hadn't really spoken to him for about a year when he rang me up one Saturday night and told me that Tom Baker was leaving *Doctor Who*, which I didn't know, and I didn't know why he was telling me that. And then he went on to say, "How do you feel about being the next Doctor?" Well, there was this sort of stunned silence. I didn't know what to say. So I told him to ring me the next night. So I spent 24 hours thinking about it and also asking close friends, or people whose opinion I respected, what I should do. Then he rang me back, and I still really hadn't made any sort of decision, so he asked me to lunch the following week to discuss it.

'So we had lunch the next week, and he got me drunk, and I think about a week after that lunch, I said yes. The reason I delayed was not that it wasn't a great chance, but I did feel that it was a fairly extraordinary thing to be offered to me.' I asked Peter why he had thought that and, after taking a moment to muster his thoughts, he elaborated. 'Well, I felt, as I am sure a lot of other people felt initially and may well still be thinking, that I was fairly young for the part. The first Doctor was, sort of, old ...'

With a gleam in her eye, Sandra interrupted, 'In his prime, dear, in his prime!'

'He was a grandfather figure, let me put it like that,' continued Peter, 'and subsequent Doctors virtually got younger, and it just took me about two weeks to come to terms with it. I did come to terms with it, and I could then imagine myself doing it, and that was really the turning point.

'It also frightened me a bit, I'll admit that. Because *Doctor Who* is a very big institution in Britain. I decided finally when I sat down and I thought, "Well, if I say no to this one, then it's a great opportunity missed." Also, no-one knew that I'd been offered it, so if I'd said no and they'd got someone else, I'd have had to keep silent for the rest of my life that I'd been offered *Doctor Who* and turned it down. And I thought I couldn't bear the thought of someone else doing it. So, I said yes. And I'm very glad I did.'

Sandra interjected again, this time her tone full of pride rather than humour. 'On the night it was announced on the *Nine O'Clock News* in England, Ronald Reagan was revealed to be the new President of the United States ... and Peter got top billing!' Peter blushed....

Deciding that Peter needed a chance to recover, I asked Sandra what her reaction had been to the offer – knowing full well that she had previously been reported as having said that he could take the part as long as she was cast as his companion! 'I didn't quite know what was happening. There was this stunned silence, as Peter has said, and I said "What?" Peter put his hand over the receiver and asked what I thought about the idea of him being the new Doctor, and I said "Oh, goody-goody!"'

'No, you've missed out the most important bit of what you said,' teased Peter, obviously determined to exact revenge. 'He knows what you said, so you might as well admit it!'

'I will never admit to saying that!' retorted Sandra. 'Vicious rumours spread about me!'

Peter smiled hugely. 'I think she said it in a moment of blind panic.'

Trying to be serious for a moment, I asked Sandra if she would seriously consider playing an American companion should the opportunity arise. 'Would you like me to be frank about this?' she said, almost earnestly. I nodded. 'I think the charm of *Doctor Who* is in its Englishness, so from that point of view, I think not. It's a really English programme, real neat, and I think if somebody did touch it by making it not English, then it wouldn't be quite as right as it should be. That's how I'd feel, I suppose.'

Returning to the question of the big offer, I asked Peter if he had been daunted by the prospect of inheriting Tom Baker's well-worn shoes. 'Oh, yes. I mean, that was part of it, you see. It doesn't hit you until you sit down and try to rationalise it. Tom had done it for seven years, and that, I figured, meant that no child under the age of ten – in Britain at least, because there aren't the sort of repeats there that there are in Australia – would have ever known a Doctor other than Tom. That was one factor. And because he was so identified with the role, you tended to forget about the other ones – even though I had watched *Doctor Who* from the age of 12. It wasn't until I sat down and thought that William Hartnell had played it for three years, Patrick Troughton for three years and Jon Pertwee for five, that I saw myself in that context and was able to rationalise it. But it certainly did worry me, yes.'

I wondered if Peter had ever met Tom Baker, apart from when he recorded the final shots of *Logopolis*. 'I'll tell you about the two times I've met Tom. The first was just after I'd started filming. It was in the bar at the BBC and he'd either just got married or just got engaged to Lalla Ward, I'm not quite sure which. I went into the bar, and there he was with Lalla. Lalla had been at drama school with me – she had been in the year above – and I was really amazed to see her. She gave me a little kiss on the cheek, and due to a combination of that and the fact that the BBC bar is awfully noisy, I couldn't hear the one piece of advice Tom gave me about *Doctor Who*! It was one of those times when someone says something to you, and you know that what they've said doesn't require an answer, so you say "Oh, right," and nod. Just by reading lips, I think he said "Enjoy yourself," but I didn't hear it. The other time I met him was at a Douglas Adams party in Islington, and he served the drinks all night. He just stayed behind the bar and served champagne. It's his new-found role.'

I next asked Peter if, once he had accepted the role, he had sat down with John Nathan-

Turner and discussed the way he would approach it. 'No, there was never any talk really about characterisation. Because when you're cast as Doctor Who, that's the decision the producer makes about the characterisation.'

Had any of the scripts for Peter's debut season already been commissioned in advance of him being cast as the Doctor? 'They had all been commissioned, and some drafts were in, written on the assumption that it would still be Tom as the Doctor. In fact, I think the whole first season was already in draft form, and I am absolutely certain that the first three stories were written for Tom. But that didn't matter materially. In fact, I quite liked that, as I didn't want the scriptwriters to make any prejudgements about the way I was going to play the role. I evolved the character as I went along. I asked John if I could have some tapes of the old Doctors, so he got them, and I sat down and I watched. I wanted to take elements from their characterisations, especially the first two, because they were the ones I'd watched the most as a viewer. Also, I felt there would be a big Tom Baker "lag" anyway, so I would be on dangerous ground if I tried to take anything from Tom's Doctor. So I really concentrated on the first two. The gruffness and slight bad-temperedness that I wanted to get from William Hartnell fitted very well with the character of Tegan. I was able to give her a hard time! And Patrick Troughton had a certain vulnerability, a certain quizzical attitude that I liked. I wanted to give the impression that you could never be quite certain if the Doctor was doing the right thing. And there was the compassionate side.'

I wondered if Peter had found it difficult to come into Doctor Who when there were already three established regulars by the time he joined, or four if one includes Anthony Ainley. 'There was fairly instant acceptance from the companions, really. Except for Matthew Waterhouse, who is a very nice chap, but he does say some of the most ... not tactless things, but he kept saying things like, "Oh, Tom used to do this" and "Tom used to do that". Eventually I felt like going ...' Peter proceeded to do a rather vivid mime of boxing Matthew Waterhouse around the ears. Sandra giggled at the thought; for that matter, so did I! 'Of course, he didn't mean it the way it came out. Something similar happened when we had Richard Todd playing Sanders in Kinda. Richard is a very well-known British film star of the '50s and early '60s. And one time Matthew apparently took him aside and tried to explain to him how to act on television and where the cameras would be, that sort of thing.' This time Peter joined in our giggling. 'But that was all, really. You have a slight – I'll rephrase that – an enormous inferiority complex when you follow somebody who has done Doctor Who for seven years, but apart from that, I had no real problems.'

In all innocence, I inquired if Peter liked the costume he wore as the Doctor. 'You think this is bad?' he asked, indicating the familiar tailored cricket outfit that was sitting somewhat uncomfortably on him in the Australian heat. 'You ought to have seen the polo outfit!' Enjoying my discomfort, he elaborated. 'There was endless talk about the costume, absolutely endless. And at one point, they wanted me to walk around in a polo outfit – boots, jodhpurs, striped shirt, a riding crop, and all sorts of hats ... Although the cricket context was my suggestion, this isn't what I would've chosen. I would have preferred a slightly more off-the-peg kind of look. But John wanted a designed look. I would've preferred the Doctor to have gone into the TARDIS wardrobe and picked out an ordinary black frock coat and a cricket jumper. I wanted a frock coat, because it seemed to me that was a Doctor Who "thing". I know Jon, and sometimes Tom, had a short jacket, but I felt the image of the Doctor was slightly more "frock-coatish". So, I would have preferred a black frock-coat, white cricket jumper, cream cricket trousers and my shoes. Tom had the question-marks on his lapels, and that's apparently the reason I was given them.'

Before I could ask my next question, Peter read my mind. 'And please don't ask me what the significance of the celery is, because I don't know. John decided that the costume needed something on the lapel, and he came to me one morning, a couple of days before we started filming, and he said to me that he had a great idea for what I should wear on my lapel. I said "Yes", and he said, "A stick of celery". I said "Oh". He's promised to explain it at some point. I'm looking forward to it as eagerly as I am sure you are!'

I pressed the point by asking if he could have vetoed the celery, if he had wanted to. 'It's a difficult thing, really. I've a certain amount of influence in *Doctor Who*, but no real power, and all I can do is suggest things. There are no arguments about things I don't agree with, but there are discussions. If I don't think something is right, I say "Why don't we change it?" But it's really up to John, who is producer.'

The obvious implication was not lost on me, but I persevered by asking exactly how much control John Nathan-Turner exercised over the production. Did he supervise everything from start to finish? The scripts, the costumes, the design? Peter's reply was immediate. 'Absolutely! He's really very, very good, because, unlike some producers, he's there all the time. He's at every day's filming that there is, every studio recording that there is – he takes a hand in everything. That's the way he wants to operate, as total overlord of everything. His dedication to the series cannot be denied.'

Given this high degree of control by John Nathan-Turner, I wondered if this meant that there had been a corresponding tightening up of on-the-set discipline. Did Peter and his fellow regulars indulge in the same kind of practical jokes that had, by all accounts, occurred during the Pertwee and Baker periods? 'Not really. Enough things happen without practical jokes being played. The problem with *Doctor Who* is that once you get in the studio, you are working under such a tight schedule to get the thing finished at all that you are in fear of your life if you waste any time. That's the unfortunate truth of it. In other things I have done, that probably hasn't been there, and practical jokes are played. But with *Doctor Who*, you are under such pressure that you don't try anything.'

All this sounded quite draconian, and a far cry from Tom Baker's description of recording during his era being 'such fun'. I asked Peter to elaborate on the show's recording pattern. 'Well, it's not generally recorded sequentially. "Castrovalva" is the only story I have done that was recorded sequentially, and that was because the first two episodes took place entirely in the TARDIS and the last two episodes took place either on the way to Castrovalva or in Castrovalva itself. This was quite exceptional for *Doctor Who* – it is not at all unusual to start with the last scene and work from there.'

Bearing this in mind, I inquired how rehearsals were carried out. How did the actors establish the continuity needed to convey the storyline, given the discontinuity of the recording? 'This is up to the director,' Peter said, matter-of-factly. 'Some directors have the theory that it's best to rehearse the story in recording order. But normally we block our moves in story order first time through, and that rehearsal lets you know what the story's about and compensates a bit for recording out of order. However, that doesn't work, because you don't record the whole thing together. We have two recording sessions of three days each for a four part story. In the first you record all the scenes in certain sets from two episodes, and in the second you record the remaining scenes from the same episodes on the other sets. So, even though you rehearse in story order to begin with, the story still doesn't make sense, because you're missing great chunks out of it. Even though we record in two sessions, we don't record two episodes per session; we record the equivalent of two episodes, so it could be ten minutes from the beginning, large sections of the middle and some before the end, and so on.'

I asked how long they took rehearsing for each recording session, and was a bit surprised to learn that the answer was a mere ten days. This meant it took about a month to record a four part story. But how far in advance of each recording session were the cast provided with the scripts?

'It varies enormously, really. If the script comes in and is liked by the production team and doesn't require too many rewrites, we get it a fair way ahead. If it comes in and is not liked and needs a lot of rewriting, we get it a bit later on. It sometimes happens that a script comes in and then is either completely changed or re-commissioned or whatever, and we are lucky to get it for the day of the read-through! I've rarely had time to read a script ahead of time anyway, even if I've got it a month before we do it. We're usually concentrating so much on the one we're doing that we don't read new scripts until we actually have to read them.'

This all seemed a bit depressing, so in an attempt to change the mood, I asked Peter what his feelings were about the Daleks. 'I'm in two minds about Daleks,' he said. 'I would be disappointed not to do a Dalek story, but I do think they have to be handled very carefully, because Daleks are in a slightly precarious position. Although in Britain they are the most popular and best known *Doctor Who* monster, they are, I feel, a bit more inhibited than, let us say, the Cybermen, for various reasons we won't go into here.' Pity, thought I. 'But, at the same time, I would be very disappointed not to do a Dalek story. I don't think they have had their day, and I do envisage my doing a Dalek story.' Extending the topic naturally, I quizzed Peter about his, and Nathan-Turner's, attitude to the reappearance of old enemies. 'Well, "Earthshock" was my favourite story from my first season, and one of the reasons for this was that it gave me the first "old enemy" I'd faced, apart from the Master. I think old enemies are good. I think that possibly in my second season there weren't quite enough really, but that was not the fault of anybody except the people behind the standard BBC strike that seems to come once a year, usually at Christmas time for some reason. Anyway, we were four episodes short, and they would have featured old enemies.[33] I think it's nice to have old enemies back.' And so say all of us.

I next turned to the subject of the Doctor's companions. Had it been planned from the start of the season that Adric would be killed off in 'Earthshock'? Peter smiled broadly. 'To my knowledge, the idea evolved as the season progressed. John may have had plans to blow him up right from the beginning, but I don't know. I think he was going to get rid of one of them by the end of the season, and he didn't know which.' Some indefinable note crept into Peter's voice, and I was sure there was more to the story, and equally sure I shouldn't press the point. Turning to safer ground, I inquired if Matthew Waterhouse and Sarah Sutton had left the series of their own volition, or if they had gone unwillingly.

'I would say neither of them went willingly,' responded Peter, 'but neither really went screaming or shouting either. I don't know whether the problem with Matthew was that he didn't want to leave or that he didn't want his character to get killed off. I said to him, and I think it's right, that if he was going to leave, then being killed off was quite a good way to go. I know it precludes you from coming back, but I do think it was quite a good thing to blow a companion up. It's something that will not be forgotten. You don't forget a companion who

---

33 The story cancelled due to strike action was to have featured the Daleks, and was eventually reworked as 'Resurrection of the Daleks' the following year.

was blown up! A lot of companions have left and *not* been blown up. Also, it actually makes the companions more important, adds a bit of depth to them, because it means they are vulnerable, they can be killed off. The thing with *Doctor Who* and continuing characters like the Doctor and his companions is that, although you have cliff-hangers and their lives are always in danger, if you know nothing will happen to them, then something is lost. I know that you know nothing will ever happen to the Doctor, apart from the odd regeneration or four, but the fact that it's a possibility a companion could die, I think it adds to it. And what a way to go, as well, saving the Earth like that. Or trying to, anyway. It was an heroic effort.'

Resisting the temptation to comment on the demise of Adric, I turned to the topic of Tegan Jovanka, the Doctor's first Australian companion. Within seconds, Peter was denying responsibility for her name. 'Nothing to do with me,' he stated firmly, and then the familiar friendly grin cracked his features. 'I don't know whether John thought it was a common Australian name or what. I've no idea at all. He likes interesting names, and you can't deny that Tegan Jovanka is an interesting name…' I refrained from commenting that 'interesting' was but one of many appropriate adjectives and instead asked Peter how much of a say Janet Fielding had over the dialogue Tegan uttered, thinking in particular of her 'Rabbits!' expletive and her easy rendering of 35,000 year old Aboriginal in 'Four To Doomsday'. Laughing heartily, Peter replied:

'Well now, I do remember "Rabbits!" actually. It was something even sillier before that, and there was a problem with the exclamation. So they said to her, "Come up with something Australian", and she said it was very difficult to come up with an Australian expression that wasn't obscene! But, taking the ground from under her feet, I think "Rabbits" was the best she could come up with, and I don't think she was very happy with it. And the Aboriginal thing, I can't remember her saying anything about it, but it's difficult to remember. The Aboriginal part was written in and she was meant to figure out what he was saying – I'm trying to get out of this the best way I can! I agree the line "I am an Australian" is a bit silly on reflection. Maybe she'd been in England too long, I don't know.'

Deciding it was best to let sleeping Daleks lie, I asked Peter if the Tegan voice was Janet's normal speaking voice. 'No, no, no, it's not. She says she's forgotten how to speak with an Australian accent. She speaks better than I do. And she keeps reminding me, she does!'

There remained only Nyssa and Turlough to discuss. I told Peter that Nyssa had been voted most popular companion in a recent Australian fan survey and asked him if he thought her character was meant to be the heart of the series. He scratched his chin for a moment and seemed to be pondering his answer more than usual. 'I don't know whether I should be frank about this or not, really. It might not be expedient to say too much about this. Let me say this. The idea was not to keep Sarah's part on beyond about the first story of my first season. Sarah's was meant to be the first character to go, and she was meant to go fairly early. And this is the influence I have had on *Doctor Who*. This is the one thing. I managed to keep her on for as long as possible, and that's the only thing I can claim. John thought that Janet was meant to be the companion. However, I did feel, and still do, that a companion has to be "sympathetic", and I thought that Sarah's part was the most sympathetic that there was in the TARDIS at that time. So I said that I didn't mind who he got rid of, as long as it wasn't Sarah. Oh dear, I'm really putting my foot in it here!' I nodded, and he smiled. 'No, I agree with your survey. The character of Nyssa has been my favourite *Doctor Who* companion, and I felt that it was a character not so much underplayed as eclipsed a bit by Tegan and to a certain extent by Adric. I would say this too – and if what you have told me about your survey is right, then it seems to be true. It's a popular misconception that having an Australian companion makes the series more popular in Australia. I think that is why an Australian is in the series.'

Suddenly he leaned forward, his eyes glinted and he became by far the most serious I had seen him. A new note of vehemence coloured his voice, and as he spoke, I was reminded of Sandra's comments on the possibility of an American companion. 'I would ask you, and anyone else who agrees, to write to John Nathan-Turner and tell him that Nyssa was the most popular companion. Not because of Janet – there's nothing wrong with Janet's character – but I just wish you would tell him that Sarah's was the most popular. Will you?' Without hesitation I agreed – and I trust that others will follow Peter's wishes ...

Turlough was Peter's fourth companion, and I asked him what he thought of that character as a successor to Adric. 'They are so completely different,' he mused. 'I suppose potentially the character of Turlough is very different from any other companion ever. He starts out being not awfully nice. So, potentially, the Turlough character is probably more interesting.'

Side-tracking for a moment, I wondered if Peter regretted not having worked with K-9. 'Well, it wasn't my decision to get rid of K-9; he was gone when I started. But I don't regret him going, really. I wish him all the best. There was a pilot, *K-9 and Company*, which didn't do well enough to be made into a series, unfortunately. But the problem with K-9 was that he did solve too many problems, and in the end he had to be disabled all the time so he couldn't solve all the problems before the end of the first episode! So it got a bit silly, and they got a bit tired of writing K-9 in and out of the series. That's the story I was given for K-9's end.'

Returning to the topic of Peter's female companions, I asked him what the intention had been behind the rather odd decision to leave Tegan stranded at the end of "Time-Flight" only to pick her up again in the next story. 'There was never any doubt about her returning. The idea of it was to provide the series with a cliff-hanger. But, as I mentioned at the time, no-one seemed to notice she'd gone until she reappeared! The idea was that the Doctor didn't realise she wasn't in the TARDIS when he left at the end of "Time-Flight". Because the authorities at Heathrow were going to ask too many questions, he nipped inside and pressed the button before anyone realised that Tegan wasn't inside, and of course once you've done that in the TARDIS, the possibility of ever getting back to the same place inside ten seasons is fairly remote, so that was all right. I did say that maybe we ought to mention Tegan at the beginning of the next season, but you'll find there is no mention of her until the Doctor finds out where she is. And the reason for that is that the Doctor wasn't allowed to say anything that would pre-empt her return.'

I mentioned that the one discernible advantage of Tegan's abandonment seemed to be that she was allowed to change out of her air hostess attire. 'I'll tell you what happened there, seeing as we're being frank,' he said, a twinkle of mischievousness dancing happily across his eyes. 'When I joined, because I was younger than Tom, it was felt that there was a danger that people would think there was hanky-panky going on in the TARDIS. So, you'll notice that both girls are fairly well covered up from head to foot in their differing outfits. The idea was that it would simply stop everyone from thinking about it – you know, what the eye can't see etc, etc. But it was pointed out in one or two letters to the *Radio Times* that a lot of the male population quite liked looking at the female companions from time to time, and a bit more of them than they were seeing! So, it was decided to give them both new costumes.' I wondered how the girls had reacted to that. 'I don't know. They were in two minds about it. On the one hand, it can sometimes be very cold recording *Doctor Who*, and I don't think they appreciated the fact that they were walking around in slightly skimpier outfits – in one case, a very much skimpier outfit! At the same time, I guess they hadn't been entirely happy with the costumes of the first season. I think Janet was quite pleased to be rid of the air hostess outfit, but I don't know how pleased she was to get into the costume she ended up with.'

The notion of three companions for the Doctor appealed to me, so I asked Peter if there was any chance of him working with such a number again. 'Well, again, I really don't know. I think the feeling was that there was one too many and it just got too complicated to keep track of three companions. I didn't mind it actually. *Doctor Who* started off with three companions, and that's the way I looked at it. It was simply going back to square one, to grass roots. I didn't mind it. You can be nastier to more of them if you have three of them!'

Having talked briefly with Peter about his first story, 'Castrovalva', I asked him what he thought of it. 'The thing about "Castrovalva" was it was really the second part of "Logopolis", and it was quite confusing. It was in fact the fourth story I recorded; the first was "Four To Doomsday". That was so that I could find my way around the part a bit more before doing my introductory story, and also, I think, because "Castrovalva" wasn't quite finished when recording was scheduled to begin. What can I say about it? I don't know – I tried to do little things in it, like the little impersonations of the other Doctors.' He broke off to snigger, giving the definite impression that he considered his impersonations not very good. 'One thing, though,' he said, after composing himself suitably. 'I don't know that I like the sorts of times when the Doctor is confused, and I seem to have done a lot of scenes like that now, where the Doctor is being diminished, or parts of him are being taken over, or he's falling over! Maybe they think I'm awfully good at falling over, or perhaps they think I am best out of the way, I don't know. But anyway, there was a fair amount of that in the first two episodes of "Castrovalva".'

Since 'Four To Doomsday' was the first story he had recorded, I wondered how difficult it had been in terms of establishing the character of his Doctor. 'Really difficult! I was just thrown in at the deep end, really, and I was just finding my way around the part. And in instances like that, where you don't know how you're going to finish up, you start off with a sort of non-committal attitude. I didn't want to make any kind of decisions about exactly what I was going to do, so I sort of blandly wandered about for a while. I don't think it was by any means the best story of the season, and that didn't help either.'

I inquired how the scenes involving the Doctor's space-walk had been recorded. 'It was actually done by several means. At one point, I was dangled on what they call a Kirby wire, which is an extremely uncomfortable thing. I was dangled by two steel wires from the top of the studio, a belt around my waist, and I swung uncontrollably! The actual throwing of the cricket ball and the initial swing back was done on the Kirby wire. The rest of the swim through space was done by me pushing myself across the studio floor on a stool. Both the Kirby wire recording and the stool bits were put into the story through CSO, Colour Separation Overlay. The stool for instance was covered in green, so it was all basic CSO. It took a long, long time to do.' The tinge of ruefulness in his voice was unmistakable.

'How did Stratford Johns enjoy playing Monarch?' Peter began in reply to my next question. 'I think he had a lot of fun doing it. The guest stars who come in invariably have a good time. They all like to do it. You can really get some excellent people in *Doctor Who*, because they do see it as a chance to let go in many ways. There's not many times Stratford Johns gets to dress up as a frog!'

I asked Peter what his opinion was of his third story, Christopher Bailey's 'Kinda', which had arguably represented a departure from the usual line of *Doctor Who* scripts. 'I think the good thing about Christopher Bailey is that he creates in his own mind a whole world. The mythology of Deva Loka was very firm in his own mind, and I liked that an awful lot. It was confusing, but it was precise. In many ways, the faults with some *Doctor Who* stories come from the fact that they aren't well enough thought out. "Kinda" was well thought out. Now, there may have been a difficulty with everyone else actually following it, and that's the problem that comes from that thinking-it-out process, but I was very impressed with the actual writing and the thought that he had put into it.'

I wondered if the sequel had been planned at the same time as 'Kinda'. 'I don't think it was, no. I don't think there was a plan to do a sequel at all until "Kinda" went out. It was quite well liked when it went out in Britain, and I think that was what prompted the sequel.'

As 'The Visitation' was the next story in his first season, I asked Peter how different was the recording of pseudo-historical stories from straightforward science fiction sagas. 'In a way, it's easier to do an historical one, because when you are dealing with history there are facts that can be used and twisted to a certain extent – as, obviously, in "The Visitation", where we ended up starting the Great Fire of London! I quite like doing them, because the trouble with the futuristic ones, and I think "Four To Doomsday" suffered from this to a certain extent, is that there is a danger that you view the future only in terms of today's technology. In "Four To Doomsday", the writer was writing about something meant to be happening way away into the future, with an advanced technology that was capable of crossing the vastness of space, and yet they were still dealing with silicon chips – and who knows, silicon chips may well be obsolete two years from now. They may be obsolete now, for all I know! So that's the difficulty with doing futuristic ones, whereas you can play around a bit more with historical ones. I liked the Terileptils, too. Very good costume that.'

As the dreaded sonic screwdriver had met its fate in 'The Visitation', I wondered if Eric Saward had been given an instruction to achieve that end specifically. 'Yes, I think it was part of the brief he was given, as there was no mention of the device in any of the later stories. You know,' Peter added, almost apologetically, 'Eric Saward is one of my favourite writers. It's just a personal opinion, but I like the twists he does at the end of them. I liked "The Visitation".'

Turning to the next story, I mentioned that the fifth Doctor's interest in cricket had really come to the fore in 'Black Orchid'. Peter laughed. 'I had a rough time with that. The cricket scenes were done in one afternoon, and it was pouring with rain, it was absolutely pouring! The thing with filming is that you can't see rain unless it's very, very heavy. So there was the problem of saying to the director, "Shall we assume it's raining in the story, or shall we pretend it's not?" Well, it wasn't really raining heavily enough to say it was raining, and they would not have been playing cricket in the pouring rain anyway, so we had to film it in the pouring rain – and that's my excuse for my bad play! I know I look very good – well, I look all right – but that was only after they cut out all the times the ball fell out of my hand when I was running up to bowl! If ever you get to see the out-takes …!' He shook his head and gulped ferociously, clearly amused by his memories of the day's sport, or lack thereof. 'At one point, I swung at the cricket ball that was being bowled at me, missed the ball entirely, and the cricket bat flew out of my hand and ended up at mid-wicket! But my one claim to fame was captured on film by accident. The cameraman, who wasn't a cricketer, was told to frame-up on me running up to bowl, so that they could use it as a shot just of me running up and delivering the ball; nothing else was meant to be in shot. And we had a batsman standing there, as we were going to do the batting shots next. So I ran up to bowl, and I bowled it – and I bowled him out! And I was really disappointed. I turned to the director and said, "If only the batsman had been in shot!" And the cameraman said, "Oh, he *was* in shot; I didn't know I wasn't meant to keep the ball in shot.' He didn't know a thing about it; he didn't know one end of the cricket pitch from another. So it's there, and if you look carefully, you'll see that it's no trick shot. I run up to bowl, bowl the ball and bowl him out. I never did it again! But it was fun to do, yes. I felt almost like a good player.'

I commented that 'Black Orchid' had centred on the Doctor more than any other story of the season. 'Yes, it's been said that the story was about my character, but I still don't think it set out to be that. It really set out to be an experiment in a two-parter, because they hadn't done one for a while and because there were money problems. The trouble with the BBC is that if a series does well, they don't give it any more money, because they assume that if it did well on the money it had, it can do just as well on the same amount of money the next year. Unfortunately costs do go up, and it meant that John had to cut the season from 28 episodes to 26, which meant having either a six-parter or a two-parter in there, and he chose the two-parter. It was more of an experiment, because it wasn't a traditional *Doctor Who* story at all. It was almost an Agatha Christie type of set-up, but I was never aware of anyone saying to me, "This story will give you a chance to play cricket," or "This story will be centred on you." I think it's just the way it worked out.'

I asked Peter if his rendition of 'I Want to be Happy' in 'Black Orchid' indicated that his Doctor would be prone to burst into song occasionally, perhaps in the Pertwee mould. For a moment he could not recall having sung, but then his face lit up with recollection. 'Ah, yes … I forgot about that, because it was a bit of adlibbing, actually. I was standing outside the door on the set and I just did it for something to do. The trouble with things like songs is that, because of copyright, you always have to pick something that's more than 50 years old, otherwise the BBC has to pay ten pence – and that's not on! I think that will probably be the extent of my musical career in *Doctor Who*.'

Peter laughed again, and through the laughter managed a question: 'Have you ever heard the record Jon Pertwee made?'[34] I winced and nodded. 'Yes, I heard it too! Someone sent it to me, asking me if I would consider doing my version! But I thought no. I think I'll leave that as Jon's classic.'

Quickly I asked another question, regarding the Cybermen in 'Earthshock'. How had the team found that people had taken to the new-look Cybermen?'

'You know, I read a letter in the fanzine here, I think, commenting about the new Cybermen, and the fact that you could see their chins, but the thing I actually liked was the idea that, rather than a totally inanimate face, you could see the hint of something moving underneath. Because there is meant to be something inside the suit: Cybermen are not actually robots. I liked this new side of them. Actually, one of the old stories I was given to look at right at the very beginning, when I was looking at how to approach the role, was the very first Cyberman story, "The Tenth Planet". And in that one they had this enormous sort of stocking mask over the face of the actor, and this enormous head light on top, and a big contraption on the chest. It was very funny, because the voice of the actual actor wasn't used. Obviously the man playing the part would open his mouth, but the sound would come from somewhere else! The mask-mouth wouldn't move; it stayed still the whole time. And the voice was wonderful as well – not at all like the latest Cybermen voices, which I feel are a bit too Dalek-

---

34 Davison was referring here to 'Who is the Doctor?', a spoken word piece performed by Pertwee over a version of the *Doctor Who* theme music and released on Purple Records in the '70s.

like. In the first story, the accent was always on the wrong words. It was really quite jolly! Anyway, the Cybermen had to be re-designed, because they didn't have enough costumes of the old Cybermen to dress them up that way! So they were redone, and I thought they looked really very good. There was the perspex chin, of course, but what was underneath it was quite complicated – maybe you didn't see enough of it? I thought it gave an impression of this shrivelled thing under there speaking. I told David Banks, who played the Cyber Leader, about the early voice, and I thought he was very good, because he incorporated that approach within the modern treatment, and I thought he came up with a very good cross between the slightly strange jolliness and the later Dalek-like voice.'

Peter broke off to double up with laughter again, and I began to wonder if one could take seriously his claim that *Doctor Who* was such hard work. 'I got too close to David in one of the scenes in "Earthshock", and my voice got "Cyberfied", because the sound treatment of the voice is all done at the time of recording. He had the microphone just inside his headpiece, you see. And there was this one scene where we were really face to face and I was shouting at him, and we had to re-do the take three or four times, because each time I got too close to him and came over like a Cyberman!'

Dreading the prospect, I raised the subject of 'Time-Flight'. 'What can I say to you? I thought the problem with "Time-Flight" … It was really many problems. We had got to the end of the season, and the Cyberman story had been expensive to do. Also, some of the earlier stories were more expensive than they were meant to be, simply because of filming problems; we filmed in bad weather a couple of times and had to spend more money. And you really are limited to a budget, so the constant threat is there that if you spend too much money on the earlier programmes, you have to do the last story in front of black drapes …' And call it 'Time-Flight'? Peter gave me a quelling it-wasn't-that-bad look and then laughed before continuing. 'The problem with "Time-Flight" was that they tried to do the exterior scenes interior, and also there was this very unsatisfactory thing of cutting from an exterior of Heathrow Airport to an interior at Studio 8, Television Centre, and it was meant to be the same place, billions of years earlier. I think that makes a tremendous difference to a programme. It's really very hard to get a believable story in those circumstances. You're all meant to be in this vast area, and the point of horizon is ten yards away! It was a shame the story was written on too grand a scale for the money we had available. Potentially, it was a well designed set, done to scale so that it was meant to look as if it was fading away into the distance, but it just wasn't possible to do it.' Looking me straight in the eye, he concluded, 'I think you would have felt differently about it if the exteriors were filmed properly.'

I quashed any notion of a reply, and steered the conversation to Anthony Ainley's Master, who had made his second initially-disguised appearance in this story. Was it a policy of Nathan-Turner's to have the Master appear in disguise? 'I think it is a policy, yes. I think John thinks it's a neat idea.' I brought up the green slime death scene in 'Time-Flight' and asked Peter how that could be justified. 'I think maybe that wasn't entirely satisfactory; maybe we didn't do it well enough. The idea was that he had fallen down and fooled us into thinking he was dead, and it was all horrible, and he came back on that trick and was suddenly the Master. When we were filming it, it looked quite revolting, and the poor person inside the outfit – because it wasn't actually Anthony Ainley at that stage – nearly choked on the green slime. Maybe they didn't do enough of it. I mean, they recorded enough, but maybe they edited a bit too much out of it, and so you didn't get to see the full effect of it. I honestly can't say.'

Given the strenuous requirements of a season's recording, I asked Peter how much of a break he had had between finishing work on 'Time-Flight' and starting on 'Arc of Infinity'. 'When did I start this last one?' he mused, speculatively. 'I think we went almost straight into it, actually. There was no real break at all. But there was a break mid-way through my first season, because I went off and did another season of "Sink Or Swim", to which I was contracted before *Doctor Who* came along.'

Did Peter have a favourite story in his second season? 'My probable favourite is the Mara sequel, "Snakedance". I don't really know why it's my favourite; I just liked it as a story. Collette O'Neil was a wonderful guest star; she's terrific. As a sequel, it was almost part two of "Kinda"; it was almost commissioned as an explanation, because the feeling was that there was a lot of potential in "Kinda" that wasn't well explained, not as amplified as perhaps it should and could have been. So Christopher Bailey was given the chance to do a sequel for those reasons, and also because, as I said, the first one was popular when it went out. Actually, we were working so solidly through on the second season that when that story was transmitted, I didn't have time to see it!'

Mention of the tight schedule reminded me of the various reports carried by *Doctor Who Monthly*[35] about the industrial problems that had beset the recording. I asked Peter about this, and he became almost angry as he spoke. 'We lost an entire story and had to re-cast parts in "Enlightenment" after we had done the filming.[36] Fortunately, no-one who was in the filming couldn't do it again. If that hadn't been the case, I don't know what we would have done. We had to recast both the Captains, and the female Captain's chief officer. The strikes disrupted the whole thing, making for an unsatisfactory ending to the season, I think. I mean, it would have been so nice to do the last story, as even though I never got a script for it, I always looked upon it as the climax of the season. To finish with a two-part story was not all that satisfactory.'

Mention of 'The King's Demons' led inevitably to the subject of the robot Kamelion. 'Well, I didn't like it an awful lot,' Peter confessed. 'Apart from anything else, it was just that, in the end, it did not work all that satisfactorily. It's a very, very clever piece of technology, there's no denying that. It's a computerised robot that moves on its own. Its voice is recorded, obviously. But when it comes down to it, it means you are incredibly limited, because you have to fit your lines in before the taped robot voice speaks to you, and it's just getting back to the K-9 situation. As far as I know, it will not continue in the series – it certainly is not in the special.'

Taking my cue from Peter, I asked him about the 90 minute special 'The Five Doctors', which he had completed work on just prior to jetting over to Australia. He took a deep breath. 'Well, all the Doctors are in it, except William Hartnell, who is dead. They got an actor called Richard Hurndall, who is not the spitting image of William Hartnell by any means, but who, with the white hair, resembles the first Doctor enough, I think. I think it would have been a mistake not to have had the first Doctor in it, and there was no way, this time, that they could cut in old footage, because there's not much around, and what there is is black and white filmed video, which is not awfully good quality. So they recast it, and I think Richard did a good job, really; not a straight impersonation of William Hartnell, but his own job of the first Doctor, with many of the Hartnell elements.' He paused for breath and then continued. 'Carole Ann Ford recreates Susan, not as she was then, but her age now. She doesn't look that

---

35 The forerunner of *Doctor Who Magazine*.

36 The shooting of film inserts for a story was almost invariably done before the studio videotape recordings.

much different, really. Patrick Troughton is in it, and he's very well. In fact, he's completely unstoppable! Because of the publicity on "The Five Doctors", we did a couple of television appearances, one with Patrick. You cannot keep Patrick Troughton quiet in a television studio! He just will not stop talking. These poor people were trying to present their breakfast television programme, and the girl presenter was talking away into the camera and Patrick was saying things like, "My, she does look different from the side," disrupting things like that. And if that wasn't enough, we did another one, an evening news show broadcast with Jon Pertwee, Patrick and me, and it was even more chaotic! I think the three of us have been banned from television shows in Britain. I don't think they got a sensible word out of the three of us all evening, but it was great fun! We just ate jelly babies throughout the interview – and Patrick Troughton wants me to bring this message to the world: he introduced jelly babies to *Doctor Who!*' We both laughed.

'Tom Baker didn't actually take part in the special, although he's featured in it via a clip from "Shada", which was another *Doctor Who* story to be cancelled by the traditional BBC strike. The clip is used very cleverly, I must say, and apart from the fact that, for Tom Baker fans, he won't really be in it, the clip fits very well into the story. I don't want to say you don't notice he isn't in it, but the story stands up very well as a "five Doctors" story even though only four Doctors take the main parts. It's a very clever story. I think when it's all stuck together, it'll be very good. Terrance Dicks wrote it, and it involves all the Doctors going toward the same goal. We are all put into a situation not of our own doing and we have to achieve the same end. It's rather like a puzzle, and we all meet up in the end, and there's only a couple of pages with us all together. But my Doctor meets the Hartnell Doctor earlier, so there's a bit of contact. Old companions are in it too; Carole Ann Ford is with Richard, Nicholas Courtney is with Patrick Troughton, Lis Sladen is with Jon Pertwee and I have Turlough and Tegan. There are other companions who appear in sort of cameo roles, but those are the featured companions. The Master and the Cybermen are also in it, but not in star roles, so there is an awful lot going on. I can't tell you any more about it, really, because John Nathan-Turner would kill me! The security on the set was amazing – even Sandra wasn't allowed on the set, which was ridiculous, because I could easily go home and tell her everything that happened! It was really a closed set!'

Leaving that particular closed subject, I asked Peter about Patrick Troughton. What was he really like? 'The nicest person you are ever likely to meet! Let me say that. His attitude towards *Doctor Who* promotional appearances stems from his not liking to be put under pressure.[37] He took part in "The Five Doctors" with considerable enthusiasm, so it's not the association with the series that he doesn't like. It's just that making public promotional appearances is very much like hard work. We did actually force him, by twisting his arm, to attend the *Doctor Who* celebration weekend at Longleat, which was a fairly massive event. He was reluctant to come, for the reason I've said, but we persuaded him, and he really enjoyed himself once he got there. But he's a very, very nice chap, and in a way you can't blame him. He had a heart attack a couple of years ago, so he's got to be careful about pressure.'

I asked Peter how audiences had accepted Anthony Ainley as the new Master. 'There hasn't really been a problem, because, obviously, Roger Delgado was killed. There wasn't any choice if one wanted to bring the character back. I think he does it extremely well. The way he's made up, he does resemble Roger Delgado, and he keeps saying that that was the only reason he got

---

37 At this point in time, Patrick Troughton generally refused to attend *Doctor Who* conventions or make other public appearances.

the part, but it wasn't. He's very, very good. A marvellous part, and we get along very well. We did a pantomime at Christmastime together. He played Baron Hardup, I was Buttons, Sandra was the Fairy Godmother and it was directed by John Nathan-Turner. It was a very successful production of *Cinderella*. It played at Tunbridge Wells, which is a fair way from London, but we still had packed houses most of the time. It was very good!' I asked if there were plans to remount the production this year, and Peter blanched noticeably. 'Oh, I hope not! It was hard work. Pantomime's gruelling, really. Good fun, but really gruelling work.'

A little reluctantly, I asked Peter the inevitable question as to how long he envisaged staying in the series. 'Well, I'm certainly doing next season, and at some point I will have to make a decision about the following year, and when that time comes, I'll make the decision. But I'm doing the third year. I'm taking it year by year, which is what every Doctor has done after the initial two year contract has run out.' Bearing in mind the speedy departure of Mary Tamm, minus regeneration, I wondered if there was a you-will-record-a-regeneration-scene clause in the contracts of the Doctors. Peter shook his head. 'No … I think you'd rarely fall out to such an extent that you would refuse to do a regeneration scene. It wouldn't happen, because it wouldn't be advisable from anyone's point of view. I will say this, though: when I go, I don't think I'll fall off a radio telescope. I'll go nice and quietly!'

I asked if a change of producer would hasten Peter's decision to leave. 'I don't think so,' he replied slowly, obviously thinking about it as he spoke. 'I think once I would have said yes. But I think I am sure enough about it all now to be able to cope with a change in producer.'

Remembering the earlier comment about secrecy on the set, I wondered how Peter felt about security leaks with regard to the plots of stories. 'As far as I know, John goes out of his way not to tell anybody anything! Obviously information is gleaned – fans are a devious lot, and they usually know what's going on before I do! Nicholas Courtney was telling me he was getting letters of congratulation about the return of the Brigadier in "Mawdryn Undead" long before he had agreed to do it! It's very difficult to keep things secret when you are recording something and there are people in and out all the time. That's why the special was closed. A case in point would be "Earthshock" and the return of the Cybermen. John tried to keep it secret as long as he possibly could, but the information got out fairly quickly.'

On the subject of leaking information, I asked if Peter knew anything about the third season he was to make. 'Not much, no. I've not seen any of the scripts yet. I think the story we lost from the last season will be used again for this season's line-up, but I'm not sure. John and Eric are continuing with the series. I think Janet will probably leave during this season, but again I am not certain. You'll probably be able to tell me more than I can tell you; I'm only in it!'

Remembering the April Fool's story in *Doctor Who Monthly* about the remake of a partially completed Hartnell story, I asked if any project like that had ever been suggested. 'There was talk at one time of doing a story that was written for William Hartnell's Doctor but never made. But that's the closest we have come. I don't know if the plan's still in John's mind or not, but I wouldn't be averse to it. As for remakes, in a way it's a shame not to have those old stories now, because they are lost forever, but at the same time, would it be good for another Doctor to remake something that was done for William Hartnell?'

That was too important a question for me to venture an opinion on, so I let it be. I ended by asking Peter if he agreed with the opinion expressed by Tom Baker that *Doctor Who* is essentially for children.

He breathed in deeply and exhaled slowly, with a whistle. 'I think in order to appeal to children, you have to make it adult. Children are very adult about what they watch. And I don't think I believe Tom, if he has indeed been quoted as saying that, because I don't think he ever actually made it for children. Well, certainly the last three or four years I saw weren't aimed at children. I think you should always aim it at the adult, and if you do, the children will watch it. Douglas Adams imparted to me a piece of wisdom that I think is absolutely accurate. He felt that the challenge on *Doctor Who* when he was script editor was to make the stories complicated enough to keep the children's attention but simple enough for the adults to understand! I think that's really true. Children pick up everything. Parents in Britain keep saying to me, "How can you expect our children to understand what happens when we can't?" So there we are ...'

And there we were. My time was up, and the Myer personnel were standing gargoyle-like at Peter's side, desperate to whisk him away to another venue, where doubtless hundreds of paperbacks were waiting hungrily for a few strokes from his pen. Wearily, the two whistle-stop tourists collected their goods and chattels and stepped resignedly into the grip of the Myer escort. I managed only a hasty goodbye to both Peter and Sandra; there was no time to express the real gratitude I felt at their having given so generously of their time, not just over the interview but throughout the whole visit to Australia.

Stephen Collins

INTERVIEW: ANTONY ROOT-SCRIPT EDITOR

Antony Root was temporarily assigned to Doctor Who *as a script editor during Season 19. He has rarely spoken about his work on the series – in fact, the following interview, conducted by Philip Newman in 1991 at the offices of Working Title Films and originally published in Issue 21/22 of* The Frame *in Spring/Summer 1992, was the first he had ever given. He has since continued a highly successful career as an executive producer on a wide variety of TV projects, including* Tales of the City *(1993),* Cold Comfort Farm *(1995),* The Grand *(1997),* Far from the Madding Crowd *(1998),* The Lady in Question *(1999),* The Great Gatsby *(2000),* Princess of Thieves *(2001),* Second Nature *(2003) and* Touching Evil *(2004).*

Q: How did you come to join the BBC?

A: When I left university, I worked in live theatre for five years, initially as a theatre manager and then as a publicist. Then, at age 25, I decided that I didn't want to stay in live theatre any longer and got a holiday relief job for three months as an assistant floor manager with the BBC. I suppose that must have been in the summer of 1979 – and, funnily enough, the show I did was a four-part *Doctor Who* directed by Ken Grieve[38]. At the end of that holiday relief period, they advertised some permanent positions. I applied, and became a fully-fledged assistant floor manager, a job I did for about 18 months to two years I guess. After that, I started an internal training course as a script editor and subsequently went on to do programmes.

Q: Many script editors – or, at least, many of those who have worked on *Doctor Who* – have started out as script writers rather than in production jobs such as AFM ...

A: I don't write. I never write scripts. I suppose I'm one of the old-fashioned story editors who believe that story editors are sometimes better when they don't write, because what they're actually doing is, like a publishing editor, trying to get the best work out of other people; helping them achieve what they want to do. I know *Doctor Who* has a tradition of writer/story editors, but I was not one of those people.

Q: How did your first script editing post come about?

A: What happened was that I went to the person who was then Head of Series and Serials, Graeme McDonald, and asked him what the opportunities were. He gave me some advice that led to me approaching the TV Drama Script Unit, where I got what was called a 'training attachment' as a script editor. This involved a period of time – about three months, I think – at the Script Unit followed by a spell back in the Drama Series and Serials Department as a trainee.

Q: When did you hear about the possibility of a placement on *Doctor Who*?

---

38 'Destiny of the Daleks'.

A: Well, at the end of my time at the Script Unit, Chris Bidmead decided to leave *Doctor Who* and they needed someone to 'plug' the script editor job for a limited period while they found a replacement. I arrived back with perfect timing and was asked if I would do it – which, of course, I did.

Q: So you knew it was going to be only a temporary job?

A: Oh yes. It was always going to be temporary. I don't think I commissioned any new work; I inherited a lot of it. I think I was around for about two stories with John Nathan-Turner.

Q: *Doctor Who* was still considered quite a major programme in the BBC's output at that time. Did you have any trepidation in approaching the job?

A: Yes I did. I have to tell you – and you can publish this! – that it was one of the worst jobs I could imagine a story editor having to do, because the weight of history was so great that it was actually totally stultifying. I was used to working to a fairly broad brief about what one might do in a script, and I was very excited about the possibilities of doing almost any story one could envisage and shaping it within the mould of *Doctor Who*. But then, within 24 hours of arriving there, I was introduced to the *Doctor Who* mail, which would often come to the script editor to advise on what the reply should be. You know, you would look at 50 letters that said something like, 'Sprodget Number Five in the TARDIS cannot be pressed to do the function that you think it can!' It seemed to me that the weight of history wasn't working to the show's benefit. So I approached it with great hopes but found it an extremely difficult thing to engage with.

Q: Had you ever watched the programme before actually working on it?

A: Oh yes! I'd been a great fan since childhood – absolutely! I remember hiding behind the sofa when William Hartnell went on, like everybody else did!

Q: At the time you joined the show, it was undergoing a great metamorphosis, in terms of production ideas, scripting and cast. Was this apparent in the working atmosphere, that a 'new era' was beginning?

A: Well, I don't remember that, but of course John Nathan-Turner had seen out Tom and was seeing in Peter, whom he knew extremely well from having been production associate on *All Creatures Great and Small*. I think that any difficulties were to do not with the casting but with the usual thing in TV series, like 'The production starts shooting in three weeks' time – which script are we going to do?' But Barry Letts was executive producer at that time, so he was always there to turn to.

Q: You said that most of the scripts were presented to you as 'faits accomplis.' How much input did you actually have on them?

A: I remember I spent a lot of time with Eric Saward on his 'Great Fire of London' story[39],

39 'The Visitation'.

though I don't know that I made any real contribution to it. The other story I remember, with great affection, was written by somebody called Christopher Bailey and entitled 'Kinda'. I thought that was really a very interesting script indeed, because it had shades of Buddhistic philosophies as well as being quite entertaining on the surface. I have vague memories of the first one we did[40], by Terence Dudley, and another about a cricket match set in the 1920s[41], but that one was done mostly after I'd gone.

Q: How do you see the script editor's job – is it literally to edit scripts, or to work through and develop ideas with the writers?

A: I think my job at the time was to firefight and to make sure that there were scripts ready to achieve the production schedule that was set. It was a very, very intense time of sleepless nights – I do remember that. I felt like I'd been thrown in right at the deep end. But, as always with script editing, it was about delivering up to directors and production teams, on the day they were meant to start, material they could use that fitted the brief. And obviously I wasn't working solo but with John Nathan-Turner on that.

Q: Do you remember working on the *K-9 and Company* Christmas special?

A: Yes. I think John had the original idea. We got it going, got a draft script in from Terence Dudley, then that would have been about the time that I moved on to work on *Juliet Bravo*. It's strange, I thought the K-9 thing would spin off much more successfully than it actually turned out to do. I thought there was almost a series in that.

Q: So you moved from *Doctor Who* to the police series *Juliet Bravo*?

A: Yes. What happened was that my attachment expired at the end of the *Doctor Who* period and I was told that I would have to go back to being an AFM because, after all, that was technically what I was, as far as the staffing of the BBC was concerned. I said that I didn't want to do that, and that I would be leaving the Beeb if that had to be – although I understood the reasons why, if it did. A couple of days went by and then they called me in and asked if I'd like to work on *Juliet Bravo*. So I went and worked on that for a season under Joan Clark, who was the doyenne of series story editors. I then went on with the same producer, Terry Williams, to do the second series of *The Chinese Detective*. Following that I worked for a couple of years on various things as script editor to a former *Doctor Who* producer, Philip Hinchcliffe. I finally left the BBC in 1984 to go to Euston Films, where I'd been offered a job as their script editor. I accepted it for a number of reasons: first, I wanted to do film drama as opposed to naturalistic studio drama, which was still being required at the Beeb then; secondly, there was in those days a much higher salary in commercial television and I could use the extra money as I'd just got married; and, thirdly, I sort of feel that you should move when you're asked rather than touting for work when you're bored.

Q: What did your work at Euston involve?

---

40 'Four to Doomsday'.
41 'Black Orchid'.

A: For the first year and a bit, I was dealing with the material that was coming in, being offered to the company, and offering my boss, Linda Agran, reports and comments on work to be commissioned and made into programmes. Then there was a change of regime and I was made script executive, with a greater commissioning function, working on a number of projects. These included a five-part gangster series called *Fear*, which I commissioned and ultimately co-produced. A couple of years later, I was asked if I'd like to come over here, to Working Title, because they'd just set up a television arm and wanted someone from TV drama to get the drama up and running. Since then, for the company, I've co-produced *Newshounds* with the BBC – that was a Les Blair film that won a BAFTA award – and a children's film, *Lorna Doone*, with Thames – that won the European Children's Festival's Best Film award. Also I've just produced *Edward II*, a Derek Jarman film, which was financed principally out of television. In 1992, we've got a six-part series for Channel 4 and another Derek Jarman film, I hope.

Q: Was it a natural progression, going from script editing to producing?

A: I only ever wanted to produce. Script editing was always the means to that end. Having had some production experience on the floor, the obvious thing to do was to try to get a script editor's job to learn that side of the business and ultimately put those two things together as a producer.

Q: Is that quite a common career route to becoming a producer?

A: Well, traditionally, in the Beeb, it was. It was what Philip Hinchcliffe did – he'd been story editor at ATV; Jonathan Powell and Sally Head too. That was the way in the BBC. To that extent, John Nathan-Turner was slightly different, because at that time, there were fewer people going from production associate to producer.

Q: How do you feel about the fact that the show's future is once again in the balance at present?

A: Well, interestingly enough, when I heard about that, and about the fact that the BBC were looking for an independent company to take over production, I immediately wrote to say that I thought that we could do a good job on it here at Working Title, and that I had some ideas about it. But Peter Cregeen, Head of Series, said that he'd already secured the company that was going to do it.

Q: Really?

A: Yes. That was about six months ago, and I keep expecting to see an announcement.[42]

Q: If Working Title did manage to get the rights to produce a new series of *Doctor Who*, in

---

42 This was at the time when the BBC was in discussion with Steven Spielberg's company Amblin about the possibility of a deal to co-produce a new, American-made *Doctor Who* series. Although Amblin would later drop out of the picture, these discussions would ultimately lead to the *Doctor Who* TV movie starring Paul McGann, transmitted in 1996.

what sort of direction would you like to see it go?

A: I think it has to be fundamentally reassessed. I think one needs to have a significant period discussing, with the BBC and any other interested parties, exactly what a *Doctor Who* for the '90s would be. I don't think that people can simply look at, as it were, the back catalogue of episodes and come to some conclusion about what ought to be done. It has got to be: 'How does one make a lower budget science fiction family show work for an audience in the '90s?' The difficulty is that we all enjoy the naivety of things like *Thunderbirds*, which we watched when we were young, which have now become cult TV, and I'm sure early *Doctor Who* would be viewed in the same way, but you can't offer that stuff up as new programming. It would be laughed at, and people simply wouldn't watch it. Going back, I think the other thing about the time I worked on the series was that there was then – and frankly it's still to be resolved – a crisis about what you could actually do with television science fiction post-*Star Wars*. On *Doctor Who*, you used to be able to get away with an exploding wall and a weird monster, but once you'd had the cinema, with its massive special effects pictures, showing people what could be achieved, you had to find something else for the show to do, some other way in. So I suspect that a new *Doctor Who* would have a greater dimension psychologically. I don't mean that in any heavy sense – you'd try to get feelings and emotions passing through the show as well as the action/adventure that is at the heart of all those sort of things. That said, I fail to see how you could bring a new twist to yet another story set aboard an alien spaceship. There's only so many of those you can do, unless suddenly, like Stanley Kubrick, you have a vision of a new way of doing it and do a *2001*. But I don't think that that's what *Doctor Who* is there for. It's certainly not meant to be repetitive. Maybe what it wants is a strangeness – to major on the quirkiness?

Q: Do you think it would work better on film?

A: I don't think anyone could ever afford to make it all on film – it's not that kind of show. I don't think that's the issue. I think it's back to stories; back to ideas! So what I would be doing is selecting a team of writers and brainstorming for really quite a long time about what one could do with the show, to be inspired by its best and its potential idea, to make it really work for an audience now.

Philip Newman

INTERVIEW: ROSALIND EBBUTT—COSTUME DESIGNER

Early in 1989, David Howe visited senior costume designer Ros Ebbutt to interview her for The Frame – *the resulting piece subsequently appeared in Issue 10, published in May of that year . At that time, Ros was on maternity leave, having recently given birth to a baby girl, but was due to return to the BBC in June to resume work. Since then, she has continued a highly successful career in costume design, with credits including* House of Cards *(1990),* Moon and Son *(1992),* Gallowglass *(1993),* A Dark Adapted Eye *(1994),* The Buccaneers *(1995),* The Tenant of Wildfell Hall *(1996),* The History of Tom Jones, a Foundling *(1997),* Vanity Fair *(1998),* Oliver Twist *(1999),* Anna Karenina *(2000),* Sword of Honour *(2001),* Foyle's War *(2002),* Servants *(2003),* Messiah III: The Promise *(2004),* To the Ends of the Earth *(2005) and* Murder in Suburbia *(2005).*

Ros Ebbutt joined the BBC in 1974 as a costume design assistant after working at the Royal Opera House as a costume production assistant. She worked at the BBC for one year on shows such as the first episodes of Terry Nation's *Survivors*, and *Poldark*. After this, she left to run the Costume Department at the Scottish Ballet. As she explained, 'At that time, I wasn't sure if I wanted to do theatre or TV costumes.' She returned to London in 1977, got married and then re-joined the BBC, again as a costume design assistant. She finally became a fully-fledged costume designer in 1980.

'The first thing I designed was the Dominic Hyde play, *The Flip-Side of Dominic Hyde*. I also designed the follow-up, *Another Flip for Dominic*. Both of those were with make-up handled by Dorka Nieradzik, whom I had also worked with on *Poldark* when we were both assistants.'

Ros went on to design the costumes for a production of Stravinsky's *The Soldier's Tale*, which starred Wayne Sleep. Because of her love of the theatre and ballet, she found this a wonderful thing to work on. 'I'd love to do another ballet, but nowadays the BBC tends to film those that have already been staged, and a costume designer is rarely required.'

Moving on to the subject of *Doctor Who*, 'Black Orchid' was the first show that Ros was involved with. She explains, 'I was allocated to it just like any other programme. When you are fairly new as a designer, you get allocated to work on programmes, then, when the directors and producers get to know you, they ask for you specifically. For example, John Nathan-Turner asked for me specifically to design the most recent one, "The Greatest Show In the Galaxy".'

I asked if Ros had seen *Doctor Who* prior to working on it. 'A little. I wasn't an enormous fan of it when I was young. We didn't have a TV at all when I was very small, and I simply grew up without being especially hooked on television programmes, though of course I knew about *Doctor Who*. Indeed, I was very aware of it going on when I was first at the BBC. It was a programme that lots of young designers worked on. They used to like to mix the less experienced designers together with the very experienced ones. It had the scope to allow them really to experiment and use their imaginations, and a lot of people did.'

'Black Orchid', of course, turned out not to have any science fiction trappings at all. Had this disappointed Ros?

'Not really. I obviously knew as soon as I saw the script that it wasn't going to be a fantasy-based programme, but the lovely challenge was to create 1920s fancy dress costumes. Finding things that would have been seen as fancy dress at that time. It was a very enjoyable show to do, and had a very good cast.'

How had Ros approached the costumes?

'We hired in most of the standard 1920s clothes, and others came from stock. It was the fancy dress that caused a bit of a problem. Every period has its own interpretation of the past and what people wore then. In the '20s, fancy dress parties were very popular, but there was a definite '20s interpretation of what period costume was, particularly if it was meant to be fancy dress. I tried to get that sort of look to it. If you look at old theatre pictures or photographs from that period, the shapes of the clothes and the styles of the time were reflected in the fancy dress. For example, the dropped waists for the women.

'I used a lot of things for reference: pictures of people in fancy dress at the time; some things of my grandmother's; and also pictures from that time of people in plays. The plays were set in the 1800s, but the interpretation of them was very much 1920s. All those things helped. Basically, the conclusion I drew was that everything was very stylised, and that was the sort of thing they went for in the fancy dress – very stylised interpretations.'

The three main fancy dress costumes were Nyssa's Butterfly, Tegan's Rose and the Pierrot. I wondered if these had been based on anything in particular.

'Nyssa's costume had to have a mask. That was a requirement of the script. The Butterfly idea was very popular at the time, and as I had to have a head-dress that could incorporate a mask very easily, it seemed obvious to make it an insect head. The Pierrot was again from the script, and Tegan's costume was simply taken from the idea of the flower.'

Had any problems arisen while working on 'Black Orchid'?

'The weather. It was frightful when they staged that cricket match. In the end, they had to curtail it because the weather was so poor. It was a great pity, because a lot of work had gone into those costumes. We had all the spectators as well as the cricketers, and we had found two teams' worth of period cricket gear! There was a lot of time spent on it, and really, the weather was so awful that we didn't get good value from the cricket match. During the buffet scenes, too, the wind was freezing. We were shooting those scenes in Tunbridge Wells in October. It could have been mild, but we had an absolutely biting cold wind.'

Having finished 'Black Orchid', Ros went on to design the costumes for *Diana* in 1983, *Bergerac* in 1985 and *A Perfect Spy* in 1986, which kept her busy for much of the time. Her next association with *Doctor Who* was on the Season 25 adventure, 'The Greatest Show In the Galaxy'. I asked her what her reaction had been on reading the script.

'I thought it was very strong and had a lot going for it. I also thought that I didn't have a lot of time, and that I had better get cracking!

'It actually took us five weeks to complete the designs and costumes before the first location shooting. My assistant, Sarah Jane Ellis, and I started by exhaustively researching clowns. I did a lot of research into the background and history of clowns, while Sarah Jane looked into clowns as they are at present. Conveniently, there was a conference of clowns going on in Brighton, so she went down there and took hundreds of photographs to give us an idea of the wide variety of clowns – the designs, the colours and the costumes.

'I discovered that there are two different strands of clowns: first there are the white-faced ones, some of which go right back to 15th Century Italian theatre and clowns like Grimaldi at the turn of the 19th Century; then there are the red-nosed clowns, or Augustes, which eventually became the butt of the white-faced clowns in early circuses.

'There is, in fact, a third type of clown, the hobo clown, which is an exclusively American invention. They weren't mentioned in the script and so we left them out. It would have been a great deal harder to make masks for that type of clown, if we had used them. In fact, Charlie Chaplin and Buster Keaton, who are associated with the hobo clown, are actually versions of the white-faced clown – look at their make-up, which is much more like a white-faced clown than a hobo clown. One of the red-nosed clowns at our circus was based on the Charlie Chaplin character.

'When we had pooled all our ideas together, I started to think through the Chief Clown, who was indicated as being a white-faced clown in the script. We did a lot of research into what fabrics were available, mainly because there wasn't going to be time to have the fabric made specially. I found two different sorts of fabric, both based on designs of black and silver. One, a sort of silver pebble design, was appliquéd onto the other, which was a predominantly black fabric with a spidery silver pattern, when we made the costume.

'For the other clowns, we found samples of different fabrics and, having decided which I wanted to use, I went away and designed using all the samples as reference. We were very lucky finding the colourful material for the basic costumes, and I appliquéd onto it some glittery metallic organzas that I found in an Indian shop in Southall. Overall the effect was just what I had hoped for.

'There were four different designs of red-nosed clowns, and we made eight costumes in total, two of each design. Similarly for the white-faced clowns, we made five costumes from my three basic designs.

'We also made some additional costumes for Visual Effects to use on the robots that were to blow up. I used some of those costumes, re-sprayed, for the scenes in the clown workshop.'

An important aspect of the clowns was that their costumes had to match up with their masks. How had this been approached?

'I worked very closely with the make-up designer, Dee Baron[43]. It had to look as though the costumes and masks were worn by robots and not people, so we worked out a sort of Balaclava affair that went underneath the masks and over the tops of their faces so there was no risk of ever seeing their skin. The actors had to don a Balaclava, a mask, a wig and a hat to play the clowns and, exactly the opposite of the situation on 'Black Orchid', the weather was sweltering. It must have hit 100 degrees in the quarry we were using for the location. Everyone, but especially the clowns, got so hot.

'Another consideration for those clowns that had to perform was that, in order to grip their props correctly and do their acts safely, they needed leather gloves. So I had white leather gloves made for them all, with long sleeves to cover up the skin on their arms.'

Moving on to the other costumes seen in 'The Greatest Show in the Galaxy', Ros told me that the undertaker costumes had been hired in from Bermans and Nathans, the theatrical costumiers. 'The costume implied in the script was modern-day undertakers' morning coats and trousers. However, I thought that this would not look convincing, as they were supposed to be worn over the clowns' clothes. I suggested the long, Victorian-style coats as they would look better and more sinister with the top hats, and you could believe that the clown costumes were underneath. I was very pleased with the end result.'

Another concept worked out in collaboration with Dee Baron was the punk werewolf, Mags. 'The main part of the transformation was Dee's fantastic make-up, but we co-operated on the colour ranges that Dee used in the hair. The actress Jessica Martin's own hair was slightly streaky, so Dee used that and added all the colour and extensions. We very luckily

43 See the interview with Dee Baron elsewhere in this book.

found a green and black flocked organza that made a perfect semi-animal skin print skirt, which I then followed through with the animal print leotard that she had on underneath it. We decided to go for the slightly old-fashioned punk look with the fishnet gloves and tights because it looked more feminine, and also because it was easier to incorporate the rest of her transformation into that. If we had used a heavy leather jacket and trousers, we would have had a problem when we tried to change it into an animal.

'The transformation was kept as simple and as straightforward as possible. If we had been recording in the studio, there would not have been the time to take Jessica off for complete costume changes as well as the make-up work. As things turned out, we had a little longer than we had expected, because we were not in the studio but in a tent in Elstree. Nevertheless, we had an enormous number of scenes to do in a very short time, so I knew we couldn't do anything very elaborate. What we actually came up with, and the way it was shot and edited, worked very well.

'We had two skirts, one just plain and one with fur applied all round. I gelled and streaked the fur in the same way as Dee had done with Jessica's hair. The leotard had two half-zips sewn in on the front, and I put fur on the other half of the zippers so we could just zip them on. We made a second pair of earrings with fur on, and another pair of gloves with fur on too. The whole basis of it was simplicity.'

Most of the other characters' costumes presented problems of varying degrees of difficulty.

'With Nord the Vandal, the problem was in trying to get the wings on the helmet to look right. Originally I had envisaged a motorbike helmet with a chin guard so that you wouldn't see any of his face. This is what is on the design. However, this was changed because, with the wings on, the helmet wasn't going to be of much practical use anyway; and the director wanted the audience to see the actor's face. I was worried that if the actor fell off an ordinary motorbike with that winged helmet on, it could be quite dangerous. In the end, though, the bike turned out to be a three-wheeled one, which was much safer, and I wasn't so worried. The final helmet was still based on a motorbike helmet, and the idea came from a small transfer of a winged skull that Dee provided. We made the helmet look like bone and the wings like bone and leather to match the transfer.

'For the family, I wanted them to look like a very boring, 1950s advertisement-type family, almost like the Ovaltine parents. That kind of feel – really dreary looking. Luckily we found all those costumes in stock.

'I felt the Captain ought to look like a stereotype explorer, simply because that was what he was. We made him a little bit different by giving him a very bright cravat. I also wanted him to look a bit sadistic – I felt that was quite important – so I gave him leather boots.

'With Whizzkid, we moved to the 1960s with the glasses, bow tie and jumper, which I had made. He was the sort of boring enthusiast type that you used to find in the comics of the late 1950s, and that was the look I decided to go for.

'Then there was the Ringmaster. The director, Alan Wareing, didn't want him to be a red-coated ringmaster, and funnily enough I discovered that the majority of ringmasters used to wear a Victorian riding coat, which was blue or black. It was only a ringmaster in Barnum and Bailey's circus that wore red, so there isn't a long-standing tradition that the ringmaster has to wear red. I luckily found a red and black checked silk and checked glitter lurex, so we were able to introduce a splash of red into the costume without making it exclusively red. The topper was a beautifully made period one, which I found in our stock and which was exactly right. It's amazing what you can find when you search through the store.

'With all these different characters, we had to make a lot of not-too-obvious character statements about the people, and there were a lot of different threads of design that went into it. I didn't want the hippies, for example, to look either threatening or wimpish, so I had to research their look quite thoroughly.'

David J Howe

INTERVIEW: BARRY NEWBERY-DESIGNER

Barry Newbery is Doctor Who's *longest-serving scenic designer. After his work on the series during the 1960s and 1970s – as covered in the first two volumes of* Talkback *– he had a break of several years before returning at the end of 1983 for his final story, Season 21's 'The Awakening'. Barry is now retired, and lives with his wife Zena in the London home they have shared for many years.*

We asked Barry what shows he had worked on during the period before he returned to *Doctor Who* in 1983.

'Amongst other things, I'd done three important serials: *Prince Regent, The Lost Boys* and *The Citadel. The Lost Boys* was produced by Louis Marks, who asked for me to be assigned to it as he was so pleased with the work I'd done on "The Masque of Mandragora", which as you know he wrote. I was very grateful for that. He also brought in Rodney Bennett to direct it, which was another link to "The Masque of Mandragora".

'I suspect that some designers might have thought it a bit of a come down to return to *Doctor Who* after a few years spent mostly on more major productions, but I didn't, because it was always so much fun to work on. I certainly couldn't complain, having done three such prestigious shows in the interim.'

The location filming for 'The Awakening' took place in the picturesque village of Shapwick in Dorset.

'I was on location for most of the filming but had to return to London before the end of it to get on with preparing for the studio recording. I left my assistant, Jonathan Taylor, down there to keep an eye on things.

'For the scenes outside the church, I had to provide a little lychgate – which is probably the most well-remembered aspect of "The Awakening" due to the famous outtake where it was demolished by a horse and cart! I also had to supply a large gravestone for the cemetery and one or two other bits and pieces, such as the village maypole. Apart from that, my main concern was to see the exteriors of the buildings for which I would have to create interiors in the studio. There were some scenes involving a barn, for instance, for which I knew I was going to have to match studio interior to location exterior so that viewers would believe the scenes were shot continuously on location.

'One exception to that rule was the Colonel's house: the house we shot at on location was Georgian, but the parlour interior had to be Tudor, as the Colonel was supposed to have had it specially refurbished in that style. The upstairs room where Tegan was held prisoner, therefore, I did keep Georgian to match the style of the house.

'Of course, I'd done Tudor sets before on other programmes – they're quite a common requirement. Even so, I still did some research. I would always look at visual references – photographs or paintings – as I might be able to pick up some interesting ideas from them. It's always better to have more information than you actually need than to be short of it.

'Some of my requirements for that set I was able to meet from stock: the BBC had one or two items of stock scenery that were actually quite good Tudor design, and also a lot of wood panelling which was suitable to use. There weren't any doorways I liked, though, so I had some quite nice arched ones made.

'I remember that when I arrived in the studio on the morning of the recording day, I looked at this Tudor set and thought, "Oh yes, that's fine, everything's going very smoothly." What I didn't know was that Jonathan Taylor had arrived in the studio an hour or more ahead of me, had seen that the set had been erected in the wrong place and had contacted the manager responsible. The set had been pulled down and put back up again on the correct marks! That's how good an assistant Jonathan was. Had the set just been left where it was, it would have created enormous problems for other members of the team such as the lighting man, who naturally had arranged his lights according to the planned position of the set and of the actors within it. There would have been dark areas, boom shadows and congestion with cameras in nearby sets.

'The largest set in "The Awakening" was the main church interior, which took up the full length of the studio. It was quite a tall set, too; the three stained glass windows above the altar were about 25 feet from the studio floor, as I recall. Some of the walls were designed to swing open so that the cameras could move into the set to get the required shots. Some were simply painted cloths. The pulpit was a stock one, but I had a carving of the Malus added to the side of it as referred to in the script.

'The Malus itself, behind the church wall, was provided not by me but by Tony Harding, who was again the visual effects designer on this story. He was also responsible for the effect of the wall crumbling as the Malus emerged: I sent him the part of the set that he needed to work on, to add his specially-made sections to achieve this effect. He prepared three or four spares to allow for retakes.

'In addition to the main church interior, there had to be a small side room leading to the secret passage that the Doctor discovered. I did this as a raised set, four feet high, so that the characters could be seen climbing down into the passage. The passage entrance was behind a carved flagstone, which was hinged so that it could be raised up. The carving was an image of the Malus, which I designed. I was very pleased with how it looked on camera.

'The other area of the church for which I had to create a set was the crypt where the TARDIS arrived. I provided all the rubble that was strewn about the floor, but the rubble that fell from above was the responsibility of Visual Effects. That might seem odd, but if my "rubble" had fallen on anybody it wouldn't have been covered by the BBC's insurance, whereas it was all right for Visual Effects to drop "rubble," as they were trained to do it!'

As Barry told us, 'The Awakening' was not only his final contribution to *Doctor Who* but also his very last production as a BBC designer.

'Sue Spence, a colleague of mine in the Department, had managed to get herself early retirement and, knowing that I would be quite happy to leave the BBC, she suggested that I try to do likewise. She didn't tell me exactly what the financial arrangement was, but I knew that if it pleased her, it was likely to please me too. So I went along and put my toe in the water, so to speak, and was made a very attractive offer, which I accepted. I had a lot of leave outstanding, which I took, but there was then a period of uncertainty, when I wasn't quite sure whether I was going to be leaving or not, because it was up to my Head of Department to give the okay. In view of this, I obviously couldn't be placed on any production that was going to be a long-term project. "The Awakening", on the other hand, was only a two-part story, and that made it an ideal assignment for me to handle while I was waiting to find out what was going to happen. It was actually around the time that I was working on "The Awakening" that I received confirmation of my early retirement.

'I left not because I had lost interest in designing but because I was becoming increasingly frustrated and dissatisfied with the situations in the BBC. During the '60s and '70s, it had been a marvellous organisation for designers. Although we hadn't been able to choose which shows we did, we'd had almost absolute control over our work and over how things looked on screen. By the early '80s, however, things had started to change. It had started to become like the commercial world. The organisation of methods and processes to produce programmes was constantly being altered, supposedly to achieve greater efficiency. I found it confusing.

'What happens now is that designers have to be interviewed by the directors and producers for their ideas on a programme, and can be rejected if they're considered unsuitable. Admittedly it works both ways: designers can turn jobs down if they don't want to do them. But the point is that they now have to compete with each other, to sell themselves. Selling yourself is no proof of artistic ability.

'In my day, the Head of Design relied on reports from his senior designers so that people were given work according to their recognised abilities. Designers were encouraged to do their own thing. They could develop without having to sell themselves in this way. And people who would never have survived in a commercial environment turned out the most marvellous work. To be honest, I'm very glad I left when I did.'

To conclude our interview, we asked Barry which of all the many productions he had worked on over the years was the one of which he was most proud.

'I think it would have to be a Louis Marks production of Sheridan's *The Critic* that I designed in the early '80s. It was a very costly, high quality production, and a very challenging one for me, as amongst other things I had to recreate the Drury Lane Theatre as it had looked in 1784. Unfortunately, it was given only one transmission, on a hot Monday evening in August, so hardly anybody saw it!'

Stephen James Walker

Interview conducted by Stephen James Walker and David J Howe

INTERVIEW: NICOLA BRYANT—COMPANION ACTRESS

When we came to plan the final issue of our fanzine The Frame – Issue 23/24, published in 1993 – David Howe and I decided that an ideal subject for our 'star interview' would be Nicola Bryant, who had played the Doctor's companion Perpugilliam Brown – Peri for short – from 1984 to 1986. Although Nicola had given many interviews before, David and I both felt that we still knew very little about her as a person, as previous interviewers had tended to focus solely on her Doctor Who work and had rarely touched on her life outside the series. We therefore decided to take the opposite approach and steer clear of covering Nicola's time as Peri in any depth, so as to avoid retreading familiar ground. Gary Leigh, editor of the fanzine DWB, later speculated that she had refused to answer any questions we put to her about Doctor Who, but this was certainly not the case – she had been happy to talk about anything we wanted, and it was our own decision to focus on other aspects of her life. Consequently the following interview is still, to my mind, the most insightful that Nicola has ever given.

The interview was conducted early one Saturday morning late in October 1992. 'How about breakfast?' Nicola had suggested two days earlier; and, only slightly daunted by the prospect of a very early start, we ventured up to Ladbroke Grove in West London, en route for a rendezvous at a small café, the name of which Nicola hadn't been able to remember, but which she had been sure was in a small turning off the Grove. Sure enough, when we arrived, the café was there – but, for the time being, Nicola was not. David wrestled his car up onto the pavement in the only available space, and we sat for a few moments wondering what to do, as the café was not yet open. Almost immediately, however, a car horn hailed us as Nicola pulled up, opened her car door and invited us to move across into her passenger seats. Marvelling at her adeptness in manoeuvring rapidly through roads flanked with parked cars, we were treated to a guided tour of the area as Nicola tried to find a parking space of her own. Half an hour later, we were still driving around, by now somewhat frustrated. Acting on impulse, Nicola headed for an old haunt and finally found somewhere to park. Five minutes after that, we were ordering breakfast in a small Italian coffee-shop. Nicola went for orange juice, cappuccino and a hot croissant with honey and jam, while David also opted for the cappuccino and I indulged in some hot chocolate.

We then got down to business with the interview, and spent a very pleasant hour or so discussing Nicola's life and work. What could not be adequately conveyed on the printed page was the great range of expressions and accents that Nicola used while speaking; as she told us, she has a knack for picking up different dialects and vocal mannerisms. From Liverpudlian to Cockney, from little girl to old hag, they are all effortlessly summoned to her lips in the course of conversation.

One other detail that has always stuck in my mind is that, although it was a rather grey, overcast day, Nicola was wearing a pair of very dark sunglasses when she met us, and initially kept these on even when we went inside the coffee-shop. I must confess I started to think that, given the earliness of the hour, she might be concerned that she did not look her best. However, David then asked her if she would mind taking the sunglasses off, explaining that he found it disconcerting to have a conversation with her when he could not see her eyes; and when she readily agreed, it turned out that her make-up was immaculate and she looked as great as ever.

Nicola continued a successful acting career for several years after this interview was conducted. Around 2000, however, an accident on stage left her with a back injury, which has seriously limited what she has been able to do since, both personally and professionally. She has, though, *regularly revisited the role of Peri in the series of* Doctor Who *audio CD dramas produced by Big Finish; and in February 2006, after a change in medication that brought about an improvement in her condition, she was able to return to the stage in a New End Theatre, London, production of the play* Taboos.

I was born in Guildford in Surrey, so it'll be very strange going back to do pantomime there[44]. There's a saying that you'll never be recognised in your own home town, and I'm half-afraid that no-one will turn up to see it! I'm looking forward to going back and revisiting my old school and my childhood stamping grounds. My mother still lives in Guildford – my father died some years ago – and she's "well chuffed" that I'm appearing there. She's told all her friends!

'I was actually brought up in a tiny village just outside Guildford. It was the sort of village where everybody knew everybody else, and you daren't go out and play up because someone would tell your mother what you'd done: "Saw your daughter picking blackberries today!" Anything you did, everybody would know about. My father's central heating company was there, and my mother's family had lived there all their lives. The central heating company's still going, and for some reason or other they ended up doing a lot of work for stars: Elton John, Dirk Bogarde, Barbra Streisand; people like that. There was no entertainment background at all in my family, except for that my uncle, my father's youngest brother, was very big in amateur dramatics – he met his wife while playing in *The Pyjama Game*. I thought he was very funny, and I remember as a kid going to see him and thinking, "That looks fun," even though I wasn't interested in being an actress at the time. I wanted to be Margot Fonteyn Mk II. From as early as I can remember, my very first thoughts were of dancing. I always had a creative streak, and I remember telling my sister Tracy, who's a couple of years younger than me, bedtime stories. I was about five years old, and I used to make them up, because I couldn't read properly. We had wallpaper covered with pictures of different animals, and every night she'd point to one and I'd say, "Once upon a time there was a great fat hippo called Henry …" Each character had a different story: there was George the Giraffe, Ellie the Elephant and so on. I'd do the same in the bathroom too. She'd point to the plastic duck and I'd say, "Once upon a time there was a big fat duck and she sank the boat …!" I was constantly telling stories and making things up, and I considered that to be part of being a dancer too, because when you dance, you are *expressing* a story. Actually, as I look back in my "mature wisdom" – ho, ho! – it may have had something to do with the fact that my mother was deaf. Dancing was a very natural way of expressing stories without words.

'I started taking dancing lessons at Bellairs Dance School when I was three. I didn't even know right from left, and my mother used to tie my right ballet shoe tighter than my left so I could close my eyes and work out which was which. Dancing was all I wanted to do right up until I was 11. I started going to classes every Saturday morning, then went three or four times on Saturdays, then started some evening classes, and eventually ended up going every evening as well as at the weekends.

'When I turned 11, I said to my family that I wanted to go to ballet school. My father thought, "Let her audition and she'll never get in. Then that'll be the end of that and she can come and work for me in the heating trade." That was what he wanted me to do when I left

---

44 At the time of the interview, Bryant was about to begin a season starring as Dandini in *Cinderella* at the Civic Hall, Guildford.

school – take over the running of his central heating business! Anyway, I auditioned and, contrary to my father's expectation, I got in. Unfortunately my father then said I couldn't go, which completely devastated me.

'Choosing a career at the age of 11 is a very difficult thing to do, and dancing was a very precarious business, so I don't blame my father for putting his foot down. However, all I had ever wanted to do was dance. Some children grow up wanting to be a bus driver one year, and the next year they want to be a doctor, and the year after that they want to drive a fire engine. This is a normal part of growing up. I, however, always wanted to be a dancer.

'So the next term I happily went back to my dance classes, and the teacher was surprised to see me because she thought I was going on to the ballet school. I was really puzzled as to why she thought I shouldn't be there. My father's refusal to allow me to go had been so traumatic that I had completely blocked it from my mind. When Mum picked me up afterwards, I remember telling her that the teacher had been in a funny mood all day and I didn't know why. It only came back to me about six months later when my godmother took me to see a performance of *The Nutcracker Suite* at Christmas. The minute the dancers appeared on stage, I burst into tears and cried throughout the whole of the show. My godmother didn't know what was wrong and took me home afterwards. I went up to Mum and Dad and sobbed, "I know what's happened ... It's awful!" I then went upstairs and bawled my eyes out for what seemed like days.

'This was the first scarring trauma of my childhood! My mother, being such a wonderful woman, realised that I was actually in a very deep depression for a child. She spotted in a newspaper that a local amateur dramatics society were auditioning for parts in *Fiddler on the Roof*, although you had to be 16 to join and I was much younger. I was moping in bed and she put this advertisement in front of me and said, "Why don't you have a go for this?" "Because I'm not old enough!" I retorted. So she said, "Well, do you think you can act?" "Of course I can!" I said, as disdainfully as I could muster. Her response was, cleverly, "Why don't you act you're older, then?"

'That laid down a challenge, so I went for the audition. When they asked what O Levels I was doing, I made them all up. I ended up getting the part of the second youngest daughter, and the lady who played my youngest sister was 18! They had absolutely no idea I was so young. I had to grow up very fast, because we used to have lunch in pubs. I was a fairly well developed young lady at the time and didn't look or act like a child. I suppose because I knew what I wanted to do with my life from the age of three, I started behaving like a grown-up early on. I'm trying to make up for my lost childhood now, however!

'My mother had been deaf for as long as she could remember. She lost her hearing when she was about four years old. When I was about 14, though, she was suddenly offered the opportunity to have an operation that could allow her to hear again, and she decided to go through with it. This was a very brave decision, as there was a chance that it might not work and disfigure her, and it was a major operation. She was in bandages for months, and it was during my school summer holidays, so I was with her the whole time. After the first operation, on one ear, she was captivated because she could hear a bee buzzing. I remember chasing this bee around the room, and when it landed on the window sill, my mum was close to tears because she couldn't hear it and thought that maybe she'd gone deaf again. I hastily explained that bees stop buzzing when they land – something that is totally taken for granted by a hearing person. A year later, she had the same operation on her other ear. You have to wait a year, because it upsets your balance so much and you can't walk. Even after the operation, my mother couldn't walk properly down stairs, but of course she would rather have that than not be able to hear.

'Anyway, I took all my O Levels and A Levels and did well, and my father was very pleased. I worked hard, all through the holidays. Boyfriends used to come round and knock on the door and ask if I could come out, and I'd say, "Oh, not now, I'm doing my Chemistry." I didn't want to go out with boys; I was busy working. I took A Levels in Geography, Economics, English and Home Economics – I just bunged that last one in 'cause I liked cooking! I also did ten O Levels and one O/A Level when I was 15 – I was a proper little swot!

'Eventually I gave up dancing, because the class started doing modern dance and tap and I didn't like it. I was classically trained and wanted to be a classical dancer, and as far as I was concerned, anything else was just secondary. Either you're going to be Margot Fonteyn or you're not. I was not going to be a Tiller Girl, and I just didn't get into it in the same fashion. I used to go and dance once a week, but I continued to appear in plays put on by the local company. After *Fiddler on the Roof* I did *The Sound of Music, Snow White* ...; all musicals, simply because I enjoyed them.

'It nearly got me thrown out of school, however, which was amazing. My music teacher saw me in one of these productions and, as she was quite chuffed that one of "her girls" was singing on stage, she mentioned it in the teachers' common room. The news got back to the headmistress and I was called to her study. This was quite a big deal, because no-one went to see the headmistress unless it was important. I stood there and she said "I understand that you are doing amateur dramatics." I thought that maybe she wanted tickets so I said "Yes?" She frowned. I had obviously blundered here. "This is time when you should be at home, studying." I couldn't believe it, so I pluckily asked, "Well, is there something wrong with my grades?" I thought that she'd got a right to drag me into her office if I was failing everything, but "If there are no problems, then I'm afraid, madam, that it's none of your blooming business" – not that I would ever have used such a word as "blooming" back then! She told me that if my grades went down at all then I'd have to give up the acting! I think my headmistress was a reincarnation of Jane Eyre's old schoolteacher. When I came to study for my O Levels, I did stop for the duration; but at the time, I wondered what the problem was.

'I chose the A Levels simply because they were what I felt like doing – there was no career plan, because by now I wanted to be an actress. Every year they used to give us forms to fill in – "What job do you want to do?" – and every year I used to write "Actress". My teachers thought that this was a waste of an intelligent young woman. They couldn't understand why I wanted to be an actress. In their eyes, the least I should do was to marry the chairman's son and become a bilingual secretary for two years before settling down and having lots of babies. But I couldn't lie and pretend that I wanted to do something that I didn't.

'There was an unwritten agreement in our household that, now my dancing career had been strangled at birth (no, I'm not bitter about it at all!), once I had done my O and A Levels, my parents would support me in whatever I wanted to do. And what I wanted to do was to go to drama school. I wrote to all the accredited schools and got auditions for every one, but they were all sneering of my age. They said "You can't come here at 17. We want experienced people, people who have been through things in their life." As if I hadn't! They weren't really interested in how good you were, just in how old you were.

'Now, when I went to the auditions, I noticed what type of person each school wanted; you're sitting around waiting before it's your turn to audition, and you see the people in the school going past on their way to classes or whatever. You look at the photographs on the wall

87

and you can see who has got which part; it's all a case of how observant you are. After I had been turned down, I reapplied to them all three months later and was accepted by them all. The reason was that, the second time, I acted my interviews. In other words, I acted the parts of the people I now knew they were looking for. The two most extreme were Central and Webber Douglas. For Central, I frizzed my hair, wore black eyeliner and jeans that I'd slashed holes in long before it was fashionable – way ahead of my time again! – an' I torked like tha'. An' I effed an' I blinded 'til I woz like, ya know. There were set speeches, and I had to do Julia's ring speech.[45] I grabbed a chair and kicked it into the middle of the room – attitude, man: I'm a girl wiv balls, ya know? – an' I said, "For those who bloody well can't see, this is a tree stump. Right! Can I start now?" They all looked at me saying, "Yes … right… this is very healthy … very healthy indeed. We can do something with this energy."

'In contrast, at Webber Douglas, I wore a full length practise skirt, put my hair in a bun, wore no make up, and was a very classical, serious young lady. Even my modern piece was classical really. I did Henry James, and everything about me was frightfully, frightfully classical. When they mentioned my age, I very seriously turned to them and said "I'd just like to ask you … please don't judge someone by the number of birthdays they've had, but by the events that have occurred between them." That was very smart of me. I couldn't say something that intelligent nowadays, as my brain's gone to goo, but they thought that was very impressive.

'So I acted interviews at Webber Douglas, RADA, Central, Guildhall and LAMDA. There was one particular director called Roger – I can't recall his surname – who was on the board for both Central and Webber Douglas. After I'd done my audition pieces at Webber Douglas, I sat down and looked across the table and there was this man who, only two weeks earlier, had seen me audition for Central! He looked at me and I looked at him and there was a sort of non-verbal communication to the effect that he wouldn't blow my cover. So I went through the whole of the rest of the audition with my nails pressed into my palms under the table, channelling all my fear and nervousness there while the rest of me was really relaxed. Months and months later, I happened to meet him again in a pub, and he told me that my audition was the most amusing thing that had ever happened to him. He said that he had been on the point of falling asleep before I came in, and that there was no way he was going to blow my cover, as if I could do that for an audition, then I could act without a doubt.

'I ended up at Webber Douglas, although the one I had really wanted to get into was LAMDA. What happened was that Webber Douglas gave me their acceptance and asked me to join in the April. LAMDA gave me a recall, and said they'd let people know in April for their September intake. So I had to decide. I opted to go to Webber Douglas, and two weeks later I got a letter from LAMDA saying that I'd been accepted for their September intake. I couldn't by then change, because the whole thing was grant-based and I couldn't switch my grant from one to the other.

'I'm not sure what drama school teaches you. I suppose that if you can survive three years there then you can probably survive anything that gets thrown at you in the business. However, I came out after three years thinking that if that was what the acting business was like, then I didn't want to go into it. I found it so aggressive and bitchy, and it was very hard to strike up friendships with people, because everyone was so fiercely competitive. Maybe part of my difficulty was that I came from a very close and loving relationship with my mother, very intimate and supportive, and I was as a result much more aware of people and feelings. I pick up things about people and what they're thinking. I have very, very sensitive hearing. I

---

45 From Shakespeare's *The Two Gentlemen of Verona*.

can tell when my boyfriend rings me from his office rather than from his home, because it has a different sound. I can walk into a familiar room and tell if the battery needs changing in the clock, because I can hear that the ticking is in a different rhythm from the week before. I actually have to sleep with ear-plugs in, because I hear so many sounds. One benefit of this is that I have perfect pitch and can pick up accents easily.

'My drama school would never cast me as a female lead, which is the most obvious thing that I would be. Ten years later, I've still got *ingénue* stamped all over me – Young Female Lead, Flirty Girly Thingy – and yet I was always cast as pensioners or men. I got to the end of my final year at drama school and they decided that instead of casting the end-of-year production in-house, which would have meant that certain people who were "teacher's pets" got the best parts (that's a bit like real life, isn't it!), they were going to get someone in from outside to put us through full auditions and make the decisions. I had started in musicals when I was 12 and had always considered that I could sing. I wouldn't say I was brilliant, but I could sing in tune and I could hold a tune, but Webber Douglas had never given me a singing tutorial. They had this stupid idea that you had to audition for them and not everyone got them. So if you were completely and utterly tone deaf and couldn't sing a note then you'd get one, because they thought they had to do something, but I've got perfect pitch and therefore in their eyes I didn't need any training.

'The end-of-year play was the musical *No, No, Nanette* – rather twee, but there you go. This chap came in to audition us, and we had about a week to prepare. I looked at the book and thought that I was typecast for this: sweet, innocent – I *was* Nanette! But as far as singing went, forget it, because I had had no training. My fiancé at the time – Scott Kennedy, a Broadway singer who had played the lead in two or three Broadway musicals and who was at Webber Douglas doing a post-graduate course – said that of course I could do it and that all this drama school stuff was absolute rubbish. So he coached me for a week and I just went for it. I auditioned and I read the piece, and I sang the song. I didn't really think anything of it, because I didn't think they'd give me the part – but of course they did!

'At this, there was uproar at Webber Douglas: "How dare you give the lead to someone who hasn't had a singing tutorial for three years." There was definite dissension in the ranks, because the girl who was Webber Douglas's singing favourite, who had had all the tutorials going and who had played the lead in just about every other production, ended up playing chorus – because, I'm afraid, in the real world, she would not have been up for the part.

'I then had to try to play this part with everyone hating my guts and resenting me. I hated it so much, and used to come home and cry into my pillow. I thought that if that was what it was like out there, then I didn't want to act. I didn't have the backbone to get me though that sort of bitchiness. In the end, I talked to Scott, and he was very supportive and encouraged me just to give it a try to see how it went.

'I was very lucky that I landed the part in *Doctor Who*, because it gave me back a sense of family. Colin [Baker] and Peter [Davison] were so nice, and especially John [Nathan-Turner]. John was very paternal and took great care of me. I had three and a half years to develop a thick skin and to realise that there are lots of nice people out there. I might come across a couple of right so-and-sos, but the majority are all right. I think I was so lucky, because otherwise I might have given it all up and tried to do something else: married the boss's son or something.

'I was married to Scott at 18, incredibly young, a year before I left Webber Douglas and walked straight into *Doctor Who*. I think I told John that I was 21 – I was trying to be older than I was – and I think it was odd for someone who looked even younger to be settled down and married. When I played Peri, I wore my wedding ring on another finger, but I never lied about being married. If I was ever asked, I wouldn't say yes or no, I'd simply say that there was just one person in my life.

'When I auditioned for *Doctor Who*, John had no idea that I was not American. I have dual nationality through my marriage to Scott, although we're now separated, and my room-mate at boarding school was from New York, so I had picked up her accent. I had been playing an American in *No, No, Nanette* and an agent, Terry Carney[46], who came in to see it, assumed that I was American. He called me up and asked me to go and audition for *Doctor Who*. He didn't want to take on someone new out of drama school unless I had a job, so this was in his interest as well as mine. I told him that I wasn't strictly American, but he told me to do it American. So I went and I did it American, and I thought that if they weren't happy with my Americanness, they'd never find out anyway. There was someone from Denver at the office and I thought that if I convinced him, then I wasn't letting anyone down.

'So I went through several auditions and finally got the part. Then I had to try to get my Equity card, because they wouldn't let me have the part unless I was a member of the union. I then had to get all my friends together and do cabaret work around some clubs to gain enough work experience to qualify for membership.

'My first day's work on *Doctor Who* was actually an interview on breakfast TV. That was really bizarre. The first money I ever earned was from an interview on breakfast television! Funnily enough, Terry Carney hadn't wanted to draw up a contract with me at first, but when he saw me on TV in front of the cameras, he rang me that morning asking me to come in and sign a contract. Of course, I signed. They never teach you about contracts, payments and the like at drama school, and yet it's absolutely essential knowledge. I've actually thought about putting a talk together and going back to my old school to tell them all about the real world. For example, they still talk about working in rep, but the rep system doesn't exist any more. Their attitude about television was that you don't need to know that much about it, because your first job will be saying "He went that way" or dying before the titles. And it's simply not true. You have no idea what you might get.

'I loved television. I loved the process and the people. What I don't like is when people come up to me and ask, "Are you Nicola Bryant?" I'll say [in a broad Birmingham accent] "You what? No, I'm not, no. Lots of people often mistake me for her, you know. But I think she's a lot older than me, and a lot taller, and a lot better looking." I just pretend to be someone else, because I hate all that "Excuse me, can I have your autograph" stuff when I'm out on my own. I just want to be private. At conventions, however, I really enjoy it.

'When I started in *Doctor Who*, I didn't think that the programme would end up placing so much emphasis on me and my role in it. It was one of those fortunate – for me – bits of timing that the show went through a period of change just before I joined. There had been five companions – Nyssa, Turlough, Adric, Tegan and Kamelion – all working with one Doctor, and in a very short space of time it was back to just the one. Me. So I didn't have to share my dialogue with several others, and my first story[47], shot in Lanzarote, represented an obvious injection of money and enthusiasm into the show. It consequently gained a lot of publicity, most of which featured me. What an incredible launch for any young actress's career!'

David J Howe

---

46 Son-in-law of first Doctor actor William Hartnell. He had also been Hartnell's agent.

47 'Planet of Fire'.

INTERVIEW: COLIN BAKER—DOCTOR

The sixth Doctor has always, to my mind, been somewhat underrated. Whenever a 'favourite Doctor' poll is conducted, he generally ends up languishing near, if not at, the bottom. Fortunately, opinions have started to turn more in his favour in recent years, as a run of strong sixth Doctor stories in Big Finish's audio CD drama range have led to a growing acceptance that the problem with his era on TV lay not so much in his character as in the scripts with which he was burdened, and in other aspects of the series' production. Even back in 1989, Colin Baker was winning over new fans with his well-received return to the role in the Terrance Dicks-scripted touring stage play Doctor Who – The Ultimate Adventure. *Jon Pertwee had intially taken the lead in this play, but Colin had succeeded him part-way through the run and continued to the end of the tour. The following interview, conducted after an evening performance of the play, originally appeared in two parts in Issues 12 and 13 of* The Frame, *dated November 1989 and February 1990 respectively.*

As a rule, Eastbourne is not the most interesting of places to visit on a Friday night. Fortunately, Friday 18 August 1989 proved to be an exception – for us, at least – as we were in town to interview Colin Baker following his latest performance in *Doctor Who – The Ultimate Adventure* at the town's Congress Theatre.

When Colin was free to join us, we left the theatre and wandered the near-deserted streets for a while until we found a chic local eatery in which to pass the remainder of the evening. Ensconcing ourselves in a secluded corner, with pop-star posters staring down at us from the walls and the sound of Dire Straits droning quietly in the background, we set the tape recorder running.

'This might well be my last *Doctor Who* interview for a long time,' Colin confided, between mouthfuls of humous. 'But David Banks and I have just interviewed each other, and it will be coming out as a tape on David's Silver Fist label. Do you ever listen to that programme *Loose Ends* on Radio 4? Or *Stop the Week*? It's a bit like that – a bit *Stop the Week*-ish. We ramble on for an hour, talking about our early lives and so on. It's called *The Ultimate Interview*. I was also interviewed for a Myth Makers video about a year ago, and that should be out soon.'

Colin was a little disappointed that we hadn't actually arrived in time to see the show that evening: 'You would have doubled the audience, if you'd been there!' This prompted us to ask what sort of business the play had done generally during its run.

'It's varied enormously. Usually, if you open to a certain advance booking at a theatre, you can gauge from that how you're going to do during the week, because you know a certain proportion of people will just turn up on the night. With this show, though, it seems we always open quite low, then gradually build and build and build. By the end of the week, we're doing quite well, because the word's got round, but then we go on somewhere else. We just haven't been able to sell it properly in advance, and I don't know why. The hot summer might have had a lot to do with it, or perhaps people have the wrong impression of what *Doctor Who* will be like on stage.'

We were curious to know what had tempted Colin to accept the role of the stage Doctor, only three years after his unhappy departure from the TV series. 'I saw the show in Wimbledon, shortly after it opened, and I wasn't particularly impressed. Then I saw it again four or five weeks later in Bristol, and it was much, much better. Even when I saw it the first time, though, when it was a bit of a shambles, I realised – with no disrespect to Jon whatsoever

– that it was particularly suited to my Doctor. That's because my Doctor is a "stage" Doctor – he's flamboyant and over-the-top. Jon's dignified portrayal was brilliant on television, but as the centre of a busy show, he had a problem, and the script didn't serve him as well as perhaps it ought to have done. My Doctor, on the other hand, can rush around and do a few more things, and I thought, "Maybe I can contribute something to this". So that was one aspect. Obviously the negotiations came into it too – the fact that I was well paid for it. And it fitted in with all the other things that I wasn't doing!'

To what extent, then, had the play been adapted to suit Colin's Doctor?

'When I was rehearsing, we took the opportunity to make a few changes to the script. In the swordfight, for example, I wanted to have the Doctor saying, "Now if you go over there…" – and as he pointed over there with his sword, he deflected one blow – "Or is it over that way?" – and he deflected another one – so that he was totally oblivious that he was actually having a swordfight. Unfortunately, there wasn't enough time to work that out, so in the end we played it as if I was such an expert swordsman that I could actually have a conversation with somebody while fighting behind my back. I mean, it's a terrible gag, but it was a compromise.

'The other scene I particularly wanted to change was the one with the flying ant creatures. When I watched it, I couldn't believe that the Doctor just walked off, consigning these things to a grisly death at the hands of the Cybermen. So now I play it as if I'm trying to stop them from sacrificing themselves, saying "No, no". And then, as I run off, I say "Thank you". Otherwise, it made the Doctor look totally callous, actually asking them to fly down and get themselves killed!

'Since rehearsals, we haven't changed anything, apart from the small variations I put in nightly, which keep the rest of the cast on their toes! I see myself, in a show like this, a bit like a soloist in an orchestra. I mean, I've got to play the tune – I've got to say the words – but I'm allowed a little licence. I think the part, and the show, benefit if the Doctor's slightly unpredictable, and does something different every now and again. For instance, the business with Zog has grown tremendously since I started doing it.'

Zog is a character that has proved particularly popular with younger members of the audience, as Colin knows from personal experience. 'My little girl, Lucy, is obsessed with Zog. It was lovely because, after one show, Stephanie Colburn said, "Do you want me to stay in costume for Lucy?" So Lucy came backstage and there was Zog standing at the side! And you know that pouch Zog has at the front? Well, Stephanie pulled out a packet of sweets and gave them to Lucy, and they had this little conversation in the corridor. The next day, Lucy wanted to get up early and draw a picture for Zog, and I had to bring it in for her the following night! It makes it all worthwhile, that. Wonderful.

'Actually, I've just bought Lucy a set of those little Dalek toys – one of each kind.[48] I gave them to her this morning, and all day long she's been playing with them. Unfortunately, she took one with us when we went to Tesco's, and as I was walking around, I suddenly heard her calling out "I will exterminate the Doctor!" For anyone else it would be okay, but for me, that's a touch embarrassing!'

By this time, the meal was well into its main course. Other people had started to drift into the restaurant, too, including a few members of *The Ultimate Adventure*'s technical crew.

'Please don't listen to this,' Colin pleaded, jokingly, 'I'm being interviewed, and it'll sound a bit naff!'

As we set about devouring our pizzas, Colin admitted that one aspect of the tour he had

48 These were the toys produced by Dapol.

particularly enjoyed was talking to different members of the audience every night. 'I learnt quite quickly that I either spend 20 minutes signing autographs at the stage door, uncomfortably jammed against a brick wall, or I formalise it. So I formalise it, and sit at a table in the foyer to sign a few autographs after each performance. Mums, dads and children come up, and the comment I've had consistently from parents is, "Well, we only came because, you know, little Jason wanted to see the show, but we've had a wonderful time, we've loved it."'

We observed that this was rather different from the sort of reaction Colin had received from certain sections of fandom during his time in the TV series. 'Yes, funnily enough, doing this tour has helped to redress the balance. I've had young kids hugging me, in tears, saying "Why can't you come back on TV? You'll always be my Doctor". I expect every other Doctor has had the same thing, but I personally had never experienced it before. Families, too, have come up and said, "You will always be our Doctor". Okay, that's probably because I just happened to be the one who was in it when they starting watching; I realise that. But it's nice to know there are people out there who feel that way.'

Did this mean that touring with the play had changed Colin's perspective on his time as the Doctor? After all, he had once said that if he'd known at the beginning how things would turn out, he probably would never have accepted the TV role in the first place. 'You can't really wish your past life away, so I suppose it was daft of me to say that. In the same way, if I was to say now, "Right, that's the end, I'm never having anything more to do with *Doctor Who*", that would be daft as well. If this play had a re-think, had a bit more money spent on it, was re-mounted as a really big spectacular and sent out at the right time, in the Autumn, leading up to a Christmas season somewhere, I'd probably be delighted to do it again. I certainly haven't got bored with it, and usually after doing something for 11 weeks I am getting a bit bored.

'Doing this show has been like putting on a pair of comfy old slippers. I was a little alarmed at how easily I slipped into it again, and how much I enjoyed it, although it's rekindled old sadnesses as well. I won't feel particularly sad when it finishes, mind you, because I've done nearly a hundred performances, and that's enough. But it's been nice to play the part again. In a way, it's laid a ghost, it's added a coda. It's made me believe that my Doctor has a part in the scheme of things.

'Even though only a few thousand people have seen the show over the weeks, I'm quite glad about that really, because part of the worry about doing more *Doctor Who* is that it could fix me as the Doctor again in the minds of people who might employ me in something else. But that won't happen with a touring stage production.

'Really, it's just been nice to do it again. I've had a good relationship with my new companions, too. It's been a great company, and I'm glad I did it.'

As midnight approached and we finished off the main course of our meal, we asked Colin how he had originally been approached to play the part of the sixth Doctor, and how the character had been developed.

'John Nathan-Turner rang me up one afternoon and said he'd like to see me. I went in to the office and he said, "I'm not offering you the part, but Peter Davison is leaving and I wondered if you would be interested in playing the Doctor?" So I replied, very casually, "Oh, yeah, I wouldn't mind". He said, "Well, I'm going to give you a few tapes and ask you to go away and watch some of the earlier Doctors. We'll meet again in a week's time and you can tell me how you think you'd like to play him." And that's what we did.'

Searching back through his memory, Colin recalled that the tapes he had been given were of 'The Space Museum', 'The War Games', 'Carnival of Monsters' and 'Pyramids of Mars'.

'Anyway, I watched those several times, then I went back to see John and he asked me what

I thought. I said, "Well, I would obviously play the part as a kind of distillation of myself, as all the others have done, but one thing I would like to bring out is the fact that the Doctor is an alien – he's not a human being, even though he looks like one."

'I thought it would be quite nice if sometimes he didn't behave in the way we would expect him to behave. So, on one day, if a person was mown down in front of him, he might just step over them and ask somebody the time; but another day, he might go into terrible paroxysms of grief about a sparrow falling out of a tree. Obviously we'd have to be able to explain why, and what it was that was concerning the Doctor; I just didn't want him to behave in an obvious, sentimental, approachable way. I wanted him to be a little bit unapproachable. He could get extremely angry about something – a build-up followed by a sudden explosion, so that the rage might seem to be about one thing when it was actually about something that happened two episodes ago, perhaps. I think there's a danger with this kind of programme that it's all too pat, all too obvious.

'Now, John liked this idea, and in the end he pushed it further than probably I would have had the courage to do, by making the Doctor so unapproachable in that first story, "The Twin Dilemma". You had to wait for four episodes before you found out if this person had anything remotely likeable in him, and I think that was very brave, especially as it was the end of a season. I like that kind of bravery in television. It's all too easy to play safe all the time.

'So that was one thing I wanted. I also saw the Doctor as being rather austere, dressed in black. I wanted a black velvet costume, but it was pointed out to me that the Master had got in there first, so I couldn't have it. And the one aspect of my Doctor that I suppose I do regret is the costume. It works for other people and it kind of works for me now, but I would have liked it to have been something different. Really, though, the costume was, to me, a very unimportant part of the whole enterprise. This was partly because I was inside it looking out – everybody else had to look at it, therefore it meant a lot to them!

'I also suggested that the Doctor should tell really bad jokes – you know, the puns. The idea of using quotes was mine, as well. I wanted to use quotes from the English language – obviously, because we were making the programme in English! – but also I wanted to make things up that sounded like quotes from other cultures. So it might be a Venusian quote, or a quote from Alderberan 4. I thought that was a nice idea.

'There was another thing, too. I have a little bee in my bonnet about the English language. It's the richest language in the world in terms of the amount of words available, but gradually we're losing most of them. I wanted there to be at least half-a-dozen words in each episode that the viewers would have to rush off and look up, because they didn't know what they meant. If you're really hooked on a character and he uses a long word that you don't understand, then you'll go and find out what it means: it's extending people's vocabularies, which I think is nice.

'All these ideas John Nathan-Turner liked, and we both went upstairs to see David Reid, who was then the Controller. Fortunately he was watching test match cricket on TV at the time, and I asked "How's Botham doing?", or something. He said "Oh, do you like cricket?" and we chatted about cricket for 20 minutes – to JN-T's total perplexity, because he knew nothing about cricket! After that, we talked about the role of the Doctor for a minute or two, and David Reid said "Well, I think that's great, excellent". Apparently the fact that I liked cricket did it for me!

'I was then asked if I would sign a four year option, because Peter had left after three years and they wanted to get a bit more continuity. I said "I'd like that very much!" – I was thinking, "Four years, 26 episodes a year, wonderful!"

'And that's really how it all happened!'

We commented that this account seemed to disprove the commonly-held belief that Colin had had relatively little say in the formulation of his Doctor's character.

'Well, in terms of the shape of my character at the beginning, it's not that I had any say as such, it's just that they asked me how I would play it, I told them, and they liked it. I think you'd have to do that with any Doctor. There's no point in hiring an actor for that part and then telling him to play it in a way that is different from how he would naturally approach it. He's got to play it his way.

'After that, though, I certainly wasn't consulted by Eric Saward about scripts, and if ever I made any suggestions about scripts, he didn't respond very warmly to that. He was of the "writers write, directors direct and actors act" school, which to a certain extent I am myself, but I think that when you've got a long-running programme with a central actor, eventually he's going to have more input potential than new people coming in from outside. I could never make any headway with that, though.

'Actually, I found there was an awful lot of casual scriptwriting went on during my time in the series. I had terrible trouble with "The Trial of a Time Lord" in particular. I remember that the worst part was the segment written by Philip Martin. I would ask the director, "Is this the Matrix lying, is the Doctor under the influence of the process he's been subjected to, or is he lying for some reason of his own that we'll later discover?" "I don't know," came the reply, "you'd better ask Philip Martin". So I asked Philip Martin, and he said, "I don't know. Eric Saward put that bit in. You'll have to ask him". I asked Eric, and Eric said, "Oh, I don't know. Philip Martin wrote that bit"! I told him, "Look, I need to know, in order to play this scene. When I'm chaining Peri to the rock, is that a Matrix lie or am I behaving like that because I know I'm being watched?" "Oh, whichever suits you"! The thing is that no-one had ever bothered to work it out. In the end, I decided that most of it was a Matrix/Valeyard lie.

'Small continuity points don't bother me: what bother me are basic mistakes like that, which usually come from a total lack of caring. I wouldn't normally accuse an individual, but because Eric was later so vociferously critical of the programme and of me, I will say this: make sure your own slate is clean before you start criticising other people's dirty slates! He really was very casual about it. You can't blame the writers, because they get given a brief.'

Returning to the question of how the sixth Doctor's character had originally been worked out, we wondered to what extent Eric Saward had been involved in that process.

'Eric was there at the meetings when we talked about it, but he didn't say much. Subsequently, he's intimated in interviews that he didn't think it was a good idea, but I certainly didn't get that impression at the time.

'Actually, before he left the show, Eric was always very friendly towards me. He used to ring me up – not often, but every couple of months, usually about midnight or one o'clock in the morning – and he'd say, "Oh, I don't know what to do about this script", or "John's getting on my back about this; I can't cope with him". He would go on like this, and I used to calm him down. He even came to my house once. He said, "I've got to talk to somebody." He came and had lunch and we walked and talked about all sorts of things, including his problems with scripts and problems with John and so on, and he went back saying, "Yes, you're quite right, I'm being silly." Then, after he left, he came out with that outburst against the programme, which included me as well![49] I just wish he'd said to me at the time, you know, "I don't like the

49 After resigning his post as *Doctor Who*'s script editor, Eric Saward gave an interview to genre magazine *Starburst*, in which he was harshly critical of producer John Nathan-Turner and others associated with the series, including Colin Baker.

way you're playing the part," or something. But he never did. In fact, on the contrary, he was quite flattering.'

By this time, the restaurant was almost deserted and the waitress had started to clear our plates away. To round off the discussion, we asked Colin about his untimely departure from the series in 1986. There has always been much speculation as to the real reason for the BBC's decision to oust him, and we were interested to know if he could shed any light on this.

'I know what the reason was. You see, whenever Michael Grade went on a chat show – and he went on a lot! – the only thing that ever fazed him was a question about *Doctor Who*. He didn't get asked about the drama output of the BBC, or its current affairs programmes, or whatever, it was always *Doctor Who*. And every time, he slagged off the production team. He said, "We're looking at the programme and we're getting it back on an even keel." Well, he had a ten minute meeting with John Nathan-Turner – that was "getting it back on an even keel"! In the end, he'd been talking about it so much that he had to be seen to do something. Changing the Doctor was the ideal solution from his viewpoint. It got publicity, it showed the public that he'd done something, and it reassured people that the programme had a future, because a new Doctor was to be cast.

'I was offered the chance to do the first four episodes of the following season – that was actually a concession won by John – but I said, "Quite honestly, if I've got to leave, I want to leave now and start making a career." The analogy I've always used is that it's like your girlfriend giving you the push and saying, "But you can come back and spend a night with me next year"! It's just not on.

'As it was, I got more work instantly. I was doing a panto directed by John Nathan-Turner at Christmas, and very quickly after that I was asked to do the play *Corpse*, which I consider is one of the best things I've ever done – I loved it. That started in March 1987 and I was still doing it in November, because it transferred to a theatre in the West End, where it had a four month run. So I was vindicated, because if I'd said yes to those four episodes, I might have got four weeks' work that year and missed out on nine months' work.'

As we left the restaurant and made our way out onto the sea front, we asked Colin how he would sum up his time in *Doctor Who*. '*Coitus interruptus!*' was his immediate rejoinder, but then he offered a more serious assessment.

'I feel that "unlucky" is the word that sums up my tenure, really. A combination of Michael Grade – who changed the schedules, changed the length of the programme, cancelled it in the middle, then put it on after *Roland Rat* and opposite *The A Team* – together with the whole Eric Saward business, the upheaval that the BBC itself was going through at that time ... all those things conspired to make it very difficult. In a way, it was more frustrating than anything else. If someone had said, "Look, we think you're awful and we're replacing you", I would have had to live with that. But when I know it was just a combination of circumstances, and I was powerless to do anything about it ...

'You know, if someone else had been cast as the Doctor in 1984 and I was doing it now, I'd still be in that part for years to come.'

Stephen James Walker

Interview conducted by Stephen James Walker, David J Howe, Mark Stammers and Gordon Roxburgh

INTERVIEW: PAT GODFREY–COSTUME DESIGNER

As costume designer for the sixth Doctor's debut story, 'The Twin Dilemma', Pat Godfrey had the task of realising his distinctive costume from the brief given to her by producer John Nathan-Turner. She also, of course, designed all the other costumes for the production, and was later assigned to one further sixth Doctor story, 'Revelation of the Daleks'. David Howe and Mark Stammers met up with her at her home in 1991 for an interview that was published later that year in Issue 19 of The Frame. *In addition to* Doctor Who, *Pat's credits include several episodes of* Lovejoy *(1986),* Skulduggery *(1989),* Hallelujah Anyhow *(1990),* Tell Me that You Love Me *(1991),* The Hummingbird Tree *(1992),* Pie in the Sky *(1995) and* Hope and Glory *(1999) for the BBC, and* Noah's Ark *(1997) for ITV.*

Pat Godfrey has spent most of her career as a costume designer with the BBC, working on many prestigious dramas as well as some more lightweight assignments. We began by asking how she had come to be a costume designer.

'When I was five years old, I was always drawing crinoline ladies that looked like those old crocheted toilet roll holders, which my father thought was hysterical. He wanted me to go to university, but I knew I didn't have the brains to cope with all that academia, so I went to Birmingham Art College and studied to become a fashion designer. However, during my first year at college, I discovered that I was far more interested in period and theatrical costume design than in fashion, so I then went on to specialise in theatre design and period costume cutting and construction.

'When the summer holidays came around, I had to decide what I wanted to do during the break. I could have got a job in an office, but I preferred to do something relevant to my studies. So I simply wrote to the BBC and to ITV, and got lucky. Joyce Hawkins, the BBC costume designer at Gosta Green in Birmingham, needed someone on a casual basis to help with the creation of the ladies' costumes for their regional productions. (Gosta Green was the converted cinema the BBC used as a production base before Pebble Mill.) The only problem was that the job was more than just a holiday position and would sometimes require me to work during term time. Fortunately, my college principal was very understanding and saw that it was an important opportunity for me to get a break in television once I had finished my course, so I was able to accept it. I ended up working regularly in television for the next three years. As the set up was much smaller than at Television Centre in London, I got to be a dresser, a wardrobe mistress and a costume assistant. It was great experience for the future.

'After I finished college, I went to work for a theatrical hire company in Birmingham. I was actually waiting for a full-time position to become available at Gosta Green, but after three months, I was told that there was a job as an assistant designer coming up at the BBC in Cardiff. I applied, and was successful. Typically, about three months after I had moved to Cardiff, the position I had been waiting for in Birmingham became vacant! I don't believe in going back, though, and as I'd only just left home and got myself a flat in Cardiff, I decided to turn down the Birmingham job. I stayed in Cardiff for eight years, eventually becoming a full costume designer.

'The set-up in Cardiff was very similar to that in Birmingham. Consequently you got to do a bit of everything, whereas in London designers tended to get labelled as "light entertainment", "modern-day drama" or "period costume".

'In 1970, I went on a six month attachment to London, where I worked on a Jean-Paul Sartre trilogy called *Roads to Freedom* starring Daniel Massey, Georgia Browne and Michael Bryant. I thoroughly enjoyed working on such a large-scale production and decided that I wanted to move to London permanently. I was lucky enough to get a job at Television Centre as a senior designer – I was still only 28, and became the youngest person ever to be promoted to that grade. I stayed in that job in London for 15 years.'

What kind of work had she done during that period?

'Basically dramas, although there was the occasional *Les Dawson Show* thrown in for good measure, which I enjoyed doing too. The kind of productions I most enjoyed were the single period plays about real people like Amy Johnson and Stanley Spencer, which were produced by Innes Lloyd. I had to research those using old films and photographs of the people being portrayed.'

How, then, had her work on *Doctor Who* come about?

'I was simply called into the production office and told that I would be working on *Doctor Who*. I said "What!" I was absolutely amazed, because it was considered to be very high flying to get to work on the programme; it was very special to become part of the *Doctor Who* stable. For about a week, I was completely poleaxed by the thought of it, as I'd never been involved with anything that had so much publicity surrounding it. The fact that I had the responsibility of designing a new Doctor's costume made the job even more prestigious.

'I talked to John Nathan-Turner about his ideas for the Doctor's costume. John very much wanted to achieve a kind of development from one Doctor to another. He wanted to get the feel of the previous costumes by going back to a more Victorian shape, but he also wanted to make the new one look very bizarre, rather fairground and clown-like. He even suggested that I could have spotted trousers, but that was a direction we chose not to follow. John wanted a garish costume – his own words were "a totally tasteless costume" – which is actually very difficult to achieve, as you have to be tastefully tasteless.'

Had there been any other constraints on the design?

'Yes. The shirt had to have the question marks on each collar, and there couldn't be any blue in the costume, because of the problems with CSO.

'I spent about a week looking at lots of different combinations of Victorian frock coats. Then I took my rough ideas back to John and we discussed and refined them to come up with the final design.

'Costumes like the Doctor's have to be more practical than real clothes, as the actors are asked to do a lot of unusual things in them. They have to be hard-wearing and very durable. My assistant went out and did a lot of swatch shopping to choose the various materials we would use. We had to buy enough of each material to make four complete costumes, although only two were made initially. I knew that whoever came after me would never be able to find all the materials again, especially as many of the fabrics were produced for only one fashion season, and some of them we had specially dyed. I sometimes feel a little guilty about this as I get letters from fans asking me where they can find the correct materials to match the originals, and I have to tell them that they can't get them any more.

'The frock coat was made from Melton cloth, which is pure wool. A lot of the sections were specially dyed, and we used a braided trim on the edges and back slit. The trousers were made of pillow ticking, which again was dyed yellow. Pillow ticking is a very tightly woven fabric, so I knew that if it got caught on anything, it wouldn't get too damaged.

'The tailor who made up the costume was a man called Arthur Davey, who has since retired.[50] He originally worked for Bermans and Nathans the costumiers, but subsequently left and set up his own business. He was a lovely man and very talented. It's very difficult to find people who can cut period patterns.'

What kind of reaction had the new costume got from people within the production team, and especially from Colin Baker?

'Colin lived quite near me at the time, so I took my designs over to his house for him to see. He had already been told what to expect by John Nathan-Turner. I think John himself was very happy with the final costume. Most people's reaction when they first saw it was that it knocked them out, although I know that there were a lot who didn't like it.'

Had the new Doctor's costume affected Pat's other designs for 'The Twin Dilemma'?

'Yes, particularly Peri's costume. This really arose from a technicality of working in colour television. When colour was first introduced, we were trained in how to design for it. Basically, we were shown a scale of 0 to 100, where 0 was black and 100 was white. We were told that the maximum range video cameras could cope with at that time was only about 30 – in other words, the darkest and brightest colours could be no more than 30 points apart on the scale. So because the Doctor's costume was very bright, I had to move everything else up the scale accordingly. If the companion's costume had been in very subtle hues, it would have been washed out by the Doctor's, so hers had to be bright as well. In any case, the actress who was playing Peri, Nicola Bryant, had a very bright and bubbly personality, so the colours suited her in that sense. I presented a number of design sketches to John, but he wanted something very different from what I had envisaged, which happens sometimes. He wanted to have her in shorts instead of trousers.'

What was the concept behind the Jocondan costumes? Had they always been intended to be bird-like creatures?

'With the Jocondans, the idea was to use metallic-looking fabrics to give them an alien appearance. The costumes were made from heavy-duty lining fabric mounted on calico to give it a bit of weight. The idea for the face make-up came slightly later, during a production meeting. The make-up designer, Dee Baron, made the feathers the same metallic colours as the tunics, so that they would blend well.[51]

'The Americanised space cop uniforms were very basic overalls that we bought in. We just added large cardboard badges to them. Azmael, played by Maurice Denham, was a more important character, so I made his costume white to ensure that it would stand out from all the others. I used a textured fabric, to which I had planned to add an extra layer; however, we ran out of time, so we just had the texture. The twins' costumes were kept very simple and plain for monetary reasons. I think I had about £7,000 to spend on "The Twin Dilemma", which was higher than the usual budget as it allowed for the expense of the new Doctor's costume.'

How had Mestor's costume been created?

'I knew the monsters were supposed to be gastropods (slugs), so I did some research, looking at pictures of slugs and basing my final design on them. I then rang Richard Gregory of the Imagineering effects house, who had been recommended to me because of his earlier work on *Doctor Who*, and he made up the costume for me. The body was a cross between a bag and a sack. It consisted of three layers of material mounted on calico, the top layer being

---

50 Davey had previously made the early costumes for Jon Pertwee as the third Doctor.

51 See the interview with Dee Baron elsewhere in this book.

organza to give it a shiny look. The back was covered in a textured latex with a fibre-glass carapace, which was also covered in textured latex. The arms were extended rubber gloves with more textured latex on them, and the feet were wellie boots finished in the same way. Edwin Richfield, who played Mestor, wore the costume only for short periods at a time, but whenever we removed it, he and the costume would both be soaked in perspiration.

'One comment I saw in the press that made me laugh was from the *Daily Mail*. It said that the slug costume was a good idea for a child's fancy dress outfit. If only they knew the time and effort it took to make, and how uncomfortable it was to wear! I think the complete costume cost something like £200 or £300.'

After *The Twin Dilemma*, Pat's next association with *Doctor Who* came at the end of the following season.

'About a year later I was asked to do "Revelation of the Daleks". The brief for that story was very precise. The Doctor had to have a cape, which had to be blue as the colour was mentioned in the script; and in fact the majority of the other costumes had to be blue as well. The mortuary workers' uniforms were all dentists' tunics, which again was specified in the brief. We had to send them all out to be dyed professionally to make sure that the colour was consistent. As these plain costumes would have been fairly boring on their own, I came up with the idea of a cap with coloured stripes on it that would continue down onto the face. I had recently read an article about face painting in an issue of *Vogue*, so I worked with the make-up designer on that story, Dorka Nieradzik, to produce the right effect.

'Eleanor Bron's character was originally called Zara, but this was changed to Kara because Zara is the name of Princess Anne's daughter. Kara required two costumes, as the script specified that she had to change for a burial ceremony. Bostock (John Ogwen) and Orcini (William Gaunt) I wanted to give camouflage jackets, but it was decided that they should be more "Che Guevara"-type characters, so we hired their costumes from a costumier and just added some small details to them.

'Davros's costume was from stock, so we just patched it up and made it reusable. We also had to supply the rags for the mutant seen at the beginning of the story. In all, I think the costume budget on "Revelation of the Daleks" was about £5,000. This had been worked out at the beginning of the season, before the scripts had been completed, and as it was a Dalek story, they'd thought that they wouldn't need too many extra costumes. Unfortunately, there turned out to be a lot of characters in the cast, so money was very tight.'

Pat left Television Centre four years ago, after working for the BBC for 24 years.

'I had been doing the same job for a long time and wanted to spend more time at home, so when I saw a job-share based at the BBC in Bristol, I decided to take it. I now work for six months a year. I get to do two or three jobs from a choice of five, and can choose to spend the whole six months on a series like *Casualty* or to do a number of one-off dramas, which I prefer. It also means I can keep in touch with all my friends at Television Centre. I am allowed to do work outside the BBC as long as it's not in direct competition, so I can do adverts or films for independent production companies. It stops you getting tunnel vision about costume design, and definitely keeps you on your toes.'

Mark Stammers

Interview conducted by Mark Stammers and David J Howe

INTERVIEW: DENISE BARON—MAKE-UP DESIGNER

In the spring of 1989, David Howe and I visited the BBC to interview Denise Baron – known as Dee to her friends and colleagues – for Issue 10 of The Frame, *published that May. At the time, Dee was hard at work on* Doctor Who's *twenty-sixth season – she was make-up designer on 'The Curse of Fenric' (as covered in a bonus feature reprinted later in this book) – but she kindly found time to tell us about her previous contributions to the series, and about her career to that point. Her subsequent credits included* The Chronicles of Narnia: The Silver Chair *(1990) and the TV movie* Old Times *(1991), but it appears that she left the business in the early 1990s.*

We began by asking Dee how she had come to work as a make-up designer for the BBC .'I came straight from art school,' she told us. 'I took a Fine Art degree – painting and print-making – and joined the BBC after that, in 1978.

'You have to join as a trainee, no matter what you've done before. You have to go through the BBC training school – you do three months there. Then you work for two years as a trainee, before you become a make-up assistant.

'After four years, you can apply to become a supervising assistant. You don't necessarily get it after four years, but luckily I did. Then, after five years, you can apply to be a designer. Again, I was very lucky and got to be a designer in five years. That would have been around 1983.'

The first production Dee worked on as a fully-fledged designer was *Only Fools and Horses*. On shows such as this, the make-up artist's job is to give the characters a 'naturalistic' look on camera, which can include providing such things as wigs, toupees and moustaches.

'If make-up is really good, you shouldn't be aware of it. That's why I'm so pleased that *Tumbledown* won this year's BAFTA award for make-up. As a make-up artist, you sit and watch programmes and, no matter how good the make-up is, you tend to think "Oh, that's a good make-up", or whatever. But with *Tumbledown*, I watched all of it and didn't even think about the make-up; I just accepted that the injuries were real.'

On *Doctor Who*, of course, the demands are somewhat different from those of the average drama production. A frequent requirement is for a distinctive alien appearance for another of the Doctor's monstrous adversaries. As an assistant, Dee worked on several stories featuring Tom Baker as the Doctor, including 'The Ribos Operation'. However, the first *Doctor Who* she handled after promotion to designer was Colin Baker's debut outing, 'The Twin Dilemma'.

One of the more striking make-ups featured in this story was that of the Jocondans. As Dee recalls, their unusual, bird-like appearance evolved during production, and the final look was not the product of any detailed research into bird characteristics but came directly from her own imagination – although, as is often the case on *Doctor Who*, she had to scale down her original ideas for reasons of cost.

'Even then,' she adds, 'to keep the cost down I actually had to make all those bird heads myself. An outside company would have charged my entire budget for all 13 heads just to make one of them!

'I think we wanted to give the Jocondans some sort of wings as well, but couldn't afford it.'

Each of the heads was made on a wig foundation, with the feathers – real ones, bought in from a specialist supplier – all sewn on individually by Dee. The horns were modelled in clay, cast in plastic, and inserted onto the base of the wig frame, while the beak-like noses were made in a similar way and given a hard, metallic finish. The beards were created like ordinary false beards, but using feathers rather than hair. All these different pieces were then fitted to the actor's head after the basic blue/grey face make-up had been applied. The moustache and eyebrows were added, and lastly a few more feathers stuck on to cover up all the joins.

'The trouble we had each day was finding feathers that looked the same for continuity purposes. Once you've stuck feathers on and ripped them off again in the evening, you can't re-use them. It drove us crazy! The same with the feathers on their hands.

'I had about 13 assistants on that one, and I remember saying to them on the morning of the first day, "Now, you've got to find six sets of continuity feathers." They just looked at me as if I was mad!'

The other aliens in 'The Twin Dilemma', the Gastropods, were largely the responsibility of the Visual Effects Department, although for the creatures' leader, Mestor, Dee had to take a face-cast of actor Edwin Richfield for Visual Effects to work from. One other piece of special make-up she remembers handling for this story was the gash seen on actor Kevin McNally's forehead after his character, Hugo Lang, escapes from a crashed spaceship. She would have liked to have made his injuries appear more extensive and realistic, but it was agreed by the production team that this would have been too horrific.

A similar problem arose on the next story Dee worked on, 'The Trial of a Time Lord' (first four episodes). Here, she designed some very effective 'scorched' make-up for the faces of the Tribespeople killed by Drathro – including Joan Sims, playing the Tribe's Queen Katryca – but it looked too gruesome and the sequence was re-shot without it.

Of course, a lot of make-up work was also required to create the Nordic appearance of the Tribe, including the use of beards, wigs and other hair extensions – and, in the case of Broken Tooth (David Rodigan), the distinctive feature that gave rise to his name! Dee also designed the unusual sideburns worn by space pirates Glitz (Tony Selby) and Dibber (Glen Murphy), along with the pallid complexions of the underground dwellers in Drathro's domain.

'We called those characters the Jelly Baby people, because they had no eyebrows – we painted over them with gelatin!'

Like many *Doctor Who* stories, 'The Trial of a Time Lord' involved a fair amount of location shooting. We wondered if working on location posed any particular problems for the make-up artist.

'I actually prefer working on location – most people do, because it's a nicer atmosphere. You don't have people hidden away in a gallery – your director is right there next to you, and it's much more personal. Also, because you're away in hotels with all the actors, living together for however many weeks, you build up a good team spirit.

'On the other hand, working in a make-up room in TV Centre is a much more controlled environment than working out of a caravan. In a caravan, you're all squashed up; and every time someone walks in, the whole thing jolts up and down. You're always hearing make-up assistants shouting "Don't stamp on the steps!" or "Don't slam the door!"'

Talk of caravans led us nicely on to circuses and 'The Greatest Show in the Galaxy'. We asked Dee at what stage she had first become involved in the production.

'I think I joined it about six weeks before shooting – about the same time as Ros Ebbutt.[52] The director, Alan Wareing, would have started before us, of course, and the set designer would also have started a few weeks before us.'

---

52 See the Rosalind Ebbutt interview elsewhere in this book.

The first thing Dee turned her mind to, after reading the scripts, was Mags's transformation into a werewolf. Her first thought was to create an effect something like the one in John Landis's 1981 movie *An American Werewolf in London*, as this seemed to be what writer Stephen Wyatt was aiming for. In the end, though, this idea had to be dropped as it would have been too time-consuming and expensive. So how had the final effect come about?

'Alan Wareing and I talked about it a lot, and he was very sympathetic to my ideas. I definitely didn't want someone disappearing behind a sofa, or whatever, and coming up wearing a mask! That would have looked ridiculous. So, because of the nature of *Doctor Who*, and how quickly it's shot, I thought it was better to go for something simpler; and, as Mags was a sort of punky character, I suggested extending the "punkiness" when she changed – making more hair shoot out of her, changing her eye colour and so on.

'These were cosmetic changes that could be done quickly, for example using contact lenses for the eyes – although poor Jessica Martin, the actress, had to have them three weeks beforehand, to get used to them. We had originally intended to go for full, cat-like eyes, taking up the whole eye-ball, and Jessica was brilliant when we tried them out – she had no problems when these great big lenses were put in her eyes. But they were painful to wear, and we would have needed an optician standing by in the studio to put them in, so in the end we decided to do something a bit simpler.

'That's the lesson I've learnt over the years – keep it simple and it'll look better. The same applies to the werewolf make-up generally. What we did looked very good on screen. But if I'd tried to put on a prosthetic in ten minutes, when it actually needs two hours, the result would have looked really bad – lifting, peeling away and so on.'

Even with this emphasis on simplicity, the werewolf scenes were by no means easy to shoot, and Dee is full of admiration for the way Jessica Martin coped with them. Quite apart from any discomfort they might have caused, the special contact lenses restricted the actress's range of vision, which made life difficult when she had to run up a spiral staircase and take part in a fight scene with Sylvester McCoy. More problems were caused by the long fingernails she had to wear.

As if all this were not enough, Jessica had also had to pay several visits to Haynes and Kulp, a firm of dentists used regularly by the BBC, to have three sets of special teeth made up for use in the different stages of the transformation, as well as a set of 'plumpers' – dental appliances designed to puff the cheeks out and give the face a more rounded look. Small wonder, then, that when it came to recording the scene, things did not go entirely smoothly.

'We had a terrible problem when one of the teeth snapped off! The top fangs were so large that Jessica couldn't close her mouth, but it was very difficult, in all the fighting and so on, for her to remember that. Unfortunately, she bit down, and one of the teeth fell out. So there was a great scramble with people from Costumes, Make-up and Visual Effects all desperately trying to find this tooth in the sawdust! Luckily we did find it, but there was a big hold-up while we glued it back on.'

This was not the end of the story, either, because when the scene came to be re-shot, Alan Wareing thought he had seen the tooth fall out again. A minor panic ensued until one of Dee's assistants pointed out that the tooth was actually still in Jessica's mouth!

Apart from Mags's transformation, the other major job Dee had to tackle for 'The Greatest Show in the Galaxy' was the creation of the clown masks. It had been decided at an early stage of production to aim for something resembling a 1950s Earth-type circus rather than a futuristic, alien one, so this was the starting point that both Dee and Ros Ebbutt worked from. They gave each clown a number, so that it would always get the correct combination of mask and costume. We asked Dee how she had gone about researching the masks.

'Well obviously I looked at lots of clown books, but the interesting thing is that when I was at college – not so much when I did my degree, but when I was doing the foundation course – I used to draw lots of clowns. So the Chief Clown (played by Ian Reddington) was evolved from a design I did when I was at college. And then they decided to use the mark on his forehead for the kite mark, which was quite nice.'

In fact, Dee also used this kite motif as a design on the character Morgana's hand, between her thumb and forefinger, but this was only just visible on screen.

One thing Dee and Ros Ebbutt agreed upon right from the start was that the clowns should all be the same size and height – unlike in some programmes where actors of very different builds play supposedly identical robots!

'For the white-faced clowns, I cast Ian Reddington's face, then I modelled up slightly bigger than that and took another cast, then I took another cast from that – a long process! – and then finally I vac-formed them over at Visual Effects, with the help of a visual effects assistant. So they all had Ian's basic face shape.'

After all the masks had been made, the next stage was to add the actual designs to the faces.

'I got each of my assistants to paint some of them up, because I thought, "The only way they're going to look different is if we all do two or three clowns each."

'Although you saw only one mask per clown on screen, each one actually had ten masks. So something like a hundred masks were made altogether. We had to allow for them breaking, we had to allow for actors doubling up, we had to allow for it raining, for some getting lost … My one brief to my assistants before they started was: "Just remember, you've got to paint ten like that, exactly the same." So we kept them quite basic and simple.'

Dee wanted the clowns' eyes to have an eerie, metallic look to them, so she went to Visual Effects and obtained some foil-like material with similar properties to a two-way mirror, which she stuck over the eyeholes in each mask. The only problem with this was that the eyes tended to steam up on location owing to the very hot weather, even though pin holes had been punched in the polystyrene-like material of the masks to let in more air.

'I was getting really worried, because I knew that later they were going to have to do things like back-flips and walking a tightrope! Luckily, one of the clown extras came up and said, "Hey, try this stuff Dee. I use it on my motorbike visor." It was a sort of gel that you can buy from motorbike shops, and fortunately it solved our problem.'

Quite apart from Mags and the clowns, Dee also had to handle all the other make-up required for the story – for example, she had to arrange for wigs and hair piece extensions to be made for a number of the characters. All in all, it must have been quite a daunting task, but Dee says that she likes the challenge of working on *Doctor Who*. Along with *Alas Smith and Jones* and *Fools on the Hill* – a play about the early days of the BBC – she counts it among the most enjoyable programmes she has been involved with.

'*Doctor Who* is one of the few programmes where you can really let your imagination go.' And with all her imagination and skill now being applied to the first story into production for Season 26, it seems certain that we have another visual treat in store for us.

Stephen James Walker

Interview conducted by Stephen James Walker and David J Howe

INTERVIEW: BONNIE LANGFORD – COMPANION ACTRESS

Bonnie Langford played Mel Bush, companion to the sixth and seventh Doctors, but was already a household name before she joined Doctor Who, *having first come to prominence as a child star at the beginning of the 1970s. Her early career is described in the following interview – the first she had ever given about her* Doctor Who *work – which was conducted by Tim Robins in 1987 and originally published in Issue 3 of* The Frame *that November. Since then, Bonnie has continued to work highly successfully as an actor and entertainer. In 2006 alone, she was a celebrity contestant on* Dancing on Ice *(ITV1), appeared in an episode of* Agatha Christie's Marple *(ITV1), had a stint playing murderess Roxie Hart in the long-running musical* Chicago *in London's West End, continued performing with Sandi Toksvig in their regular two-woman theatre show* Short and Curly *and prepared to begin a run as Adelaide Adams in a new tour of the musical* Guys and Dolls. *Since 2000, she has also made regular return appearances as Mel in the* Doctor Who *audio CD dramas produced by Big Finish. Despite her very varied career, however, her prevailing public image is still that of a bubbly 'song and dance' performer – an issue she was keen to address in her interview for* The Frame …*

'People seem to think I eat, sleep and drink dancing, and that I get up bouncing,' says Bonnie Langford. 'Whenever anyone asks me to do a publicity picture they always say, "Jump for joy, Bonnie." So much so, in fact, that, as my car number plate is NMJ, I've named it "No More Jumps"!'

Considering the picture often painted of her by the popular press, Bonnie can understand why her joining the cast of *Doctor Who* was greeted with scepticism in some quarters. 'I do have this image that wherever I go, so does the song and dance. Quite honestly, that's not the case at all. I don't find it necessary to sing and dance in everything; that's just normally what's required of me. In fact, the reason I adore doing musicals is that they require me not only to sing and dance, but to act as well. I find if I don't have something acting-wise or drama-wise to get into, then my thought processes aren't developing.'

So Bonnie welcomed the chance to play the Doctor's current companion, Melanie Bush, and hasn't found appearing in a straight drama series at all limiting. 'It's a change for me, and it's great fun to be doing something that's different. I don't feel as if I'm in a strait-jacket. I probably have *more* freedom, in fact, because I've managed to discover a lot more in me without having to kick my legs in the air! I can run if I want to! I can stand still if I want to!'

Bonnie laughs, then notes, 'The things I enjoy doing most are when I can actually get my teeth into something, find something new and go off in a different direction. Variety is the spice of life as far as I'm concerned.'

So far, Bonnie's life has had plenty of variety. She has enjoyed great success in virtually every medium of the entertainment industry.

Amongst her television work, Bonnie has co-hosted *Junior Showtime* and *The Saturday Starship*, played Violet-Elizabeth in *Just Willliam*, co-starred in *The Hot Shoe Show*, guested on shows such as *Give Us A Clue* and *Saturday Royal* and, in 1986, was the subject of *This Is Your Life*.

On stage, Bonnie has appeared in four hit West End musicals – *Gone With the Wind*, *The Pirates of Penzance* (which also had Sylvester McCoy in its cast), *Cats*, and *Peter Pan – The Musical* – and starred on Broadway in a revival of *Gypsy*.

Bonnie has also made inroads into films, guest-starring in *Bugsy Malone*, and the music industry, with the single *Just One Kiss*.

In fact, at 23, Bonnie has had the kind of showbiz career that would take many people a lifetime to achieve. But then she did have a head start: she made her stage debut at just three months old.

'My mother ran a dancing school, and every year the school presented a lavish show at Richmond. This particular year, they needed a baby on stage … so rather than use a doll, they picked me.'

At the age of six, Bonnie made her television debut on *Opportunity Knocks*, singing the number usually associated with Shirley Temple, *On the Good Ship Lollipop*. 'It's funny, but I didn't particularly want to go on the show,' she recalls. 'But a family friend got me the audition and I suppose I couldn't back down once they wanted me to appear. But I only made one appearance, even though I was voted into joint first place and was asked back the following week. The dancing school had planned a big stage production in Richmond on the same day I was due to appear. There was a great clash of interests. So I decided that as everything had been planned for the Richmond show so many weeks in advance, I couldn't let them down by not appearing.'

Opportunity Knocks brought Bonnie to the attention of the general public, but at first her parents weren't particularly keen on her becoming a child star. 'I think they had seen all the pitfalls in others and didn't want me to follow. But I soon got the taste for entertaining and, after that, you couldn't stop me.'

However, Bonnie's career did stop her doing one thing – watching episodes of *Doctor Who*. 'I did see a few of them, but I was never able to watch regularly. When I was very little, I was too scared of it. Then, when I did get to an age when I knew it was pretend, I was doing things like shows, which do require you to be there on Saturday afternoons and on Saturday evenings. So to me, *Doctor Who* was like *Dallas* and *Dynasty*, in that I was aware of what it was all about but I never really got into it.'

It was during a gap in Bonnie's busy schedule that she was given the role of Melanie. 'It was Christmas time, about December 1985, just before I had to do *Peter Pan*. I'd been on tour with a show and had been out of London quite a bit. The first day I came back, I went to see John Nathan-Turner and I read this piece of character analysis. That was it really.'

The analysis outlined the character of 21 year old Melanie ('known as Mel') Bush that viewers have now become familiar with. 'It said that she was a health and fitness fanatic, that she was a computer programmer and that she was bright and very energetic. It also said that she was to just appear on the programme; you didn't find out how she got to travel with the Doctor, which was apparently quite unusual, because normally there's a sort of introductory meeting and then the Doctor asks the companion to go on the travels with him. That didn't happen in my case.'

Not having watched a lot of *Doctor Who*, Bonnie feels unable to compare the character of Mel with other companions, but she does note: 'I met Nicola [Bryant] and we got on very, very well. Whether the characters we play are the same, I don't think so, and I hope not, because we're all different people and there's tremendous scope. Obviously the relationship between the companion and the Doctor is similar, because the companions are there to help and assist the Doctor's role. Also they are required to translate the Doctor's complicated language so that children and other people who follow the programme can understand.'

Bonnie's first work for *Doctor Who* was on location for episodes 12 and 13 of *The Trial of a Time Lord*. This, she remarks, involved 'a lot of explosions, screaming and running about.'

During the trial itself, Mel described herself as being: '... as truthful, honest and about as boring as they come'. It was a line delivered with obvious irony. In fact, Bonnie sees Mel as anything but boring. 'I think she likes adventure and loves a challenge. She is quite a go-ahead girl. I think she gets very bored very quickly, particularly about anything everyday. Words like "sitting and waiting" are not in Melanie's vocabulary. She will say, "Come on, let's get on and do something exciting."'

Mel's energetic character has sometimes led to a slightly antagonistic relationship with the Doctor. 'I think it's very easy to be nagging to the Doctor, especially when there was this part of my character that was meant to be nagging him about his health. I'm conscious of the fact that I don't want to become a nagging old mother, saying "You must do this and you must do that."'

Mel's health and fitness regime would seem to have worked beyond her wildest dreams. With the twenty-fourth season, the Doctor has emerged quite literally as a new man. But while Sylvester McCoy's Doctor may be less portly than his predecessor, his eccentric character has still provided something of a contrast to that of his companion. Particularly considering Mel's abilities as a computer programmer.

'The thing I've discovered is that computer programmers are tremendously dedicated people, terribly devoted to whatever they're doing at the time. Usually, with things like computer programs, they will stay up all night for a week just to get something right. And they're very logical people as well. I suppose, you see, the Doctor is not that logical in a way, is he? He goes off at a tangent at times. I think sometimes Melanie can put the logical argument to something – not that she really realises it. She just says something that seems totally obvious and might be very mundane, but in fact it's something everyone else has overlooked.'

Mel's adventures have certainly shown that she is capable of taking care of herself. However, Bonnie believes that the ultimate authority in the stories must be the Doctor. 'I think the Doctor definitely is the commanding power, very obviously. I think Melanie knows she can very easily overstep the limits, but she knows what the limits are, so I think her nagging is somewhat tongue in cheek. Melanie likes to tease, and the Doctor rather likes that. He cares about her tremendously and wouldn't want anything nasty to happen to her. He would go all out to help.'

Less than helpful were some of the comments made in the press about Bonnie's suitability for a drama series like *Doctor Who*. She is quick to respond to those who would cast doubt on her ability to act. 'It's sometimes very irritating when people say, "All she can do is sing and dance." I mean, how do people think I got through *Peter Pan*, which is a two and a half hour marathon performance, without being able to act? How do they think I got from one song to another? You've got to be convincing somewhere along the line.'

Multi-talented Bonnie believes she is more than able to demonstrate that people are wrong to pigeon-hole her, but admits there can be obstacles. 'You can only prove to people that you can do something different if there's absolutely no trace of anything you've done before. If there's any kind of dancing or suggestion of me dancing in *Doctor Who*, then people will say, "Oh, she's put that in because she can't act, she can only sing and dance". They won't look at other parts of it. This makes me sound as if I'm terribly annoyed. I'm not. It's just at times I think, "Hang on, I've got wider scope."'

These comments take on added significance, bearing in mind developments during the twenty-fourth season and Bonnie's imminent departure from the series (which had not been made public at the time this interview was conducted). It is certainly a pity that the scriptwriters have not been able to make more use of the scope to which Bonnie refers. The character of Melanie has a lot of potential, combining '80s interests in health, fitness and information technology with more traditional characteristics of a *Doctor Who* companion – notably the ability to give voice to an ear-piercing scream at the least sign of danger.

However, there is one tradition of *Doctor Who* companions that Bonnie surely will not be following. Now that she has finished work on the series, she will not be disappearing into obscurity. 'I like to keep branching out, trying new things. That way, I can only progress and develop, and there's far less chance of being stuck in one particular kind of role or situation. I love new challenges, I like to be as versatile as I can in my career. I just hope that I can meet any new challenge that comes along.'

Tim Robins

INTERVIEW: GARETH EDWARDS–GRAPHIC DESIGNER

The final title sequence of the classic Doctor Who *series, used on all three of Sylvester McCoy's seasons as the Doctor, was designed by Oliver Elmes at the BBC, but realised by Gareth Edwards of the CAL Video graphics company. In 1988, Philip Newman spoke to Gareth at the CAL Video office in central London, and the interview first appeared in print some five years later, in Issue 23/24 of* The Frame. *Today, Gareth continues to work as a graphic designer; his credits include the* Horizon *documentary 'Supermassive Black Holes' (BBC2, 2000) and* The Legendary Lighthouse *(BBC2, 2003), and he was nominated for a Royal Television Society craft award in 2004/05 for his work on the BBC3 drama/documentary* End Day.

Q: Have you been involved in the production of many television title sequences?

A: Well, I've actually done about 250 separate animation sequences for all sorts of clients, the BBC and ITV stations included. That concentration of work hasn't been planned – I just happen to have ended up doing lots and lots of title sequences and television station idents. Some of the biggest jobs I've ever done have never been shown in Britain! There was one programme I designed, which was about Halley's Comet, for which I did a full computer-generated simulation of the comet, with clouds of gas and bits and pieces boiling off the surface. That was great fun; terrific to do. I really enjoyed that! And that was really big: it was shown in 84 countries, but wasn't transmitted in Britain because of some financial or legal battle with Yorkshire Television. I suppose the two biggest artistic successes I've had, though, were as animator on the Channel 4 winter ident in 1985 – which was highly acclaimed by a lot of people – and a sequence for a series called *Innovators*, which some people have very kindly said is probably one of the most definitive pieces of computer graphics ever produced. It was my great fortune to actually work on that; I've been very lucky to have been involved in doing the titles for nearly every single major news programme in Britain, including *Channel 4 News* and the BBC's *6 O'Clock News* and *9 O'Clock News* bulletins.

Q: How then did your association with *Doctor Who* come about?

A: Well, Oliver Elmes, who's one of the senior BBC designers – in fact, you don't get much more senior than Oliver – was asked to do the titles for the new *Doctor Who* sequence. Oliver came to see me with a couple of A3 sheets of paper on which he'd sketched his own visualisation of what looked like 'an orbit.'

Q: What sort of brief did he give you?

A: Well, it amounted to two main things: he wanted the end logo to look like the end logo, which he'd already prepared and done the artwork for, and he wanted something that felt like it was a switchback ride on a rollercoaster. He wanted that kind of feeling, particularly at the beginning when we're coming down onto the galaxy, which, incidentally, was based on a faithful model of the Milky Way, with all the little detailed globular clusters; I played all kinds of tricks with logarithmic spirals to get that just right! But Oliver kept on at me to get this feeling of movement, this rollercoaster effect.

Q: How far do you think you succeeded in achieving this?

A: Not far enough, really, although I think it does work when we come down and see the upside-down TARDIS in the bubble. If you look at it, you'll see that the TARDIS doesn't actually turn the right way up; instead, we dive over the top of it and do a 180 degree rotation around it and then pull away. The idea for the bubble with the gas around it developed as we worked together, as did many of the sequence's effects. All the stars originally started off white, but Oliver wanted some of the stars to be different, a bluey, purpley or orangey colour. So, we looked at it as it stood, which was basically a large white starfield with a large white blob and an occasional dot of colour! Then he said, 'Let's see what it looks like the other way round.' Now, when designers say things like that to me, I know that what they really mean is that they want a kind of negative. So, basically, I swapped all the colours: where they were white, I made them blue, and so on. That's why the star background has that colour. You see, a lot of this isn't planned. Another beautiful example is on the TARDIS itself. If you look, you'll notice that the 'POLICE – PUBLIC CALL BOX' signs in the sequence are white lettering on a black background, but on the original TARDIS prop, the background is blue. Well, the reference they gave me had a black insert, so I created a black insert on the computer model. However, when the producer came to see us, he said, 'It's black!' I thought, 'Oh, no!' You see, it was too late by then, because we'd already generated the computerised images – we'd actually started creating the final frames. So, as you can see, the whole sequence underwent considerable change from its start to its finish – which is right and proper. That's what creativity's all about!

Q: What sort of technology did you use to create the various components of the title sequence?

A: It was designed and animated on a Sun workstation and IRIS terminal using in-house software. I used a Quantel paintbox to add all the colours and touch up some of the images, while the Doctor's face, the main galaxy and the TARDIS were all created using a caption camera. To edit all the pieces together, I used HARRY, which is a digital editing system, on which I also created the 'laser attack' effects in the pre-title sequence of the first episode.[53]

Q: How long did the sequence eventually take to complete?

A: Well, I was taken ill about halfway through the job – I had a dreadful viral infection, which put me out of action for about two weeks – and then, a week after I came back to work, I had to go off to Australia for a fortnight! So, in the middle of the job, there was a five week break. In the end, from start to finish, I think the job was on my desk for nearly three and a half months, but I actually spent about six or seven weeks working on it. That's quite a period of time!

Q: Did you have a copy of Keff McCulloch's version of the theme music to work to?

A: Well, yes and no. The music was supplied in a very rough version quite early on, but we're

---

53 Edwards was referring here to the pre-credits sequence of Sylvester McCoy's debut episode, part one of 'Time and the Rani'.

talking *very* rough! It was very uninspiring. It was a bit like doing lip-sync hand animation without any emotion in the voices to try to give it some character. When you're doing hand animation, you tend to be inspired by the other components, including the sound, which are going to make up the whole. In this case, the sound component didn't seem to work with the pictures as well as it might. However, when it was remixed and re-edited later, it sounded far, far better; moreover, the addition of sound effects, like the TARDIS and the meteorites' 'whooshing' noises, helped a great deal. In fact, it wasn't really until I saw the final edited sequence with sound that I actually began to like the job. People may not realise this, but when you finish a job, particularly when you've been working on it for six or seven weeks, you usually hate it! I hated the job intensely for at least a month afterwards. I think that goes for everybody who's just a little bit creative; by the time you're halfway through a job, you want to be starting the next one!

Q: Were there any major problems to be overcome in the creation of the titles' many effects?

A: The only problem was getting the face laid in. When we created the sequence, I timed the dissolves on the face very carefully; I felt that the mix of the face to the background was correct. That's just to me as a creative individual. I was at art school for about eight years, I went to the Royal College of Art; I think I know how to make pictures. I won't get upset, but I feel I know what I'm talking about when it comes to my personal aesthetics. Now, Oliver and I, working together, crafted that bit very carefully, to get the balance of the face to the background just right, so that it was like a haunting face. The BBC, when it was viewed, asked for it to be modified, so that the face became far more visible. I can't actually find words strong enough to express this as I'd like, but I personally very much prefer the original mix. I really do. I was not happy that it had to be remixed. I understood the reasons why it had to be redone, but I don't think it actually improved that portion of the sequence at all. It spoilt the atmosphere as far as I was concerned … I'd better not say any more! But that was it, by the way; the only controversy. The rest of it was just great fun! Excellent fun![54]

Q: Did the fact that the sequence you were producing would become part of the history of such a long-running series affect your approach to the job in any way?

A: Well, one of the things that I was primarily concerned with, whilst I was working on it, was this sense of historical precedent. One of the images that Oliver had sketched out was this idea that after we'd met the TARDIS, we'd see the Doctor's face and stars swirling all around it. Now, when I did the blue clouds that flow around and through the face, I was consciously trying to create something that had throwbacks to the original sequence by Bernard Lodge. I really was determined to get that same kind of swirling effect, and if you look at it, you'll see that it's very similar. But that's another reason why I was so annoyed about the change in the face: it lost a bit of the drama, in my opinion.

---

54 The original version of the opening title sequence, with the more subtle integration of the Doctor's face, was in fact transmitted – in error – at the beginning of Part Four of 'Time and the Rani'. The only other difference between this version and the final one is that at the very start of the sequence, the orange 'halo' effect around the opening starburst is missing.

Q: What, for you, was the most memorable part of your work on the *Doctor Who* titles?

A: Working with Oliver; he was a damn good man to work with! I mean, people of the calibre of Oliver Elmes are brilliant at their jobs; they are extremely gifted. One of the nice things about the job that I work in is that, because it's a young industry and there are so few of us in it, I've been fortunate enough to have been allowed to work with people like Oliver, and Martin Lambie-Nairn, who are the very best – the cream of the cream – of British design. It's a great job, to be paid to do what I'd been driven to do anyway; I mean, if I wasn't doing it here, I'd be doing it at home or something! It's a lovely job and I'm very pleased with myself, but very proud to be able to do it.

Philip Newman

BONUS FEATURE: OLIVER ELMES TITLE SEQUENCE DESCRIPTION

When the preceding Gareth Edwards interview was first published in Issue 23/24 of The Frame *in 1993, it was accompanied by a brief description by BBC graphic designer Oliver Elmes of his intentions underlying the design of the Sylvester McCoy title sequence; this is reprinted below. Oliver's other notable credits for the BBC include title sequences for* The Goodies *(1970-1980),* Elizabeth R *(1971) and* The Good Life *(1975-1978), and the 'stripy' BBC2 channel ident logo used during the 1980s.*

The original thought was to explode from nothing, the beginning of the universe, making a huge great starfield. I was hoping that by using computer-generated graphics we could get right inside and move around to get a real feeling of space.

From that point, having created the universe, I wanted to get a very obscure bubble coming across the screen. Originally, it was going to become a bit more misty and gaseous, but we couldn't achieve this effect with computer graphics, so Gareth Edwards created a similar effect by using several different textured layers. We were then going to follow the bubble, go through it and look down upon it, trying to recreate, in a very dramatic fashion, the feeling you get when you go for a ride in the fairground; going up and down very quickly, with that stomach-churning sensation. We didn't actually get there in the end, because of time and money; we had to simplify the idea. But we did succeed to some extent, and when we went over the top of the TARDIS as it was actually forming – the whole picture turned upside down. To really get that feeling, though, you have to be in the cinema, because there's nothing around you to tell you where you are; in front of the TV at home, you've got things on the mantlepiece, people talking etc etc, to destroy the illusion.

Within the bubble we were then going to materialise the TARDIS, which was going to have flecks of light coming off it. Then, having seen the TARDIS go past us, we were going to see it fall into another galaxy, which would explode to form the head of the Doctor.

The idea originally was to create a skull-like shape first, which then developed into the head, which was a bit more sinister than what we eventually ended up with. But we were limited with funds, and CAL Video actually did quite a lot for us within the £20,000 budget we had. If we'd had the money, we could have spent far more time and got more out of it; we'd certainly have done more with the head. In the end, the producer wasn't too happy with the original head we did, which was rather less detailed than the one that appears in the final version of the sequence. It looked far more as though it had been formed from the galaxy we'd created, with the blue clouds swirling though it. But because he wanted a very hard image, and we'd run out of money, we had to go back and use simpler equipment to actually superimpose the head, as he wanted it over the one we'd done. I think it somehow loses some of the drama, because the head just suddenly appears.

I was very happy with the lettering at the end, and the explosion with things shooting towards us. The logo was actually just as I originally designed it, and the producer was happy with it, so few changes were made.

Andrew Cartmel was Doctor Who's *script editor throughout Sylvester McCoy's three seasons as the Doctor, and naturally had a very big influence on all the stories of that era. He subsequently worked in a similar capacity on a season of the BBC's hospital drama* Casualty *(1990), and some years later on a season of the New Zealand-shot Channel 5 fantasy series* Dark Knight *(2001). His other writing credits include original novels and novellas – including a number of* Doctor Who *titles for Virgin Publishing, the BBC and Telos Publishing – several comic strip stories, a stage play and one of Big Finish's* Doctor Who *audio CD dramas. He was also editor of the genre magazine* Starburst *for a short time in 1999/2000. In recent years, he has written two factual books drawing on his* Doctor Who *experience –* Script Doctor: The Inside Story of Doctor Who 1986-1989 *(Reynolds & Hearn, 2005) and* Through Time: An Unauthorised and Unofficial History of Doctor Who *(Continuum International, 2005). During the period when he was actually working on the series, however, and for a number of years after that, he preferred to keep a low profile, and turned down numerous interview requests from fan and professional journalists alike. The following was, in fact, only the second interview he had ever given about his* Doctor Who *work, and the first of any real substance. It was conducted at his South London home, over two sessions three weeks apart, and originally appeared in July 1994 in Issue 40 of* TSV, *the magazine of the New Zealand Doctor Who Fan Club – which is still going strong today, and has its own website at www.doctorwho.org.nz. Currently, Andrew works as a lecturer at St Mary's College, part of the University of Surrey, in Twickenham.*

Q: How did you get the job as script editor of *Doctor Who*?

A: I was working in Cambridge at a computer company. I'd never previously really had a proper job, I'd always been writing, waiting to be successful as a writer. After my dad died, I thought, 'Time's moving on, I can't just sit around writing; I've got to get a civilised, decent job.' So in the course of about three phone calls, I organised a post graduate thing in computer science, which led to me getting a job a year later in Cambridge. I was very happy in Cambridge. It was a very groovy company full of ex-hippie vegetarians, designing incredible software of a kind I'd never seen. CAD stuff – computer aided design.

One thing I had achieved while I was starving as a writer in my garret was that I used to be called in to the BBC's writers' workshops, with a bunch of other hopeful writers – the BBC used to have a thing called the Script Unit, which would read unsolicited scripts and encourage writers. A lot of whom, I have to say, have gone on to be very successful, often after being commissioned by me! There was Ian Briggs, Malcolm Kohll, Robin Mukherjee. Although Robin never wrote for *Who*, if I'd done another season, he certainly would have. I gave him his first commission on *Casualty*, he's gone on to write the Russian cop series *Grushko*, and he's basically turning into one of the best British screenwriters. Anyway, there was this cluster of writers.

I was working in Cambridge, and through having these contacts at the BBC, knowing writers, I discovered that you can get an agent. Now, according to the *Writers' and Artists' Yearbook*, the font of all wisdom, you can't get an agent until you sell a script. Malcolm hadn't sold anything at the time, but he told me that was bullshit. Instead of sending scripts into a broadcaster, you send them in to an agent. So I referred to the *Yearbook* again, and I noticed that two very respected writers, Derek Marlowe and Tom Stoppard, were both with a particular agency. So I sent some scripts to Richard Wakely there, and the agent took me on.

Well, my agent knew John Nathan-Turner, and when they were looking for a new script editor, I got this phone call while I was in Cambridge saying, 'Come for an interview'. I went and saw John at Threshold House, sat down with him, and we chatted and hit it off. And they offered me the job, which threw my whole life into a spin.

My whole life had to change, but at least my girlfriend lived in London. I prevaricated – this was over Christmas 1986, and I had to decide by the New Year. The worst part was handing in my notice at my old job. I was dreading it. I remember walking across the common in Cambridge; it was like walking to the OK Corral. I'd lost jobs before, but I'd never resigned from one. So I quit, I came to London, and I started working on the show.

Q: When you arrived, you weren't over-burdened with script-editing experience …

A: The reason John gave me the job was that we got along, and I didn't impress him as being an idiot. He'd read a script of mine, and obviously saw qualities in there that indicated I knew what a good TV script should be.

Q: When you got the job, you were how old?

A: Well, I'm 36 now, so late twenties then, I guess.

Q: So, when you arrived, what scripts were already on the shelf? How far had they got with the first McCoy season?

A: Oh God, it wasn't even the McCoy season! Well, the BBC would never decide whether they would do a season of *Who* again until the very last minute. It was either a low priority for them or they couldn't wrap their heads round it. So we always got the go-ahead at the last minute. And we also always got the same budget as the previous year, which meant our resources were actually shrinking, due to inflation.

So John had had this eleventh-hour go-ahead for whatever season it was[55]. With some money left over from the previous season, he'd covered himself by commissioning Pip and Jane Baker to do a four-parter. So what we had was Pip and Jane under commission and in the course of writing a script. And that was all there was. They were recasting the Doctor, but we didn't know who it was going to be, so it was wide open.

The first thing I did, when the job was just a glimmer, was that I started getting in touch with people I knew from the writer's workshop, people I knew to be good, because we each had to present our work there. So, there were people from the workshop who did get approached at this stage. Ian Briggs, I remember, came in quite early.

Q: 'Time and the Rani' was originally called 'Strange Matter', and Pip and Jane have said there was a little argy-bargy between them and you.…

A: There was enormous conflict between me and Pip and Jane. I was totally fresh to it; I didn't

55 Season 24.

know anything about the politics of handling a situation like that. Now, I'd be more gregarious and laid back about it.

The thing about Pip and Jane is that structurally their stuff is very sound and they touch all the bases and write well-carpentered stories. But the things I was looking for were much wackier, much more offbeat; much darker, much sharper, much harder. They came from a background of writing a lot of children's stuff, a lot of Gerry Anderson. So my style wasn't their style. The other problem was, I think they perceived me as this new kid on the block; they didn't know if I knew anything. In a situation like that now, I'd get the people on my side; win them over so we could work together. Once you make friends with people, anything is possible. I didn't make that effort, because I was young, I was green, I didn't know. I just wanted the scripts exactly the way I wanted them.

Pip and Jane, they divide the responsibilities. Jane's like the business manager, and Jane and I were just totally in conflict. So it wasn't a very happy situation, although we were terribly nice to each other, ostensibly. I had inherited the scripts. They wanted to do a standard, old fashioned story, and I wanted to do a funky new thing.

At the time I was reading a lot of Alan Moore[56], a lot of *Swamp Thing*, and you can imagine the collision of cultures between what I was wanting to do and what they were wanting to do.

What I should have done with 'Time and the Rani' was say to myself, 'Well, John's very happy with Pip and Jane, Pip and Jane do a certain thing.' I should have just stood back, let them get on with what they wanted to do, because down the line, I was infiltrating it with all my writers. I should have just looked on 'Time and the Rani' as a learning curve. It would have been much happier. I didn't get what I wanted in the end on that story anyway.

Q: In that story, it's obvious nobody has any idea what the Doctor is like….

A: Including Sylvester, because he was new to the role. I didn't like the story, because it was formulaic, people get sent from one place to another and get split up and they're running around.

Q: Not to mention the giant brain….

A: The giant brain was John's idea, I think, and a good one. John had an instinct for, if you think in terms of painting, a big block of colour, a powerful moment for the end of episode three. And it was this big, gothic thing.

I remember going on location for that story; it's a collage of memories. I remember staying in the hotel and the sound of the person in the next room, who was apparently screwing half the night and then throwing up the other half of it! That's the BBC on location, I thought.

The design on 'Time and the Rani' is interesting, even if part of the story is shot in a quarry. But we get inside from the quarry quite quickly. I liked Kate O'Mara a lot, although I didn't think the Rani was a fantastically deep character.

When we were back in the studio for the other portions of the story, there's a cliff-hanger where the Doctor's surrounded in a nest of Tetraps and he's reacting to it. We did the take, and at the end of it Sylvester said, 'That's the most ridiculous thing I've ever done!' And up in the control room, John turned to me and said, 'You ain't seen nothing yet.'

56 An innovative British comics writer.

But the first writer who sought me out, I'm trying to recall how he came to me, was Stephen Wyatt. He knew he wanted to do a *Who*, and he knew I existed, so he sent a script of his along. That was *Claws*. It was about backstabbing and treachery amongst cat breeders, and it was dark, quite funny. So I said 'Sure, come in. Let's chat.'

Stephen came in, and I was sitting at my desk in Union House. Union House was empty – the BBC was still away for Christmas – and it had like a big, glowing wintry light, the whole place like an empty school at that time of year. And Stephen, he said 'J G Ballard', and started to talk about *High Rise*, which is one of Ballard's books (and which I still haven't read). We went to the pub and the idea grew. Then he met John, and so we got 'Paradise Towers' under way; that was what inspired that. That was the first script I commissioned.

What you have to understand is the way it was structured. One of the things that John was great at was budgeting. He'd come up from a budgeting background; he'd been a production associate. The BBC always got more than they deserved out of him, because they never gave us enough money to do a series. So John was constantly – whatever the expression is – putting quarts into pint pots, making money and resources stretch so we could do as many stories as we did.

The way that worked was that we would do two four-parters and two three-parters, but with the two three-parters, one was all location, one was all studio. Due to the Byzantine structure of BBC finances, you could get the most out of the money that way. So we planned it that 'Dragonfire' was the three-parter in the studio and 'Delta and the Bannermen' was the three-parter on location at Barry Island.

Q: Quite often on *Doctor Who*, the format seems to determine the number of episodes for a story, rather than the story dictating how many episodes it deserves. For example, 'Paradise Towers'....

A: You're saying it should have been a three-parter, not a four-parter?

Q: That's probably being generous.

A: I can sense you didn't like it. Well, the three-episode story is a natural structure, while four-parters are strange beasts. You can do four-parters, but it's quite understandable if there are problems with them. So what are your particular areas of loathing in 'Paradise Towers'?

Q: Like a lot of New Zealanders, I read a lot of the later novelisations before I had an opportunity to see the stories themselves. In the book of 'Paradise Towers', the character of Pex is a hulking, huge brute, always boasting and bragging, but in the show....

A: That's interesting, because that's exactly what Stephen wanted. Stephen's gag – which I wholeheartedly endorse – was the idea that this guy was a total muscle man who fucks things up because he's incredibly stupid. He ends up being a victim. But when Nick Mallet cast it, he got Howard Cooke. Nick didn't have the same vision for Pex; he was just concerned with getting a good actor who could do the business. So Stephen was disappointed with that. It was a joke that was screwed up by the casting, but at least we ended up with a good actor.

Q: Then you've got the Kangs, the gangs of girls who speak in a sub-Anthony Burgess

Clockwork Orange slang, which annoys me, but that's a personal thing....

A: Stephen and I sat down together to hammer out the story for 'Paradise Towers' – working with a writer is always a collaborative thing – and I should say in Stephen's defence that it was me who said 'Let's have a gang of teenage girls involved in this.' That probably says more about my subconscious than it does about Stephen's.

The different colours, the different factions, reflect a future clash of youth cultures, and it kind of anticipated the colours gang thing in LA. Stephen put a bit of real thought into the sociology of the world and its slang, which is more than a lot of writers do.

Q: The story isn't helped by featuring a killer robot that's really a box on wheels armed with a corkscrew and some pincers!

A: It's time for me to make another speech here. We started with certain elements. It's set in a high rise that's become a decaying urban maze. There's the hierarchy of the people who manage the building, and the fascistic girl gangs (just to please me). But we needed a monster. And we went to see John and said, 'What about tentacles? They could come out through the ventilation grilles.' And he said 'Tentacles are difficult,' spoken with the knowing manner of a man who's tried tentacles before.

John knew the constraints of the BBC budget, and he knew what you could do with the BBC Visual Effects Department. What you're really talking about is working on a limited budget and in a limited time span. The script said 'Killer robot drags girl off,' and what you got is what you've just described. If it had been shot like a James Cameron film, you'd be reminiscing about how incredibly scary those things were. Would that we'd had those sort of budgets, or the sort of gifted design you got in *The Terminator*, which was a relatively low budget movie.

This is going to be a running theme throughout this interview. On *Who*, we had effects teams made up of a lot of people, some of whom would never have seen a film like *The Terminator*; in fact, they'd probably have gone out of their way not to see a film like that. If we'd had hungry young guys who knew what was possible, even with the budgets, they could have done fantastic things.

We did have some people like that at the BBC. Mike Tucker and Lindsay McGowan are a couple of examples. But they worked in teams, and they weren't the heads of those teams. So their contribution was diluted and filtered by the time you saw it on screen. Actually, I think I first met Mike on 'Time and the Rani', in a quarry. We were both painting rocks blue or something.

A big problem with *Who* is that people will say that they don't like a story, that the writing is crap, but what they actually mean is that the studio lighting is bad. Frequently the reasons stories didn't work were to do with the costumes or the lighting, but fans don't analyse it that way. If you work in TV or movies, you can begin to identify what irritates you about a show. It's like being a doctor; you can recognise the symptom of the illness.

Q: Again on the subject of budgetary constraints, in 'Paradise Towers' you have a monster that is two neon rings in a dark room....

A: We were lucky to have the neon rings! Thank god it was a dark room! That story had some great actors. The guy who played the Chief Caretaker's flunky[57], he was terrific. Stephen was saying at the time, 'He's only got six lines. If I'd known we'd get this geezer, I'd have written a lot more for him.' But it was fantastically well cast. I've got a lot of time for Nick Mallet as a director, especially as an actor's director. There's all kinds of good stuff in that.

Q: He was labelled as a crap director in the fan press after he did the opening segment of 'The Trial of a Time Lord' and 'Paradise Towers'. When it was announced that he would be directing 'The Curse of Fenric', the reaction was one of horror from some fans....

A: But the thing about 'The Curse of Fenric' was the lighting was better, the costumes were better. It had the tang of veracity, which is very important; it had a World War II setting. We'll come back to that later; real world settings are very important. I think the fans didn't like the other shows not because of Nick Mallet, but because of other elements of the production process. Fans shouldn't be quite so cut and dried about things.

Q: Then there's the 'pantomime actors' criticism....

A: This pantomime thing has to be addressed immediately. Whenever you work with someone, especially in a high-pressure situation like TV, there are conflicts. So there were times when I was totally in conflict with John. I don't want this to be like, 'Everybody totally loves each other,' some luvvie thing. But John has real virtues that nobody appreciates. One was that he could do things with budgets. Budgeting is a very creative thing. You've got all this money, and you can take money from certain areas and use it in others. And John was a past master at getting incredible value for money. The BBC gave us incredibly low budgets. There would have been no *Who* at all without John to juggle the budgets.

The other thing about John is that he's fantastic at editing. What I didn't know is that probably half the battle on TV is getting the script and shooting it. Almost all the other half is that you've got the raw material, these nuggets you've mined, and you work with them. Editing is a whole other creative thing. John was fantastic at it. He'd say, 'Cut all that, reverse the next two scenes, put that there,' and it'd work. Michael Wearing is like a god at the BBC, and he's renowned for that. John has the same skill. I learned so much from watching John edit.

So when people say about it having a pantomime aspect, I say nobody ever gives John credit for the things he does strongly. As for the pantomime aspect of *Who*, let's put it like this. If you could have just brought the lighting right down, and got really imaginative, moody lighting in all those shows, instead of what I think of as like snooker lighting, I think the whole pantomime thing would have evaporated. That bright, artificial lighting gives a brashness and a lack of depth. That's what made it look like a panto. Shooting on video really doesn't help.

Q: When Richard Briers was hired, he was perceived as purely a comedy actor, although he's rehabilitated his career with a lot of straight acting since then....

A: When John hired him, he didn't think, 'Richard Briers is a comedy actor, I'll get him'. He hired him because he was a very good actor. Richard Briers was doing Shakespeare on stage at

57 Clive Merrison.

the same time we were doing 'Paradise Towers'. He is a serious actor.

I was in the control room during the recording of his climactic speech in 'Paradise Towers'. Richard is a terrific actor, but during this speech I was thinking, 'You could put a parrot on this guy's shoulder and it wouldn't look out of place.' I don't know how or why things end up as they do. We might have wanted a darker, more complex performance, but we didn't get it. I don't know if that's to do with the actor, the director or what. Again, it comes down to having very little time.

Q: How did 'Delta and the Bannermen' come about?

A: Malcolm Kohll's basically a thriller writer. After he did *Who*, he wrote a thing called *The Fourth Reich*, a political thriller for American TV with an African setting.

Anyway, we had Malcolm writing a science fiction action story, and we had Don Henderson as Gavrok. Don was fantastic; he lends real authority to that performance. Also, we worked on that nostalgia thing. You might say it was pantomime, going for the '50s look. But what we were going for was rooting the story in reality, in recognisable history. They were the good things about 'Delta'. There were a lot of *Hitchhiker's* kind of jokes, and I think they can co-exist with a dark and scary story. Like in music, you've got to alternate moods.

The thing I remember about Malcolm and 'Delta' is that occasionally you get to make somebody's dream come true. Malcolm, as well as being a good writer, is a motorcycle freak. I don't know anything about them, but apparently Vincent motorcycles are like an incredible collector's item. So he included this god-like Rolls Royce of a motorcycle in the script and, bless them, the BBC got the motorcycle. So Malcolm got to sit on it and even ride it. That was fun.

Q: Around this time, Bonnie Langford decided to go...

A: Yeah, that was interesting. There was a lot of fan hatred for Bonnie Langford and Colin Baker. Some of the shows they were in were quite light and comic, which I think is one reason why they got this hate projected towards them. Having worked on the show, I have this terrible quandary, because I met Bonnie Langford. I didn't really know her, that she came from this 'I'll scweam and scweam and scweam' background, but my impression of her was that her life was totally dedicated to the professional thing. She'd been in show business since she was tiny. Much as I'd like to join in the simplicity of hatred, she was just a nice person, as was Colin Baker.

But in terms of the show, we were stuck with Mel as created by the previous team. I was much more moving in the direction of darker, dirtier, funkier, nastier, and that certainly isn't Bonnie's thing at all. So they were looking for a new companion. And we had Sara Griffiths, who was Ray in that story, and she was great; I liked her. Logistically, John kept his options open when choosing the new companion.

We wrote two stories, each with a potential companion in mind, so John could get them on, shoot their shows and decide from there. If he'd chosen Sara Griffiths, we could have done great stuff with her too. I'm terribly fond of Sophie Aldred, so I'm glad we chose her, but the quality she had in common with Sara Griffiths was being spunkier than Mel.

I don't know if you read *Love and Rockets*[58], but we were going for that sort of sisters-are-

---

doing-it-for-themselves kind of thing, which was not Bonnie. We wanted a post-*Alien* teenage girl – again, that probably says something about my psyche. That was something Stephen Wyatt said: 'The hallmark of Season 24 is tough young bitches.'

There are two other things worth putting on record about 'Delta'. I remember we turned up – in a quarry – to do those opening sequences where Delta was fleeing her planet and she had the natives of the planet with her. And the people who were responsible for making the aliens look alien, all they'd done was stick some cotton wool on their faces and dye it green! Then John and the director and I turned up, and we'd got the aliens running around with cotton wool stuck to their faces! When we saw those aliens, we were so enraged. We had all tried so hard, to the best of our abilities, but somebody else had thought, well, we can just get away with something. And none of this is planned; nobody wants this to happen.

I remember when we were doing the press screening of the story at BAFTA, I was sitting next to this woman journalist, and she saw this alien guy's face and she snorted with derisive laughter … People just can't take it seriously after seeing that. Someone just didn't try.

Certainly Don Henderson's performance was great, and the costumes. The Bannermen were dressed like Spanish Civil War fascists, and the costumes were as good as the make-up effects on those aliens were bad. It's not one of my favourite stories, but that's because I think various elements were pitted against it. It still had a lot going for it: the alien biology; the huge back-story of these two alien cultures at war – that was quite complex and interesting. It's worth not dismissing it out of hand.

Q: There's not a real sense of threat, despite Don Henderson's presence.…

A: Yeah, that was something we were aware of when we were working on the script; there was a tendency for it to go into light sitcom territory. I don't know why that was. Like everything else Malcolm's ever written, it was a hard-edged thriller.

Q: Yet 'Dragonfire' just seems to hang together better?

A: Everything for that season was done in a real hurry, and I remember there was a major rewrite on 'Delta', like 'Scrap all of episode two and write a new one.' I remember going to Malcolm's flat in Hampstead and we blocked out this story. I reeled out of Malcolm's flat and I got on the tube back into London and I looked up and there, three seats down, was Briggs, who was in the middle of rewriting 'Dragonfire'! I still kind of regret that I didn't go over, tap him on the shoulder and say 'Where's the next draft?'; make him think I'd been relentlessly following him all over London! But I wasn't sure his heart could stand it, so I approached him carefully and explained it was just a coincidence. But it still threw him.

Q: 'Dragonfire' has the benefit of a great performance by Edward Peel as Kane, the villain of the story.…

A: Yes, he was very icy – sorry, no pun intended. He was obsessed with his lost love, which gave him some depth. I remember the statue; it was supposed to be this object of heart-breaking beauty. We came on the set and it looked like a fucking melted lolly! What could we do about stuff like that?

Ignoring criticisms of other elements, it's gotta be said that Briggs is a really skilled writer, good on construction. I did have to keep hammering away about the thriller thing, because he came from a background of writing non-thriller material. But he's a really good writer, because he gets passionately committed to things and he writes about people's emotions. When he invents a character, they've got something going for them emotionally.

A problem was that he hadn't written science fiction before, as a lot of the writers hadn't, and I had to keep hammering that too. 'It's a thriller, a suspense story; it's got to have these punches at certain stages.'

I remember 'Dragonfire' has got one of my favourite bits of Briggs's writing, where he has the Doctor trying to go into Glitz's spaceship and discusses philosophy with the guard.

Q: And the great joke after it where Belazs says she is going to kill the Doctor, and he says she's an existentialist.

A: Did you laugh when you saw that?

Q: Oh yes.

A: Well, that was the reaction we were after. The BBC used to have this procedure where you'd go to the Head of Drama, or Head of Series and Serials in the case of *Who*, and show them the episodes. And these guys, their minds were obviously elsewhere; they had big time jobs. We showed him this episode, and he went and made a cup of tea or something. I'd expected him to roar with laughter at that scene, and instead he wasn't even in the room. I'm very glad somebody got the joke, because I loved that.

Q: The character of Ace is established well in just a few lines of dialogue....

A: Well, that's Briggs's background, writing very realistic real world characters. I can't say he created Ace, because John and I did a draft of the character, due to the BBC notion that otherwise Briggs might own Ace and get royalties. The edict was that this shouldn't happen, so effectively John and I developed a new companion. But Briggs breathed life into her. We probably had a terribly two-dimensional stereotype, but he brought her fantastically to life, so in that sense, he's responsible for Ace. And Sophie was perfect for the role, too.

I remember that in 'Dragonfire' there's a scene where she goes back to her room and throws herself on her bed, putting her hands behind her head. And there was this appalled comment from the floor manager: 'We can't use this – she hasn't shaved under her arms.' I was sitting there thinking it was quite sexy, but I was outvoted. The unshaven armpits of a female companion could bring down the nation.

One of the things we wanted to do in 'Dragonfire' was something like the cantina scene in *Star Wars*. But without a decent budget ... Excuse me, but I'm about to slip into broken record mode here. The set for Iceworld was a very imaginative set. It wasn't designed to look strictly real; there were things that were just painted. But the designer, John Asbridge, was a very skilled guy. He took a sort of expressionist approach with things, so that when correctly lit, they would look very dramatic, very real. And, of course, this is where snooker lighting came into effect. The set for the cantina scene was lit so it looked just like a set, as did all the others. Everything would have benefited from sympathetic lighting.

Q: Something that stands out in 'Dragonfire' is the music, by Dominic Glynn, quite an underrated talent....

A: Dominic and I became friends during that period, because I was always a bit of a soundtrack fan and I recognised the quality of his work. Dominic was far and away the best composer we worked with. There are two tricks to making soundtracks that work. One is to do good music, the other is to stick it only where it's necessary. He's now writing rave music – and doing quite well.

Q: There's a gaping plot hole or two in 'Dragonfire', like why Kane has waited three thousand years to send anybody down into the depths to find the dragon....

A: I can't remember the story. I could look it up and solve that plot hole for you. Or it could just have been a fuck-up! I doubt it, though. We were quite careful about things like that. For fans, the stories are constantly alive in their minds, but for people who worked on those stories, well, they've moved on.

The thing I liked about 'Dragonfire' was that there were a couple of nice revelations, like there's this monster, but it's a synthetic monster, and inside the monster is this jewel, which is the McGuffin they're looking for. Then that turns out to be the ignition key for the city, which turns out to be a whole spaceship.

Q: A lot of McCoy stories suffer from some really lame cliff-hangers....

A: The worst one is at the end of 'Dragonfire' Part One. In Briggs's script, the Doctor climbs as far as he possibly can along this path in an ice cliff, then he is forced to climb down the face of the cliff itself. This all makes perfect sense in the script – he's on his way somewhere, the path runs out, he has no alternative, he has to start climbing downwards.

But the way it's shot! He's walking along, then, for apparently no reason, suddenly he dangles himself over the edge. Someone rang me up and said, 'Why does he do this?' The problem is, when you've got the script and you know what's supposed to be happening, when it's expressed on the screen like that, you don't question it. But if you're just a viewer watching this, there's no apparent reason for his actions.

One of the things the director has to bear in mind is that viewers don't know the script. Something to do with the essential film grammar of that scene was missing.

Also, when you're editing, sometimes you'll find your intended cliff-hanger has fallen three minutes before the end of the show. So you did get some weak cliff-hangers, because they were not originally supposed to be cliff-hangers. But if you tried to re-edit to compensate, the knock-on effect through the rest of the story would make matters even worse.

Q: When Season 25 began, something had changed. Suddenly we had a Doctor who was manipulating events, doing things, this mythical 'dark Doctor'. The dark Doctor is attributed to you, Ben Aaronovitch and Marc Platt....

A: Do we have to include Ben and Marc? [Laughs] The thing about the Doctor's character ... You always learn by doing, and I'd done one season. Also, we had a new companion. When you've got Bonnie on screen, you've got a certain expectation of comedy or lightness or something. Now the whole ball game had changed.

I was learning as I went along. And I remember getting a letter from a fan during my earliest season. This guy said, 'Whatever you do, watch "The Seeds of Doom" and "The Talons of Weng-Chiang". You have to remember, I came into this thing on the fly, and when you walked into John's office, you had an entire wall of videos. What do you pick first? We were doing a certain kind of monster, so John said, 'Watch "The Caves of Androzani."' It soon became obvious to me that Robert Holmes was a special writer. Anyway, this guy's letter said, 'Watch these two stories'. So I watched 'Seeds' and thought, 'This is good. It's got a lot of *Day of the Triffids* and *The Thing from Outer Space* in it, but it's quite good.' But 'The Talons of Weng-Chiang' blew me away. That showed me how good Holmes was. It really gives you a grasp of what the Doctor's capable of. I probably would have seen that story eventually, but it was better to have seen it sooner rather than later. So thank you to that letter writer. Having seen that, I began to formulate the Doctor in a better way, or in a more interesting way.

Also, when you have super-powered characters, you really want them to appear as little as possible, because if they're there too much, they can solve all the problems in the story too easily. If you have the Doctor wandering around, manipulating everything, being responsible, in a shadowy kind of fashion, it's a great plot device. Why is the Doctor interfering? Because he's playing this chess game. It makes the Doctor an interesting character, quite potent and dark and powerful.

I remember having this chat with Sylvester, probably during Season 25, where we said that the Doctor should be like a distant mountain range, mistily seen, an imposing power from a distance. A damn sight easier to plot, too.

This version of the Doctor, I have a lot more respect for him. I always hated it when he was zapped on the head or knocked unconscious and tied up. I always thought that was demeaning to him. If he does get tied up, it should be that it was his plan all along.

In one sense, it's the cheapest, crassest plot device possible; in another, it's a stroke of characterisation that gives you chills down the spine. He should be this enigma. It all goes back to Doctor Who? The mysterious, scary, powerful Doctor.

It struck me this was the most interesting way to do the show. You could crack on and do some really exciting television.

Q: So how did you choose the writers for Season 25?

A: One of the first things I did, on my first couple of days at the BBC, was talk to this great script editor called Caroline Oulton, who had edited a series called *Inside Out*. Caroline's now an executive producer at the BBC; she's one of the head honchos in drama. One day she wandered into my office and said, 'Here's this script by this guy I think you might be interested in.' And it was a Ben Aaronovitch script. I remember reading it on the train home, and I was enjoying it so much that I just had to put it down and look out of the window so I could savour it. I didn't want it to end.

Ben had written this *Doctor Who* pilot. It wouldn't work for *Who*, but it was full of great dialogue, an obvious grasp of science fiction. All these wonderful qualities shone through – just brilliant! I got on the phone to him almost immediately and invited him into the office.

I think John suggested 'We've got to get some grand old monsters back; let's do a Dalek story.' Another of John's qualities was having faith in people. No matter if they had no track record, if he believed in them, he'd give the go-ahead. If I really believed in a writer, I could convey it to John, and he'd go with it. These people came out of nowhere – Ben had no track record, Ian had no track record, Malcolm had no track record. Having worked with other producers now, I realise how lucky I was then. John deserves credit for that, but he doesn't get it from fans, perhaps because he did too much. You can only do so much *Who* before you start drawing all the flak.

So John said yes, Ben could do a Dalek story. Ben was crazy about the notion. I was never a *Doctor Who* fan, but I remember, when I was growing up in Canada, seeing the show, and this weird black and white story with Thals wandering around – the first Dalek story. And the Daleks themselves were terrifying. I remember a scene where the Doctor and his companions disable one, and this great big mound of evil jello comes slithering out. I've never forgotten that.

So in my head, *Doctor Who* was this terrifying kind of thing, and the Daleks were a great icon to me too. Ben was delighted to do the story. What happened was that the scripts were already virtually written, John went on holiday and I sent the scripts to Roger Hancock. And he basically played games to get more money for Terry Nation, like any other agent would do. Those games consisted of saying things like, 'Ooh, not sure about these scripts mate.' And that was a terrifying thing to hear at that stage. Everything turned out fine in the end, but it was a bit of a nightmare early on. I think I should name my first ulcer after Terry Nation's agent!

Ben was not a total *Doctor Who* fan before he got work on the show, but once he was commissioned, he checked out all the tapes and assimilated it all. He knew more about the Daleks in 30 seconds than I ever would. He knew to start the story title with an 'R', he knew all about the history of the Daleks, he had the galactic map!

Q: 'Remembrance of the Daleks' has a very similar basic plot to 'Silver Nemesis'....

A: Thank you for pointing that out to me ... The script convergence. When you've got a bunch of different writers, it's like a wheel: the writers are the spokes and you, the script editor, are the hub of the wheel. Without you meaning it to, it's quite easy for stuff like that to happen. Obviously nobody sits down and says, 'Right! Let's have four stories this season and make two of them the same.'

It's not even like you suggest plot elements to a writer. They come in and you might suggest emphasising some elements – to use a musical analogy, you might say, 'Let's have more sax solo.' And lo and behold, you've done the same thing twice. I guess that's just down to my unconscious thought processes. Abject apology – sorry folks! Two good stories, so you can't complain too much.

Q: 'Remembrance of the Daleks' has some wonderful subsidiary characters, like Group Captain Gilmore and Rachel.

A: I liked the love affair between Ace and the treacherous Mike. That was really good.

Q: Ace always falls for men in uniform who promptly turn out to be the enemy, as in 'The Curse of Fenric'.

A: It's *Jagged Edge*, isn't it? At least we put that one in a different season! I wonder what we're revealing about my subconscious processes now...?

Q: Remembrance has the classic cliff-hanger of the Dalek going up the stairs. Who suggested that?

A: Probably Ben. I think he said he was sick of this thing about the Daleks and stairs; 'Let's explode everybody's preconceptions and have the Dalek go up the stairs; scare them silly in the process.' A brilliant flourish. That's pure Ben.

A flash of memory: I went with the director, Andrew Morgan, to the street where we were shooting the school, and he looked up and said, 'Oh my God, it's Macbeth Street!' He came from a theatrical background, and *Macbeth* is a jinx in the theatre. But it went without a hitch. I remember it snowed while we were shooting it, which lent it a nice aspect. It felt like grim, '60s London social realism. It proved four-parters can be done....

Q: It's got lovely lines like 'Unlimited rice pudding!'

A: Ben would just come up with this stuff; just hilarious. The whole way the character of the Doctor was handled, the humour, coupled with this vast, dark, alien aspect, he just got it spot on.

Q: In one story, the Doctor is transformed from a bumbling, spoons-playing slapstick fool into this dark manipulator.

A: It was certainly very powerful and strong. I think Sylvester was finding his footing. He was as happy as anyone to have this powerful character to play instead of this clownish character.

Q: Made a change from stuffing ferrets down his trousers....

A: I'm sure he did that very well too! But if you think about it, that background of the Ken Campbell Science Fiction Theatre of Liverpool was perfect for the role. When I started, they hadn't even cast the role, and although John had no need to do this, he let me sit in the corner while people came in to audition for the part. Ken Campbell was one of the people who came in to read for the role, and so did Sylvester, who was his protégé. The thing about Ken's audition, if you think dark and scary, he was like this bull. The kind of Doctor he would have been would be much more violent and powerful and unstoppable, and much more unsympathetic. That would have been interesting too. Colin Baker's Doctor was gentrified by comparison with this – positively cuddly! Ken's audition was dangerous. Sylvester could be dangerous, but you also felt you could trust him.

I mentioned before this BBC ritual where you have to show them every episode. At that time, the Head of Series and Serials was Mark Shivas. This episode had my favourite sequence. It's where Ace is staying in the boarding house. She's about to go out and she sees this sign in the window. She turns it over and it says 'No Coloureds'. I thought that was fantastic, because we had these sympathetic people who turned out to be racist, because of the time they were living in.

Shivas was on the phone during this bit – they were always on the phone – so I made him rewind it and watch it, because I was so proud. He was a bit pissed off, but the thing he said, and he was right, was we should have had Ace tear the sign up, because then her disapproval would have been totally concrete. As it was, there was a chance it could be misinterpreted.

That's one regret about 'Remembrance'.

Q: Next was 'The Happiness Patrol', a story apparently packed with subtext.

A: If memory serves, there were three phases to that. I remember saying to Graeme Curry, 'Yeah, yeah, make it an attack on Thatcherism, totally.' Then, of course, we'd soft pedal, saying 'No, no, of course it's not like that.' Then Sheila Hancock, without anybody saying anything to her, totally latched on to it and just played it like Thatcher. So Graeme and Sheila would go to conventions together and someone would ask if 'The Happiness Patrol' was an attack on Thatcherism and Graeme would feel obliged to waffle for a bit, knowing he might get me into hot water if he said yes, then Sheila would say 'Of course it was!'

So, of course it was. But nobody intended it to be that and nothing more. We didn't want to produce something that could function only in its period.

Q: 'The Happiness Patrol' doesn't suffer so much from snooker-type lighting.

A: Although that does turn up, in places like the Kandyman's kitchen. But you're right, it is darker in places, and the director was gunning for that. You could make the lighting guy bring the lights down, but it went against his nature. Even then, I felt it should have been darker.

Q: Upon first watching, I didn't realise it was meant to be set mostly outside on the streets at night. I thought the whole city was set inside some huge, monolithic dome.

A: The dome's a nice idea; we should have thought of that. But that's always a problem with studio-bound stories; they always look like they're indoors, no matter how hard you try.

Q: Was it a problem that the Kandyman looked a bit like a heavily copyrighted character symbolising a certain brand of liquorice allsorts?

A: The Kandyman was meant to look like a stick of candy rock or something, but the designer did a fantastic job, creating this liquorice allsorts man instead. There was a certain amount of trepidation that this might invite all sorts of litigation, but thankfully it didn't. It was a wonderful idea, but I could understand higher-ups being worried.

The problem with suits like the Kandyman had is that they completely mask the actor's features. If you give the characters very witty lines, like the Kandyman did have, they kind of get lost. The characterisation gets lost. Graeme did a nice, subtle job on the Kandyman. He was a very black, comic character.

'The Happiness Patrol' had the sinister aspect of taking all these childish things and making them dangerous; the sort of thing that sometimes gets mentioned unfavourably in Parliament! A comics writer I've always admired is Alan Moore, and when I first got on the show, I tried to get him on board. I actually spoke to him on the phone, but he was too caught up in other stuff. But one thing he said about *Doctor Who* was that it was scariest when it poked into dark nursery corners. That was harking back to the Hartnell years, but 'The Happiness Patrol' tried to probe those corners too. The Kandyman was a figure of fun, yet he was totally homicidal, and he had sweets that can kill you. That sort of thing.

It came about because I'd read a radio play by Graeme called *Over the Moon*, which was about football, of all things. But I could tell from it that the guy could write. So I got him in and asked for story ideas. It was painful at first; he'd keep coming up with stories, but we couldn't get one to click. He'd just about given up hope of ever doing one. We went all through the same thing with Robin Mukherjee.

Finally Graeme came in one day, slumped in a chair in the office, and said: 'What about a planet where everybody has to be happy, and if they're not, they're executed.' Bingo! He'd done it! There were torments and rewrites to come, but the story was on.

All the while we were working on it, we just called it 'The Happiness Patrol' to have something to call it. Eventually we had to come up with a proper title, so Graeme called it 'The Crooked Smile', but John said, 'For God's sake, call it "The Happiness Patrol".'

Fans always wanted the show to be dark and punchy, and as soon as they heard about a story called 'The Happiness Patrol', they formed preconceptions about it. Another problem was that a lot of the costumes and the elements were this kitsch holiday camp thing, presented as sinister, and I think some fans lacked the irony to see beneath the surface, to see that it was this horrible concentration camp.

Q: I loved the bit with the Waiting Zone.

A: Sort of Kafka meets the Marx Brothers – that's Graeme all over.

By this time, I'd started to think of *Who* in classic television terms, with shows like *Quatermass* and *The Avengers* in the mix. But a show I've always loved is *The Prisoner*, and 'The Happiness Patrol' reflects that.

Q: Next was the silver anniversary story, 'Silver Nemesis', a story that's mythic for the amount of material that had to be cut out of the final broadcast version.

A: Something people don't realise about the timing of scripts is it's really hard. You can have two scripts, both 63 pages long – which by convention means they should run for 63 minutes – but they can end up being wildly different time lengths. In years of dealing with directors, producers and writers, I came to realise that no-one can precisely time a script. Well, there might be somebody out there with this magical ability, but I think they're one in a million.

For me, a story is first the script, then the rushes. I might watch it on broadcast, but the material that's missing is still in my head, so I don't notice. 'Silver Nemesis' does have a lot of plot elements – the modern-day Nazis, the 16th Century pair, the Cybermen, the Doctor and Ace – but it's a fairly straightforward story, isn't it? Maybe one too many elements.

You're right, it was something of a reprise of 'Remembrance', but the thinking had evolved about the Doctor, about him being in charge of things. And in 'Silver Nemesis', you've even got the metaphor of the chessboard on screen. Perhaps I felt there was something touched upon in 'Remembrance' that could be taken even further.

Q: Elements of 'Silver Nemesis' work very well, like the Robert Holmes-ian pairing of Lady Peinforte and Richard.

A: Kevin Clarke didn't have any *Who* background at all, so that was totally original; he just wrote those characters very well.

Q: But the Nazis are just cannon fodder.

A: Well, you do need cannon fodder in some stories. Actually, we were at pains to always refer to them as paramilitaries, to avoid any kind of affront – but of course, they were Nazis.

Q: 'Silver Nemesis' isn't a patch on 'Remembrance of the Daleks'.

A: Well, I think Kevin's script was brilliant, and without naming names, if that didn't come across on screen, that's due to other factors in the production process rather than the script itself.

Q: There was a story circulating that 'Silver Nemesis' would reveal who the Doctor really is, but it proved to be a giant tease.

A: Oh yeah, yeah. Well, of course, there's no way you could really say who the Doctor truly is, that's he is so-and-so. We had begun to push towards this notion that the Doctor had god-like powers and was this vastly powerful, almost supernatural being. And John didn't like it at all; he felt this was verging on religion, the last thing he wanted to do. Kevin was all for going the distance on that. I suppose there was a collision there and it was cut back, but I could see John's point of view. It was a kids' show; you didn't want all that controversy. Having built up this great revelation about the Doctor's secret, we had painted ourselves into a corner a bit.

Just as we managed to get the motorcycle for Malcolm in 'Delta', so we managed to make a dream come true for Kevin on 'Silver Nemesis'. Kevin had this thing, 'Let's get Courtney Pine to do the music; he's Britain's best jazz musician.' I said, 'Kevin! He'll never do it!' But John said to try him, and he agreed. So there was this fantastic day one weekend where Kevin and I went into the studio to watch Courtney record the music for the show. It was a great moment, and he seemed a decent guy, too. It was fantastic.

Q: The season ended with Stephen Wyatt's 'The Greatest Show in the Galaxy'.

A. Which is the only one I've watched recently, so on your guard!

Q: That was four episodes, but could have been three.

A: Yeah, possibly. Too much running around.

Q: There's a great performance by Ian Reddington as the Chief Clown.

A: Yeah, there's a lovable kind of madness and menace to him, which the performance brings across. Again, 'Greatest Show' has that *The Prisoner* element to it. The menace is in things that should be happy, like the circus, where you're supposed to enjoy yourself. The hearse and the top hats at the start.

There were two lighting directors on 'Greatest Show', and eventually the director got more sympathetic lighting, but you can still see sequences that are quite flatly lit. Others are much more moody …

There are nice elements like the billowing white tent walls, which are like something out of a Doctor Phibes movie by Robert Fuest. The colours and the costumes for the clowns were great; the costume designer did some of the finest work I've ever seen on *Doctor Who*. The make-up was very good too.

But it also featured the half-buried robot, which I didn't like very much. Scenes like that, you hope they will be realised effectively, but that particular one wasn't. Money and personnel again …

Q: There were lots of nice cameos in 'Greatest Show'.

A: We did the rather cruel thing of destroying a fanboy. There was a lot of laughter on the set when we finally executed that character, I can tell you! Well justified. I remember sitting around on the set with T P McKenna, and him talking about working with Sam Peckinpah on *Straw Dogs*. We had people of real calibre.

One of the things we didn't do in 'Greatest Show', which I still regret, was give the character of Mags, the punk female werewolf, a thick Glaswegian accent. Fans always accuse the show of being, and John of making it, too lightweight comedy, but it was John who fought against that kind of thing, it was John who said, 'We can't have that; it's going too far.' Having watched it again, I still regret not doing that. Jessica Martin was a very good mimic and – call me frivolous, call me insane – I think a Glaswegian accent would have added a whole new element it otherwise lacked. But John felt it wasn't serious enough.

Q: The story really puts the boot into hippies.…

A: Puts the boot into corrupt, failed hippies. Hippies who sell out.

Q: Why was all of Season 26 Earth-based?

A: John favoured the more exotic settings, but I put my shoulder behind Earth-based stuff, because I felt it worked better. The other thing I always argued for, which there was resistance to, was monsters that looked like human beings. I knew that if we had a monster that was just a person with long fingernails and fangs and contact lenses, it could be done beautifully. Whereas as soon as you get into anything more elaborate, you get into a gap where make-up or effects or costumes may leave you with a monster that's just funny or cuddly. That's a big danger, cuddly monsters. For example, the Cheetah people in 'Survival'. Or the dragon in 'The Caves of Androzani'; it's a very good story, but the dragon doesn't look alive, it looks like a Chinese New Year's parade dragon. I was glad we had all Earth-based stories in Season 26, although I suspect a lot of fans weren't happy about that.

Q: There's a near-total absence of the TARDIS.

A: I did have an agenda: more Earth-based stories, more humanoid monsters, less of the TARDIS. The TARDIS is great, but the less you see of it, the better. I particularly disliked people having arguments in their bedrooms in the TARDIS. It was like *Neighbours* with roundels on the walls. The TARDIS is this spooky machine that transports you through time and space and it's bigger on the inside than it is on the outside. But beyond that, it's just a plot device.

Sure it's a cheap set to shoot, but it's terribly brightly lit and looks like a plastic control room. Also, you'd get shots of the TARDIS flying through space. Why? It's a time machine! I have a kind of revisionist view of the TARDIS.

Q: What influence did Sylvester and Sophie have over their characters?

A: All stars wield more influence the longer they're with a show. Sylvester and Sophie never got difficult, but they certainly became more comfortable with their characters.

Q: How did you choose the writers for Season 26?

A: Some of the writers I had used had moved on. Kevin was now writing for *Minder*; I had been lucky to get him in between commissions, but now he was making far too much money elsewhere to do *Who* again. Stephen had done two on the trot; Malcolm had gone on to write his American mini-series.

Ben, of all the writers, he was the ultimate *Doctor Who* writer, because he had a real feeling for *Who*. With other writers, I felt I was the custodian of *Who*. It wasn't about whether or not other writers were fans, because often fans have no objectivity; lots of knowledge but no objectivity. Although Ben in isolation could not create the perfect script, he was – at that time and place – the perfect *Doctor Who* writer. So wheel on Ben.

Q: And he wrote 'Battlefield', which apparently re-jigged elements from a previous idea he'd submitted.

A: I can't remember the exact circumstances, but I did name the story 'Battlefield'. The site of the story was an ancient battlefield, and it suggested the whole story was a battlefield, a metaphor for greater forces. But that story was also a lesson in objectivity for me.

For some reason, Ben couldn't write a particular speech for the final episode of 'Battlefield' so I ended up writing it. So I wrote this speech, and it went on for pages. It was the 'CND speech' at the end of episode four.[59] Ben looked at it and said, 'This goes on for too long.' I said, 'No! Don't be ridiculous. Every words stays!' When it hit the screen, people were falling asleep in droves, so we edited it right down. It was a very valuable lesson for me. I could always edit other people's material, but I have trouble editing my own.

Q: 'Battlefield' has a lot of returning elements from past *Doctor Who* stories – UNIT, the Brigadier …

A: Ben loved all that stuff. He knows all about ranks and how many units in a battalion. And he loves doing research about UNIT and things like that.

Q: In an interview, he said the story was originally three parts and it was padded out to four.

A: I can't remember the exact thought processes at the time, but it made sense for the two established writers – Ben and Ian – to write the four-parters while the new writers did the three-parters.

59 Cartmel was referring here to the Campaign for Nuclear Disarmament.

After a big hit, people want to see someone screw up. And after the Dalek story, there seemed to be a surge of hatred from the fans towards Ben. Briggs seemed to avoid that, maybe because he'd had one season off. He'd had a year away, and maybe expectation wasn't so high for him – 'Dragonfire' wasn't the classic that 'Remembrance' was. Although, of course, 'Fenric' reached that level.

Ben is very articulate and isn't afraid of talking to the fan press. One of the reasons I've avoided giving interviews myself is that you're asking for trouble. Say nothing and they've got to fight your Sphinx-like silence.

A lot of the shows, there are aspects of them I cringe to think about – the lighting or sometimes the costumes or make-up or a particular visual effect. But 'Battlefield' I think was well mounted, well directed. Perhaps it didn't reach some of the peaks of 'Remembrance', but as a plateau, I felt it was almost that good all the way through. The Dalek story has more ups and downs within it, but I know that is not perceived fan wisdom. In ten years time, people might look back and think 'Battlefield' was a great story.

Q: There was a rumour, usually attributed to JN-T, that the Brigadier would die in 'Battlefield'.

A: That wasn't just a JN-T rumour. All the way along, we definitely toyed with the idea; but the problem was, ultimately, we liked the guy too much. The Brigadier does arrive very late in the story. It starts and you think you're going to get the Brigadier, but you get Bambera instead. And then you get the Brigadier anyway. That kind of riff really appeals to me. It's a tease. There are elements of 'Battlefield' I thought were genuinely spooky, like where Ace and the other girl are in the chalk circle.

Q: The Destroyer is a great looking monster, but it's almost thrown away.

A: The BBC is capable of producing a great monster like that, but you couldn't predict when they'd do it. We were very conscious of alluding to *The Devil Rides Out*, witchcraft stories and pentagrams.

One of the things I liked about 'Battlefield' was this casual line by one of the characters about having to phone from the pub because the phone in the car wasn't working. Nowadays, nobody would think twice about that, but at the time, nobody had really foreseen car phones. Ben was very good at that; he could absorb the Doctor and writing for television but he also had that science fiction turn of mind. With some of the other writers, you had to try to get them into that way of thinking, or just do it yourself when editing the scripts.

A lot of would-be scripts I'd get at the *Who* office were just self-contradictory. They'd give you a future world that was inconsistent and implausible.

Costumes presented a similar problem. For years in movies and TV, if it was the future, everyone was wearing either Roman togas or white zipsuits. *Blade Runner* was a real turning point for that, because it recognised that fashion was cyclic and that people in the future would wear fashions from the past, as they already do now.

One thing I was happy about was something we did on 'Paradise Towers'. They were looking at a video recording at the start, and I inserted into the script that they should use a CD. Of course, in the future, it won't be a CD, it'll be something else, but at least it wasn't an old videotape.

But the phone in the car, and the two drinks costing five pounds in the pub, and the living currency that the Doctor pulls out of his pocket, those were the little touches that Ben was exemplary at.

Q: Next was 'Ghost Light', a story that's semi-legendary for its complexities.

A: Actually, I thought 'Ghost Light' was quite straightforward!

Q: At a convention I went to, Marc Platt was on a quiz show during the cabaret, and his first question was, 'Explain the plot of "Ghost Light" in ten words or less'. He struggled a bit....

A: Okay, let me try. Bunch of aliens end up in Victorian house! If Marc can't explain it, I certainly can't. But it's a good, moody ghost story – superficially a ghost story, but actually about aliens in a Victorian house. I think the whole evolutionary theme is that survivors succeed. It is a very ornate story.

Q: 'Ghost Light' makes a virtue out of necessity. It's studio-bound, but all takes place in one house, with a lovely BBC set.

A: Well, at least it glows like old mahogany. Marc was a fan who actually did a *Doctor Who*, and is no doubt hated and envied in fandom for that. We got endless script submissions. I can't tell you how many scripts we got from fans. The great thing about Marc was that he sent in his work cold. He was working at the BBC at the time, but there was no clue to that in his script. I liked the material and got in touch with him, and then I discovered he was working just up the road. Anybody else who was a fan and who worked at the BBC would have put that at the very beginning of their letter. So I was impressed by that.

He'd sent me this great story that was utterly unfilmable. It wasn't an early version of *Time's Crucible*[60], which is all about the TARDIS, with the TARDIS as a character – I always feel you're on thin ice with that. In the TARDIS, anything can happen. I always like to have a fairly nailed-down environment. In the TARDIS, anything goes ... It wasn't 'Lungbarrow', either; it was something that was quite a way off. 'Lungbarrow' was the first thing of Marc's that I actually groomed as a potential script to show to John. 'Lungbarrow' was the precursor to 'Ghost Light', and we almost got it on. It was all about the Doctor's family. John didn't go for 'Lungbarrow', so I regrouped my forces in my head and said, 'Why don't we do a Victorian story, with a lot of the elements of "Lungbarrow", like the creepy household?' So I said to John, 'How about it?' He went for it, so I rang Marc and said, 'You're doing this Victorian Earth-based story.'

Q: What else can you tell me about 'Lungbarrow'?[61]

A: The Doctor goes home and faces his family. It was very *Gormenghast*, full of Mervyn Peake intricacies, dark and gothic.

Lungbarrow was the name of the Doctor's home, and it was actually a sentient being. Marc had

---

60 An original *Doctor Who* novel written by Platt after the TV series ended, for Virgin Publishing's New Adventures range.
61 Subsequent to this interview being conducted, Platt wrote a *Doctor Who* novel entitled *Lungbarrow* for Virgin Publishing's New Adventures range; the novel reused the setting and many ideas from the unmade TV story.

worked out all this stuff about the history of the Time Lords. In contrast to most of the stories we see set on Gallifrey – all people in spangly togas in brightly-lit places – this would have been sort of *The Addams Family* on acid. There were a lot of great things about it, mostly the mood.

When John was presented with it, he felt it was too way-out for a lot of reasons. In retrospect, I have to say I'm kind of glad, because we then came up with another Earth-based story, and I'm very pleased we had recognisable settings. 'Lungbarrow' was the antithesis of that – the Doctor doing weird things in an extremely weird setting, even by the standards of *Who*.

The Victorian cobwebbiness of 'Lungbarrow' was one of the best things about it, so we stole that mood, that feel, and a few other elements, and came up with 'Ghost Light'.

Q: Later on, you gave the Doctor a house in England in your *DWM* comic strip *Fellow Travellers* and your New Adventure *Warhead*, and it also featured in Ben Aaronovitch's New Adventure *Transit*.

A: Yes, Ben picked up on that, bless him. Kind of validated it.

The Doctor's house is loosely based on the house where I grew up in Kent, because I'm familiar with it. I'm very fond of that English-haunted-house-in-a-flourishing-green-garden image. I think I called the house Smithwood Manor in the comic strip, but giving it a name killed it, so now it's just 'the house on Allen Road'. The local kids keep renaming it 'Alien Road', as if they're aware of something strange going on there. It's a romanticised version of my family's house.

But it's great, because although you've got these weird outbuildings and strange artefacts lying around, it's an ordinary environment, whereas the TARDIS is a weird environment. I think that keeping a weird character like the Doctor in a weird environment for too long is like putting a painting in too ornate a frame. I like having this place the Doctor can keep returning to. In fact, there's quite a lot of it in the new novel; I was just writing a section set there today.[62]

Q: 'Ghost Light' being a period story, the BBC could cope well with its needs for costumes and props.

A: That was something we'd noticed on 'Delta'. You'd get these people who didn't necessarily want to work on *Doctor Who*, that were being rotated through the BBC system and weren't enthusiastic about working for you. Some of these people respond to the challenge of science fiction by trying to do something really interesting, but others just don't have any reference point; they don't like SF, they think it's silly, they don't give it their best shot. But as soon as you say '1958' or 'Victorian England', they go crazy with enthusiasm, they love it. And you want that, you want people's enthusiasm, you want the team on your side.

Q: 'Ghost Light' suffers in the sound mixing; the music's too loud in a lot of places, and you miss vital chunks of the dialogue.

A: Perhaps there's a flaw in the scripts, because missing one line shouldn't make the whole story incomprehensible. One thing I learned was never to have important dialogue and action at the same time. Of course, in 'Ghost Light' you do get Ace cross-dressing!

There's a lovely moment where the bells chime, panels slide back and maids almost float out

62 This was the New Adventures novel *Warlock*, published by Virgin Publishing in January 1995.

from inside. That was Alan Wareing's idea, and oddly enough, his reference point for that was *The Blues Brothers*. In that, a nun comes rolling out on a trolley at the beginning. Alan was great; he'd watch other stuff for ideas, like *The Blues Brothers* or an ad where they'd made people's eyes glow, and he'd say, 'Let's do it like that.' Other directors wouldn't give you that input. Leaping ahead, when we were doing 'Survival', he actually went to the zoo and looked at cheetahs, which is more than Rona Munro or I ever did. I don't know how much good it did him, but at least he did the research.

'Ghost Light' has a lot of reference points to *Alice in Wonderland*, and a very cruel soup joke – 'The cream of Scotland Yard.' When Marc was writing that, he didn't have a word processor, so we'd get these hand-typed pages with pieces of paper stuck on top. All the writers ended up with word processors pretty quickly, after draft 97.

Q: Season 25 was the 'dark Doctor' season, but Season 26 seemed to focus more on Ace and her character, her background.

A: I think John picked up on that in Season 25 and felt it was going too far. With Ace, it was perhaps because she was from Perivale and had a real-world environment. If you had a writer who wanted to deepen the characterisation, he couldn't do a lot with the Doctor, so he had a choice of using either Ace or one of the other characters.

All the stories were Earth-based, but 'Battlefield' was the only future Earth story, and that's the one where Ace got shortest shrift. That was a tendency with historical settings; she sort of plugged into them. I don't think she's that strong in 'Ghost Light' …

Q: We discover that she is a teenage arsonist, and that the house in Perivale is the one that she'll torch in 100 years time.

A: Oh yeah. There was some cross-pollination between Ben and Marc, which is all to the good.

Q: There was the line about unrequited love and burnt toast.

A: Yeah, burnt toast – that was another great speech from Marc. Earlier I mentioned Alan Moore and dark nursery corners. That was what this was all about. We had the weird rocking horse.

Q: 'The Curse of Fenric' is probably the most popular story from your era amongst fans.

A: I remember sitting round with Briggs, working on the plot, the dark Viking curse and the World War II thing. There was a constant attempt to make things more interesting. Instead of having Germans, we had Russians, and the British were virtually the bad guys. It was a Cold War story, very sophisticated. It might end up as the best one we did during my tenure, although I also have other favourites. It scores so strongly in so many ways. I don't go a bundle on the Haemovores …

Q: The scene where they come out of the water is very dramatic, if a straight rip-off from 'The Sea Devils'[63].

63 A 1972 *Doctor Who* story.

A: I doubt Briggs or I had seen 'The Sea Devils' at the time, but we were probably aware of it.

John was conscious of not making it too scary for children, so we didn't call the creatures vampires; we had to call them Haemovores instead.

The story went through a lot of title changes. We often had trouble with this. Perhaps it was a fault of the stories; they were too complex. We were trying to decide what to call it. It had been 'The Wolves of Fenric', and finally I said, 'Why not call it "The Curse of Fenric", because that explains the whole thing, about the curse coming down through the ages.' That title solved millions of problems, because people could get a handle on what was going on.

A lot of 'Fenric' evolved from Briggs talking to me and ideas bouncing back and forth. I liked the fact that the characters, such as the different Russian soldiers, all had their own agendas, without making it too complicated.

When we were plotting it, we were stuck on some plot point. And Briggs said, 'Ah! The way to solve this is to think about the history of the characters. One of the characters is responsible for the scientist being in the wheelchair, because of a sporting injury when they were schoolboys.' I always thought in terms of plot and more plot, another piece of plot. But Briggs worked with plot springing from the characters themselves. That opened my eyes – Briggs was teaching me what he knew.

Another thing Briggs does that I subsequently used in my own writing was that he doesn't write in sequence. If he wants to write a scene from the end, then a scene from the middle, he will. He writes in a sort of patchwork fashion, and it's very liberating when you realise you can do that, because you don't get blocked writing something dull when you're rather be doing another scene further ahead that you're excited about. Or when you reach a scene you're not ready to write yet, you can skip ahead and do something else.

Q: What came first in 'The Curse of Fenric'; what was the first idea?

A: It's very difficult to recall this in exact detail. But one thing was that Alan Moore had done a story about aquatic vampires for *Swamp Thing*, so when I was knocking about looking for serviceable monsters for *Who*, that went into the mix. Briggs is very knowledgeable about Vikings and runes. World War II setting? Great; that's one of the best things about 'Fenric'. That was probably an early plank of it.

Q: There's an element of retroactive continuity: references back to 'Silver Nemesis' and the first Ace story, which Ian Briggs also wrote.

A: I remember there were things that Briggs wanted to achieve, that he felt 'Dragonfire' hadn't done. So he had an agenda. I remember we sat around for ages talking ideas. I think the setting of London during the Blitz might have been one. And there are references to the code-breaker Alan Turing, early data processing; all this went in. Briggs is an egghead. He's a very good writer and poet, but he's also an egghead; he knows a lot of stuff.

Q: 'Survival' is the final story broadcast to date. It's got some wonderful material, but it's also got that animatronic cat....

A: The aggravation we got from that animatronic cat! I won't slag off the people involved in this case, because I know the guys involved were very dedicated; they were totally behind it.

They'd worked and they'd worked, but the thing wasn't quite ready. It got to a point where we had to say, 'We'll shoot some more stuff the next day,' and they worked night and day again to get it ready. So you might be disparaging of what you saw on the show, but the animatronic cat on screen is a lot better than the one there on the first day! The problem is, you can't train a cat like you can a dog. The director said that the first time he read the scripts, he knew it was a potential problem. But yeah, the cat doesn't look real, and it blows it.

Q: What inspired 'Survival'?

A: The BBC liked to encourage new writers. I went along to a new writers' bash and got loads of scripts from people, and Rona's was the standout script. It didn't have anything to do with *Who* – it was about baby-minders – but Rona chimed because she was a good writer and because she liked fantasy.

So I encouraged her, said we were looking for a story that was only partly Earth-based, because that was as much as I could get away with. We started talking about animal experimentation. She was also into feminist/occult symbology, things that have been associated with women, wise women, down through the years, like the cat symbol, reflections of the moon in water, all this witchcraft kind of stuff. She was happy to weave that in. She also brought absolute authority to this feral aspect, to Ace getting drawn into this more feral world. I thought Rona evoked that beautifully.

Here was a writer, writing from her own obsessions and inspirations, on a path that was parallel with *Who*. That was what you wanted. You wanted to get the best out of someone and get something that was *Who*. The inclusion of the Master was, I think, John's suggestion, but Rona weaved him in, made good use of him. He's a Machiavellian manipulator who's corrupting and infiltrating yet being corrupted himself at the same time.

The whole 'survival of the fittest' Darwinian thing, tooth and claw, that all came out of Rona's head. I actually thought 'Survival' was the perfect title for it – I was into terse titles at the time. I'm not sure she liked it.

Q: Wasn't it called 'Catflap' at one point?

A: Oh yeah … Rona was into science fiction and dimensional travel, like *The Lion, The Witch and the Wardrobe*. 'Catflap' was a great title but far too tongue in cheek. The story would have suffered the same fate as 'The Happiness Patrol', fans reviling it because of its name. And I doubt even the man in the street would have had the depth of irony to enjoy it. It's probably just as well we didn't call it that. I had to say, 'Sorry, Rona, but "Survival" it is.' Rona had a catflap, and I remember her saying to me, 'You never know what you're going to get through it. Next door's cat or a dog or anything. It's a feral thing; get in through the catflap.' And that was what was happening in the story, too; all these things shifting and getting in to other dimensions. 'Catflap' would have been a wonderfully poetic title, but 'Survival' it had to be.

Q: The Master standing around stroking the kitling was incredibly reminiscent of Blofeld in the James Bond movies.

A: Yes, Donald Pleasence in a volcano has always been an enduring image for me.

Q: 'Survival' was the final story broadcast, and it ends with the Doctor and Ace walking back to the TARDIS, with an overdubbed final monologue from Sylvester that concludes the series: 'People made of smoke … Somewhere the tea's getting cold …'

A: Yeah, that obscure, Marc Platt-style burnt toast bit – I think I might have been responsible for that. I think that's why I ended up writing that speech: we weren't sure the show was ever coming back. And there was this great responsibility to leave the series open for continuation or to put some final words that would echo honestly. That was quite a sad moment. What a shame …

Q: So 'Survival' was wrapping up, Season 26 was coming to an end. How did the end come?

A: We were told to wait and see about another season, but there was definitely a flavour of 'You'll have to wait a very long time.' I was head-hunted for a job on *Casualty*. John and I could have gone on planning *Who*, but there's no fun working if you don't know anything's going to come out at the end of the day.

Q: You mentioned trying to get Alan Moore to write for the show.

A: Alan actually said yes. He'd go round to comic conventions saying he had this other iron in the fire, that he was writing for TV – meaning *Doctor Who*. But he was too busy. He's also a very nice, generous man and probably made a few more commitments than he could actually keep. If I'd got him a few months earlier, before *Watchmen* took off, he might have done it.

Then again, I don't regret it. I so admired Alan Moore and his writing, and I'm sure it would have been a rough ride. All the writers had a rough ride; it was this B-movie process of working under fire. This guy was a hero of mine. Could I have been objective about his work? I could have been, but I probably would have had some bad feelings about it.

Even just talking to Alan Moore on the phone was quite stimulating. He said he'd like to take the Time Lords and turn them into a bunch of bad guys. He'd had a lot of fun doing that with the old Charlton superheroes in *Watchmen*. He was quite happy just to sit and talk.

There was actually a ritual I had for new potential writers who weren't familiar with science fiction, to give them the *Halo Jones* books to read.[64]

Q: Any other examples of stories like 'Lungbarrow' that got a long way but never made it to the screen?

A: It was rare for things to go too far without being broadcast, because that would have involved somebody parting with some money. Money was so tight that if you paid a writer, you sort of had to go ahead with the story. There were several instances where writers came in and had discussions but it didn't go much further, or never got followed up. They included the guy who writes *Taggart*, Glenn Chandler, and Chris Russell, who later became the backbone of *The Bill*.

There was a professional writer who kept trying but just kept getting further and further from the mark, and I got to a point where I couldn't really encourage him any more. Some

---

64 These were graphic novel collections of Moore's *Halo Jones* comic strip from *2000 AD*.

people just couldn't get the mind-set. One thing I learned was, never have a meeting with someone before you read his or her stuff.

There was one writer called Charles Vincent who was very good and had the right sort of sensibility. I've often thought if I'd stayed on with *Who*, he probably would have got work. I hope he did all right. I always felt a terrible responsibility for the writers, especially those who had talent, but there just weren't enough slots or time …

Q: Virtually all your predecessors as script editors wrote for the show, either out of necessity –

A: Or avarice!

Q: Or avarice. Did you ever consider writing a story yourself?

A: If we'd done another series, I think I probably would've taken a crack at it. It's one of my lingering regrets that I didn't. The thing is, you're there, you have the opportunity to do so. Basically I was too honourable to do it. I know that sounds crazy, but I really thought I should give writers a chance. I wasn't hurting for money. There've been times since when I've thought, 'I wish I'd had that x-thousand pounds that I'd have got if I'd written it, and the residuals, and – above all – the screen credit and the experience.'

But in all honesty, I always felt that if I commissioned myself, it would be an incestuous thing to do. The only way I could have got away with it would have been if I'd written a great one. I remember trying to plot out a story for Season 27, if it happened. I was on holiday in Turkey. I'd never had any kind of trouble or imagination block suggesting things to writers. But when I tried to do it myself, I thought, 'Shit! I can't think of anything!' It's probably a good thing that I didn't, because I'd much rather not have done one than have done a bad one, or failed to do one.

Q: There seems to be a view within fandom that you'd always intended to leave *Doctor Who* after three seasons.

A: I was ready for a change. But if I'd had to do another season, I would've been resourceful, used a blend of new and old writers. I think it would've been great. We would have had a new companion, but Sylvester would've probably stayed on. We were already thinking of ways to introduce the new companion.

Q: It's been reported that Sylvester would have stayed on for a full season but Sophie was only willing to sign up for another eight episodes.

A: I think that would have been John's strategy, to bridge the way to a new companion, halfway through the season.

Q: It's also been reported that Ben Aaronovitch and Marc Platt were the most likely candidates to script stories for Season 27.

A: It's quite likely they would've done. Certainly Ben; I always felt he was the ideal writer for *Doctor Who* at that time. He could have been another Robert Holmes for *Who* …

On the list of regrets, if we had done another season, Ben and I had this great sequence that we'd cobbled together for introducing the new companion. There's a big mansion house, a big party going on, contemporary times, Britain. Full of debutantes, a costume ball, a big upper class kind of party, people dripping with diamonds. And there's this girl; this beautiful girl in a dress. She goes up this sweeping staircase. She goes down a long corridor and then into this room. She takes off her gloves and sweeps back the black curtains on one wall to reveal a huge safe. She kneels by the safe – she's a safecracker! – and spins the dial and cracks the safe. She opens the door, and there's Sylvester jammed inside the safe, and he says: 'What kept you?' Bang, straight into the opening title sequence. And the safecracker would have been our new companion.

I'm always sorry that we didn't get to use that. Sylvester being such a little guy, we could have done it.

Q: That's almost like a typical 'Mrs Peel, we're needed' sequence from *The Avengers*.

A: I used to love all that stuff.

We wanted a companion who was street level like Ace, but more of an Emma Peel, an 'aristo' character, who could be quite intriguing. I think we would have gone for a girl companion; that always seemed the best option. I love the idea of her being a safecracker. Although there's a rough edge, she's always kind of a goodie. A darker companion would've been nice …

Q: When were you happiest as script editor of *Doctor Who*?

A: I was happiest when things were going right! When I had a new writer coming on to work for the show. After the first season, I had learnt a lot, so I think I was probably at my peak at the start of the third season. I knew a lot, but was still relatively fresh. Around the end of Season 25, start of Season 26.

I have to say I thought the final season avoided the glaring errors we'd had earlier. We had 'Survival', 'Ghost Light', 'Battlefield' and 'Fenric'. There's not a real dud in them; not even one I felt had any big flaws. I felt that was a very high standard to maintain; some very mature, very adult stuff. I'm glad I did that third tour of duty, because in many ways that was a good as it was going to get.

Q: From your 12 stories, are there any particular favourites that stand out?

A: There's a heady rush for the Dalek story. The scripts were more perfect than the final, finished product. Ben had these hilariously funny lines. The scripts were funny, scary, and the Doctor had come together as this dark figure. 'Remembrance of the Daleks' was a great moment. And 'Fenric'. 'Fenric' looked like this fantastic war movie.

Q: Anything you particularly regret?

A: If I was to watch my first season again … I felt they were all flawed, because I had a lot to learn, Sylvester was settling into the role, and we had the switch from Bonnie to Sophie. Watching stuff from that season would be the most cringe-worthy. Things got steadily darker and better as they went along.

Q: Any particularly great moments?

A: Great moments were things like Courtney Pine playing live at this beautiful country pub one summer's day. I remember getting a ride back with Sophie and Kevin Clarke and listening to Tracy Chapman's 'Fast Car', which was a big hit at the time; that was a great moment. Being in Macbeth Road as it snowed on the Dalek story. Standing on North Acton tube station with Ben, waiting for a train, talking about what we would do if we got him writing for the show; that stands out.

Q: Which do you prefer – script editing or writing?

A: Oh, writing. You do a good day's writing and you feel sane and drained; you feel like you've got a place in the universe and you're doing what you always wanted to do.

Script editing is a craft, you're helping other writers, but it doesn't touch anything deep-rooted within you like writing does.

David Bishop

BONUS FEATURE: VISUAL EFFECTS OF SEASON 24

In the late 1980s, The Frame ran a succession of in-depth features on various aspects of the production of Sylvester McCoy's three seasons as the Doctor, based around a wealth of exclusive interview material. The first of these features, which originally appeared in Issue 4 of The Frame *in February 1988, focused on the visual effects of the series' twenty-fourth season. The interviewees were Mike Tucker, Susan Moore and Stephen Mansfield.*

Mike was at that time employed as an assistant in the BBC's Visual Effects Department. He had joined the Department some two years earlier, after completing a Theatre Design course at Croydon Technical College. Coincidentally, his first job had been to build a new miniature of the TARDIS for use in the opening scenes of the sixth Doctor's last story, 'The Trial of a Time Lord'. Mike went on to have a highly successful career as a fully-fledged effects designer, initially at the BBC and then, after the Visual Effects Department was closed down in 2003, with his own company, The Model Unit – which in 2006 won a BAFTA craft award for effects on the BBC drama-documentary Hiroshima. *Mike and his team supplied numerous model effects seen in the first two series of the new, Russell T Davies-produced* Doctor Who *in 2005 and 2006, and were responsible for constructing the updated Dalek props. In addition, Mike has co-written (with Sophie Aldred) the non-fiction book* Ace! (Doctor Who Books, 1996); *co-written (with Robert Perry) and written numerous original* Doctor Who *novels, novellas and short stories for the Virgin, BBC Books and Telos Publishing ranges; and written several audio dramas in Big Finish's* Doctor Who *and Bernice Summerfield spin-off series.*

Susan Moore and Stephen Mansfield were freelance model makers who worked both separately and in partnership. Susan attended Camberwell College of Art, and her first job after leaving was to produce the Starburst awards for Marvel Comics. From there, she went on to work on The Hitchhiker's Guide to the Galaxy – *both Ken Campbell's stage play at the Rainbow Theatre in London and the television series – providing masks and other special props. Her other early work included supplying props and models for various TV commercials and programmes, among them* The Benny Hill Show *and* Morecambe and Wise. *In addition, she designed and modelled Zelda and the other aliens for Gerry Anderson's* Terrahawks. *Stephen completed a foundation course at Middlesex Polytechnic and began his career in the industry with freelance prop work for* Terrahawks. *Shortly after that he joined forces with Susan to work on an independent puppet production, and then continued the partnership to take on more work from the BBC. Over the two years prior to this interview being conducted, Stephen and Susan had contributed to a wide variety of series, including* Alas Smith and Jones, Tomorrow's World, The Kenny Everett Show, The Marksman, Max Headroom *and, of course,* Doctor Who. *Much of Stephen's time, however, was taken up working as a caricaturist and modeller for Central TV's acclaimed satirical puppet series* Spitting Image.

Visual effects is one of the most important areas of a science fiction-orientated production. Without effects, the show simply could not be done. This is certainly true of *Doctor Who*, and each serial is therefore allocated a visual effects designer, whose job it is to provide all the effects required for that particular batch of episodes. In practice, however, the designer is not expected to carry the whole thing off single-handedly; the Visual Effects Department employs a number of assistants to help develop and realise the designer's ideas. Occasionally, an assistant will even be asked to work out and execute a particular effect from scratch (although under the supervision of the designer, who has the final responsibility for it). Mike Tucker,

Susan Moore and Stephen Mansfield are three of the assistants who worked on *Doctor Who*'s twenty-fourth season – Mike as an employee within the Visual Effects Department, and Susan and Stephen as freelance contractors hired to make certain specific contributions. We spoke to them shortly after the season finished transmission about their work on the three stories to which they contributed: 'Time and the Rani', 'Delta and the Bannermen' and 'Dragonfire'.

TIME AND THE RANI

Q: Perhaps the most impressive effect in 'Time and the Rani' was the spinning bubble traps.

MT: That was interesting, because they ended up being a combination of visual effects, video effects and design. All three departments had some idea of how they were going to do that effect. Geoff Powell, the set designer, had an idea of using the paintbox system to create the spinning bubble, and Dave Chapman, who is the video effects guy, agreed with that but needed an actual physical bubble on which to key the effect. So what we ended up with was making a miniature bubble that we span in front of camera for Dave Chapman to move within the picture, for the video effect to be overlaid on. That was a very good example of all three departments working on a particular effect.

We did originally consider making a full-size perspex bubble, that we would actually bump around the landscape for real, but that eventually proved a little expensive, and in retrospect probably a little tricky.

We did have a full-size bubble base, and the effect of the bubble was added by Video Effects. The base was swung in some scenes to provide the path of the bubble; and when Mel was rescued, the base simply acted as a guide for Bonnie Langford to see what she was supposed to be reacting to.

Q: On a more basic point, how do you decide how many guns etc you're going to need for a particular story?

MT: That comes down to budget. On that particular story, there were certain items that were essential and obviously one-offs. For example, a model of the Rani's citadel, model shots of the asteroid around the planet and a model of the rocket. With things like guns, it depends on how many of the monsters there are going to be – and, again, monsters are one of these cross-over areas, where they may be make-up, costume or effects. In the case of the Tetraps, they ended up as a combination of effects and costume. We provided the heads and the arms and Costume provided the body. Their budget allowed them to make six Tetraps, therefore we made six guns.

Q: The Tetraps' guns fired nets.

MT: We had one fully-practical gun, which fired charges and a net. It was operated by compressed air and was worked out by an assistant called Roger Barham. It was almost a real working prop. For all the other scenes, we had fibreglass copies of the working gun. Once the thing had been filmed, Dave Chapman added video effects over the net as it flew, and then, for the scene where it lands, obviously a cutaway, we dropped a net over the actor/actress to be captured, and again Dave added the effects in post-production.

Q: How were the Tetraps developed?

MT: Costume gave us polaroids of the costumes being built, and also copies of their design drawings, from which Colin Mapson designed the heads, which were sculpted by Stan Mitchell. Those heads were in turn sent off to Sue and Stephen for painting and the application of fur.

There were six heads and arms and one animatronic head, which was decided upon during one of the production meetings. In some of the scenes, the tongue had to come out, and it wouldn't be practical to do that with one of the costumes, so a completely mechanical head was sculpted. It was operated by three of the guys on cable controls and another providing the arms. The other change that we made was to give Urak radio controlled eyes, to give a bit more life to that mask. So we constructed a fibreglass under-skull in which we mounted four servo-motors, and at the end of each servo was an eyeball. The head was controlled by Effects throughout production. The other Tetraps didn't need anything like that kind of sophistication; they were just slip-cast latex masks.

Q: How was the Tetraps' cave done?

MT: Obviously we couldn't build a full-size cave, and we didn't have enough Tetrap costumes to do that for real, so it came down to a miniature cave on CSO with a few foreground 'real' hanging Tetraps and the foreground action. We knew that we needed at least two sizes of Tetraps, possibly three, for a forced perspective. The initial Tetrap shape was sculpted by Stan Mitchell, and this was actually done before he had seen the costumes, so he sculpted a basic human figure with the head and hands, which we had already done. That sculpture was then handed over to Sue, who will continue the story.

SM: The sculpture, as it turned out, had to be altered once the costume details were known, so we resculpted the body and made a smaller version as well. We also sculpted it with hair on already, which is a technique used when doing caricatures; you provide the bulk of the hair on the sculpture and then dress the finished item with a small amount of real hair over the top.

The large Tetraps had hair applied in all the right places, but the smaller ones just had hair on the crests of the head, because they were in the background and the detail wasn't necessary. We made 20 in all, all painted and dressed with hair.

MT: Knowing the sizes of the Tetraps, I then, under the designer's supervision, designed the forced perspective cave, which ended up measuring about ten foot square.

Q: Who created the Brain?

MT: The Brain was built in part by a gentleman called Len Hutton, an effects designer in his own right. He had done quite a few *Doctor Who*s in his career, and had gone back to being an assistant. Sadly, 'Time and the Rani' was the last thing he worked on, as he died shortly afterwards. The Brain was a fibreglass under-shell with a latex skin over the top. We taped about a dozen condoms under the skin and simply blew through air pipes to give the effect of the brain pulsating.

Q: Was the Rani's base a difficult effect to realise?

MT: We had to show the Rani's laboratory in relation to the entrance-way in the cliff, which had been constructed full-size on location. In order to match the lighting and the cliff background, we had to take our miniature on location, and the two were recorded at the same time. One camera was looking at the set of the doorway, which filled the bottom half of the screen with the top half blanked off, and another was looking at the miniature, which was in the upper half of the screen with the lower half blanked off. They were recorded on two separate pieces of tape and then combined in post-production. Foreground miniatures work when you are on film, but all the work we did here was on video, and therefore it had to be combined in post-production.

DELTA AND THE BANNERMEN

Q: Gavrok's spacecraft was very impressive in 'Delta and the Bannermen'.

MT: The original script asked for a fighter for the spacecraft, but at the first production meeting Andy McVean, the effects designer, suggested that the ship be expanded from just being a fighter to being a troop carrier. He designed it and came up with the idea of the neck moving up and down to allow the crew to disembark. I built the ship, and it was recorded entirely on video in the Effects Department during post-production. There was no filming of the model work for 'Delta', mainly because it all had to be integrated into the real settings on video – the landing by the lake, and the landing in the holiday camp.

A full-size section of the nose cone was built to take around on location, which was done before we built our miniatures, so we had to match that set when the ship was designed in full. Hence there's a corrugated effect at the rear of the miniature ship that matched their front section set.

Q: What was supplied for the battle at the start?

MT: We provided some of the guns and also the pyrotechnics in the quarry. The scene where Delta is running and there are explosions and gunshots all around her; we had to pre-plan a route and walk through it with the director. Then the effects were set in and fired off by Andy McVean.

Q: Moving onto the Chimeron baby, we believe that was contracted out to Sue and Steve?

SM: We received a drawing from the designer, Andy McVean, of a baby. It was based on an elephant shark, which has leech-like tendrils hanging down around the mouth. We were told that this creature was going to be born with loads of loose-fitting sacs of skin, which would contract and get tighter as it grew older, as it was going to do very quickly. The Costume Department would take over after the first stage of the baby and it would end up as someone in a leotard-type costume with honeycomb-like scales over the surface.

SMan: We had some rough guidelines as to what the baby should be able to do. It was required to have only a very small amount of movement, although the mechanics eventually became much more elaborate, resulting in a more mobile and lifelike puppet. We were also told that the body should have leaf-like scales on it, and that the colour should be a cabbage-green!

SM: We constructed two versions of the baby. One was operated like a hand-puppet and had a pipe that spilled gunge out of its mouth; that was the one that came out of the egg. After it had hatched, Delta was going to hold it in her arms and it had to react slightly. Stephen therefore rigged another up with cables so that both the arms and the legs moved and the head swivelled around, and the veins on the forehead pulsated and the mouth opened and shut. So they could get quite a lot of movement out of it.

Q: How does cable operation work?

SMan: The cables are basically a casing with a wire running through the middle, and you are literally pulling on the wire – much like a marionette, except of course the wires are concealed.

The baby was basically an aluminium and fibreglass armature with a latex skin. The joints inside were under tension, so that when you pulled and moved the limbs, they returned automatically to their original positions once you'd released the cable. Very simple. It's the most reliable way of getting the movement. There were also air pipes to make veins on the head pulse, the veins being simply balloons.

Q: It was obviously sprayed with something to make it glisten.

SM: Yes, it was covered with a green, Swarfega-like substance. There were a couple of takes of it hatching, and one was a bit too messy and gungey, so they played it down a bit. Originally it was supposed to have this green fluid pouring out of its mouth, but they cut that and just had the baby coming out of the egg.

Q: The space-flight scenes were very interesting.

MT: With the coach, we had to match the real one, and we had this really bizarre situation of a coach flying through space. That immediately presented problems, in that most people know what a coach looks like, but we had it in a very incongruous setting. So it made it quite a tricky effect to do, in terms of believability. That, coupled with the fact that we had a spinning police box in shot as well, made it a very bizarre scene to shoot.

The coach was about two feet long, mainly for ease of handling and because of the amount of time we had to build it. The TARDIS was the same one from the previous season; the one I built for 'The Mysterious Planet' segment of 'The Trial of a Time Lord'.

The satellite was both a full-size one and a miniature, based on a Sputnik. The rocket was interesting. They wanted a rocket that could launch a satellite, and so we took a few liberties by giving it a nose cone that opened, that looked visually interesting even if it was not historically accurate.

DRAGONFIRE

Q: How was Glitz's spaceship, the 'Nosferatu', developed?

MT: Basically we knew it had to have an undocking scene, a take off scene, a flying away scene and an exploding scene, so two versions were made; one for all the flying work, and a breakable version for the scene where it explodes.

The feel of 'Dragonfire' was that Glitz's ship should be a rusty old tramp steamer, and that is basically what I used as an influence when we designed it. It had this rusty orange colour and a ship-like conning tower at the back and cargo pods. It just seemed to suit the character of Glitz; that this was the sort of ship he would have.

Q: And Iceworld?

MT: Initially what was wanted was a planet with an obvious hot side and an obvious cold side, and on that cold side there was an icy, crystalline structure. This would be seen as simply a city, but in episode three it would be revealed to be a spacecraft. So the initial shots had to disguise the fact that it was going to be a spacecraft, but at the same time it was designed around the fact that it would be taking off into space.

Iceworld was designed by Andy and, because of lack of time, had to be made by outside contractors, Derek Hendon Associates.

Q: The *Star Wars* Cantina sequence was an obvious influence for the scenes in the Soda-bar, with lots of aliens milling around. How did those scenes come about?

SM: The make-up designer asked us if we had any off-the-peg masks that had not been used in any other TV or film production. We had a number of bits and pieces that we'd made over the years – masks and puppets and so on – and I took along a whole collection, including a few masks made by another colleague. Make-up chose a selection and used them on the extras in the background. Luckily, the director, Chris Clough, was there at the same time, and he spotted a half-mask I'd made for a party, and thought that it would be perfect for the scene where the child wears a mask to frighten Mel. He also spotted Eric the puppet, and Eric became a legend in his own lunchtime! (For some obscure reason, every creature we make seems to end up being dubbed Eric – it's a silly name at the best of times, and it seems a suitably ridiculous name to give to anything that's an alien, and supposed to be taken seriously.) At one point, the producer called down from the gallery, asking if it had a name. I just said 'Eric'. It was originally going to be in the background, but then they decided to start the scene with Eric at the table with this fish creature that we provided, and they finished the scene off with him snapping at the Doctor as well. Eric was operated by the man in the green fish mask, and everyone was very pleased with it.

Q: How was the effect achieved where the medallion and Kane's hands smoked?

MT: A combination of effects. When we could, we ran smoke pipes through the costume and out through the cuffs. For the scene where the coin was put down on the desk, we used two chemical substances that, when mixed together, smoke slightly. We sprayed one on the coin, one on the desk top, and when the two were brought into contact they smoked.

SM: The portrait on the coin was meant to be Kane's face, so we modelled a likeness of Edward Peel onto it. I hope it looked like him, because originally we were told it was just going to be handed to people in long shot, so we were surprised when it was seen so close up.

Q: Tell us about the Dragon. What did the script say?

MT: The script initially said 'a huge, fire-breathing dragon'. It turned out in episode two to be a bio-mechanical creature with laser beam eyes, breathing smoke and fire. That was handled almost entirely by one guy in the Effects Department, Lindsay McGowan. Andy McVean came up with some initial design drawings for the head, and Lindsay prepared a rough maquette of the creature – a small plasticine model about 12 inches tall – which was approved by John Nathan-Turner and Chris Clough. Then he sculpted a full-size version, which was a latex and polyurethane foam suit and a fibreglass head. There was also a separate mechanical head, the mechanics of which were done by Paul Mann, which opened up to reveal the Dragon's treasure. That suit was then painted up by Lindsay and Paul McGuinness, another effects assistant who in the previous season was inside Drathro. The head was sat on a helmet arrangement on top of the actor's head, and he looked out through the neck.

Q: The destruction of Kane at the conclusion of 'Dragonfire' was a stunning piece of effects work, which we understand was handled almost entirely by Susan and Stephen under the supervision of effects designer Andy McVean. How did that come about?

SMan: While we were working on the Chimeron baby, we were told that there was the possibility of a melting head sequence at the end of the final story. At that time, it was not confirmed that *we* would be handling the sequence, but we were asked if we thought it was feasible. We had to bear in mind the potential complexity of such a sequence and the limitations of a TV studio recording.

There were two major stipulations. As the effect had to be done on a live recording day, it *had* to melt very quickly. In addition, there were to be no red colours on the underskull, or any liquid resembling blood.

SM: So we went off and did a lot of research and found out how the similar melting effect in the movie *Raiders of the Lost Ark* was done. I spoke to some senior effects people in the film industry. Everyone said that it couldn't be done, not on video and certainly not that quickly. In spite of that, we felt the problems as we saw them could be overcome, and that it was certainly a project worth having a crack at. And, as it turned out, a month later we were offered the job.

SMan: Edward Peel apparently wasn't keen on the idea of having an alginate face-cast made, especially as it would have had to have been with his mouth open, which is doubly uncomfortable for the subject. There wasn't really the time, anyway.

Andy McVean arranged for us to meet Edward Peel at Visual Effects during a break in rehearsals. We took instant photos of him in the facial position he would assume at the start of the melting scene. I then took calliper measurements of his face, whilst Sue took more detailed photographs. We set to modelling the head from the instant photos that same afternoon.

SM: The head was sculpted in water-based clay, from which a multi-piece plaster mould was taken. From this mould, six wax outer-skins were eventually taken. As the mould was multi-piece, the original clay bust remained intact – just as the inflexible wax casts had to! Using the teeth and the top of the head as registering points, we started cutting away at the face, taking it back to what it would be if it had melted to the bone. A silicone mould was then taken of this new sculpture, and two fibreglass skulls were cast. The skulls and the skins were then airbrushed.

SMan: To these underskulls we fitted various pipes – in the mouth, in the nose and under the helmet. Because the melting had to be done very quickly, the wax skins had to be very thin.

Therefore, when they melted, they tended to give off a very thin dribble of wax and not much else. So, through these pipes we pumped a liquid coloured to match the molten wax, thus creating a more authentic, head-sized volume of wastage!

Selected areas of the glass-fibre skull were cast in latex, and acted as bladders. These sections, when inflated, helped to distort the face, and generally accelerated the degeneration process by pushing wax away from the skull. The whole lot – six skins, two underskulls, liquid etc – was finally completed with hours to spare, about 4 am on the studio day, 29 July.

MT: The head had been fitted to a support post in the studio that was the same height as Edward Peel, and Costume had provided a collar section to go around the neck – they couldn't use a real costume, because all the wax and gunge would have ruined it.

There were four of us operating it in the end. Steve provided the spit and gunge, while Sue, Paul Mann and I all wielded hot air guns and bladders. Cameras lined up on it and told us when we were in shot or out of shot. When we were all ready and out of shot, we turned on the hot air guns and away we went.

SM: There was a little bit of improvisation when the instruction came from the gallery to start dropping it out of shot. As the rig was mounted on a huge baseboard we couldn't literally drop it downwards – so we just tilted it back.

MT: What they were trying to get was the effect of a collapsing man; they wanted to see Kane shrivel and deflate as he melted, and they wanted to match this shot with one we had done of the body collapsing from behind.

Then Dave Chapman, in post-production, managed to mix in Edward Peel's real mouth, so that it actually screamed as it melted.

In the end, we did only one take on it, because it all seemed to go well and the gallery was happy with it.

SM: Ultimately it turned out to be quite an unsettling effect in spite of the lack of red colours. At one stage in the middle of shooting it, all this yellow gunge came out in a torrent, because of a blockage in the air pipe. Also, one of the wax eyes that were underneath the skin popped and ran down the face. Not a pretty sight. Needless to say, none of this reached the final programme. We were flattered though to receive a round of applause from the assembled cast and crew!

MT: What you saw on screen was a fraction of what was recorded; it was shown at about 30 times normal speed, and the melting in real time took about ten minutes, from which they chose a suitable sequence to use.

SM: I think on the whole it worked very well on screen, which is, of course, the ultimate consideration. Apparently it's the first time an effect of this type has been attempted on British television, so it's a first for *Doctor Who* – and of course for us.

David J Howe

Interview conducted by David J Howe, Mark Stammers,
Stephen James Walker and Tony Clark

INTERVIEW: SOPHIE ALDRED-COMPANION ACTRESS

In the autumn of 1990, the future of Doctor Who *was very uncertain. It was already apparent that there was going to be a hiatus following the twenty-sixth season the previous year, but how long that hiatus would prove to be, and whether or not it would ultimately spell the end of the series as an ongoing BBC production, no-one knew for sure. It was against this background that Mark Stammers and I arranged to interview Sophie Aldred, who had portrayed the Doctor's most recent on-screen companion Ace in the last two seasons. The interview was actually conducted at the second attempt. We had agreed to meet up at the BBC's North Acton rehearsal rooms – sometimes referred to jokingly as 'the Acton Hilton' – but on the first occasion when Mark and I arrived there, we found that Sophie had left a Post-It note for us, apologetically saying that she had been taken ill and had to go home. I later discovered that she had also left a phone message for me a couple of hours earlier, explaining the situation and asking if we could rearrange the interview for a later date, but sadly by that point I had already left to rendezvous with Mark. Undaunted by this initial mix-up, I spoke to Sophie a few days later, by which point she was back to full health, and duly fixed a new date for the interview. This time, fortunately, all went well, and Mark and I spent a very pleasant couple of hours in Sophie's company in North Acton. The interview subsequently appeared in Issue 17 of* The Frame, *dated February 1991.*

Sophie now balances her acting career with her family life, having got married in 1997 and had a son, Adam, in 2000 . She co-wrote with Mike Tucker the book Ace! *(Doctor Who Books, 1996) and has reprised the role of Ace on numerous occasions in audio CD dramas for Big Finish and, prior to that, BBV.*

We met up with Sophie Aldred at the BBC Rehearsal Rooms in North Acton, where she spoke to us during a break in rehearsals for *Corners*, the popular children's series she co-presents. We began by asking about her childhood. Was that when she had first become interested in acting?

'Yes, it was, really. I was always putting on entertainments in the garage and sending the proceeds to *Blue Peter*, that sort of thing. I used to be so bossy when I was little – my life was an extraordinary mixture of being bossy and crying a lot – and I got all the local kids, most of whom were older than me, involved in these vague scripts that I wrote and starred in and directed. I always had to be Prince Charming, because I got to wear the nice shirt and ride on my hobby horse!

'Gradually this carried over into junior school. I've still got some of the things I wrote, actually. I adapted the *Just William* stories and, of course, I always cast myself as William. In fact, I modelled myself on William. Until the age of about 12 or 13, I used to walk around school with one sock up and one sock down, and I loved being kind of scruffy and dirty. Mind you, some things never change!

'Also, where I was brought up – in Blackheath, South East London – there was a marvellous adult education place called Kidbrooke House[65], which had an art and drama workshop every Saturday. My mum, my brother and I went along to that and did a couple of hours of art in the morning – experimental stuff, chucking paint around, but very kind of creative – and then drama for another couple of hours later.

---

65 This has since been renamed Mycenae House.

'So that's really how I started acting.'

Had she always known, then, that she wanted to go into acting as a career?

'Well, I suppose so, although I also did a lot of writing when I was young and would still like to do more, if only I could get the impetus. I mean, I do a bit for *Corners*, but stories were more my line. I used to write them for my younger brother. I produced my first novel when I was 7 1/2 – I've still got it at home with all the pictures. That was called *The Seekrat of the Cupboard*. It was meant to be *The Secret of the Cupboard*, but I couldn't spell "secret"!

'Once I'd kind of given up on the idea of being a writer, though, I did a lot of acting at secondary school – a lot of opera, actually – and a lot of singing with the local church choir. I started playing the trumpet and the piano, too. Then in the sixth form I had a wonderful English teacher, who directed a lot of the plays that we did, and it was she who suggested that I try drama. So I ended up at Manchester University studying drama as a degree. In fact, I was lucky enough to be there at a very creative time. Ade Edmondson and Rick Mayall had recently left, and Ben Elton was still there, doing his MA. It was a real hotbed of comedians! Simon and Trev, who are on *Going Live* on Saturday mornings, were also there. Simon was my best friend in the first year. He used to come round in the middle of the night and say "Sophie, I'm hungry" – because he was really skinny and weedy at the time – and I'd make him biscuits at two o'clock in the morning.'

We wondered if Sophie had had any interest in science fiction prior to joining *Doctor Who*.

'Well, I've never read any science fiction, but as a kid I was just obsessed with *Thunderbirds*. I thought I was Scott Tracy for a while! My mum made me a little blue suit with the hat and the International Rescue sash, and I ran around saving the universe.'

Always Scott Tracy rather than Lady Penelope?

'Oh yes, always. I do remember screaming and screaming until my mother bought me a Lady Penelope doll, so I must have thought she was quite cool, but no, I was always one of the boys, I'm afraid.

'Anyway, when I was at university, somebody suggested to me that I should do a dissertation about puppets – because it was always a bit of a running joke that I was into *Thunderbirds* and everything. So, sure enough, I did my dissertation about Gerry Anderson and puppets on television. When I was working on that, I went along to a science fiction shop that had just opened in the university precinct – the first time I'd ever been into a science fiction shop, I think – and discovered the Fanderson magazine *SIG*, as it was then. I was one of the first members of Fanderson, actually. So I got in touch with a few of the fans through that, for my research.

'I never went to any Fanderson conventions, though, so it was a real eye-opener for me when I started attending the *Doctor Who* ones. I realised then that I was by no means as enthusiastic as most science fiction fans.'

Had John Nathan-Turner given her any advance warning about the series' huge fan following?

'He didn't want to shock me, obviously, but he did give me some indication. I quickly realised, though, that it was much bigger than I had imagined. To be honest, before I got the part of Ace, I hadn't really been aware that *Doctor Who* was still going on. The last time I'd seen it was when Tom Baker was the Doctor, and even then I hadn't made a point of sitting down and watching it every week, so I'd completely lost touch with the series. Once I got involved in it, though, I became fascinated again. My friends all thought it was the funniest thing on earth that I was working with Bonnie Langford on *Doctor Who*! They wanted to see the videos of all the old stories they remembered, so I'd go into John's office and say "Er, could I borrow that ...?" I'd have my friends round and we'd all watch *Doctor Who* videos!'

We commented that the way Sophie had joined the series had been quite unusual, in that she hadn't known initially that Ace was going to become a regular character.

'Yes, I've had quite an interesting entrance to and exit from *Doctor Who* – if it's to be an exit. Both totally unexpected!'

Would the traditional bimbo image of the '*Doctor Who* girls' have worried her had she been approached to play a companion in the first place?

'Yes, it would have done, I think. If they had said, "We want you to take over from Bonnie Langford and wear a mini skirt and scream," I would have thought, "Well, why the hell have you chosen me?" There would have been other people better suited to that type of role! As it was, though, I had this character in "Dragonfire", and when I read the script I couldn't believe it, because it was like reading about myself – in terms of the tomboyishness and the strength of the character, anyway – which was very appealing. Of course, when it comes down to it, I would probably have been delighted to accept whatever role they'd offered me – you don't tend to turn down an opportunity like that! – but one of the great advantages was that I really, really loved the character and very much believed in what I was doing.'

We pointed out that, unusually for a *Doctor Who* companion, she had also had an opportunity to discuss her character with the writers and to make suggestions about her costume.

'Yes, although I didn't realise at the time that it was unusual. It was only when fans started telling me this that I thought, "Oh crikey, you're not meant to do that!" You're not actually meant to tell the producer "I think I'll wear Doc Martens," or say to the costume designer, "Let's go and buy a bomber jacket and put some badges on it"!

'Actually, though, I think the degree of input that artists have into their work has changed a great deal over the years. I can imagine that, even ten years ago, working in this place would have been very different – I would probably have sat in a corner and shut up! – but in my time on *Doctor Who*, I've really felt as though John and Sylv and I, and Andrew Cartmel too, have all worked together.

'Talking to past companions, I get the impression that they took on the role thinking, "Oh great, a strong female character," and then five minutes later found themselves running around a quarry in a bikini, screaming. So I'm really pleased with the way Ace's character developed. I think the companions are also very much a reflection of their times, and that's especially true of Ace, as she was younger than most of the others. It all just seemed to come together really well – Ace's relationship with the Doctor, the fact that Sylvester and I got on so well, everything.'

We were interested to know if Sophie could recall anything specific that she had contributed in her discussions with the writers.

'It would be a bit presumptuous of me to say that I had any influence at all. It was simply that the writers got to know my personality and so were able to write very much for me. It wasn't that I went in and said, "I think I'd rather like to beat up a Dalek with a baseball bat today." The plots were the writers' responsibility. I mean, Andrew would always ask me at the beginning of every season, "Right, Sophie, what would you like to do this year?" and I'd say "Ride a motorbike!" I never did get to ride a motorbike, so that shows you how much influence I had over plotlines!

'I did feel, though, that I knew what Ace would do in a given situation. For example, there was one point in "Battlefield" where the script said "Ace screams" – I think it was in the scene where all the pub falls in. I said, "No way, I'm not doing that!" Unfortunately, in the finished programme, it sounds as though I am screaming, but it was actually Ling Tai. I was really disappointed about that! There was a bit in "The Happiness Patrol", too, where I had to slide down one of the pipes, and Gary Downie[66] said "Oh, do a few screams or something." I told him, "Gary, you know I don't scream – I shall yell"!'

Did she feel bitter about the BBC's continuing indecision over the series' future?

'Well, I just wish they'd been brave enough to have said yes or no earlier on, you know, because it's dragged on like this for ages now. I didn't even hear that there wasn't going to be a season this year until Sylvester told me, which I thought was a bit off. Then I had to wait about six weeks to get an official letter confirming it – although I knew that everybody knew that I knew, if you see what I mean! It was just embarrassing, really, because nobody wanted to probe and say "What is actually going on?" Now here we are, months later, and still no decision's been made, and still we don't know what's going on.

'It's not that I feel sorry for Sylvester or myself, because we've both been lucky enough to be in work continually since then, and at least we've still got the publicity of being the latest Doctor and his assistant – we haven't been superseded. I just wish that somebody would decide once and for all, so that I can stop thinking about it. In the back of my mind is still the idea that somebody might make another season and somebody might think, "Oh, it would be good to have Sylvester and Sophie in one more episode," you know. I mean, it'll probably come to it and Sylv and I will both be in Hollywood. Chance would be a fine thing …'

We wondered why she had decided to go back to *Corners*, having left part way through the previous season.

'I left because I got a part in panto, which was something I wanted to try as I hadn't done it before. It just so happened that when they asked me to do *Corners* this year, I was really ready to come back and do some more TV after six months in the theatre. It's going to be the last series of *Corners*, and the producer really wanted me to do it, so I thought it would just be nice to round off a phase. Actually, we've been given six extra programmes after Christmas, because it's gone down so well, but then that will be the end of it.

'As it's turned out, I'm really glad I have done this year. I've certainly not found it boring – in fact, I've got a lot more out of it. I really feel as though I've consolidated my presenting skills, and I've still had some input on the writing side.

'Also, it's worked out very well in that, because we're into the routine of it, we have two days of rehearsal, a day off, a day in the studio and then ten days free, which means that I have time to do other things. Last week, for example, I was able to take up a job with Radio 5 doing a schools programme called *Singing Together*, which I really loved. Actually, that's the first big radio thing I've done. It's basically teaching children to appreciate music, which is something I'm really keen on as I think music is such an important part of a child's development. It was nice, too, to be working with a lot of kids, because on *Corners* we don't actually have any contact with children. It was good to be able to get some feedback.'

Presumably, though, she still receives a lot of letters from *Doctor Who* fans?

'Yes, I do, which is nice, because it shows what a loyal following the series has. I'm getting a lot of mail from abroad at the moment – from places like New Zealand, Australia and America – because they're continually showing episodes over there. I think there's a sort of *Corners-Doctor Who* crossover, too, so I get quite a lot from 10-15 year olds.'

Surely it must be hard work having to deal with all this fan mail?

66 Production manager.

'It has been hard sometimes when I've let a backlog build up. At first I tried to answer every letter personally, but now that's just proved impossible. Of course, I still do as much as I can, and Mediaband are helping me out a lot with it. I do feel that when someone has bothered to sit down and write me a letter, the least I can do is send them a signed picture. Sometimes, though, I get terribly guilty about all the letters that are piling up, and the friends that I haven't written to for two years. And then there's my grandmother saying, "Sophie, why haven't you rung me for three weeks?" I have to tell her, "I've been doing my fan mail, granny!"'

Does she ever regret, then, being in the public eye?

'Well, the advantages far outweigh the disadvantages – although of course there are the boring, stupid tabloid journalists who just want to talk about my boyfriends all the time. To be honest, though, when I see myself in the paper, my reaction is a sort of weird mixture of saying, "Oh my god!" and thinking, "Actually, I'm quite flattered, people must want to read about me." That's an awful streak to own up to, isn't it, that you actually quite like being talked about!

'It does become a real pain, though, when it affects your family and friends. Last year, for example, my father was away on business, and when he got back, before I'd had a chance to speak to him on the phone, somebody told him, "Oh, there's been this thing in the paper about how Sophie had a terrible accident in a water tank."[67] I think he realised that if I'd been badly hurt he would have heard something about it, but obviously he was really worried. The awful thing is that you can't separate out what's true from what's not true. I mean, the story about the accident had a basis in truth, but there are some things that are written that are absolutely a load of codswallop, and you can't possibly ring up all your family and friends and say, "Actually, that's not true!"'

To round off the discussion, we asked Sophie how she saw her career developing in the future.

'Well, I've just signed with a new agent, and when I went to see him he pointed out that my CV is very "muddy". A director will think, "Hmm, *Doctor Who* girl, Noel Edmonds' Christmas Day show, children's presenter – equals bimbo'. Then he'll see that I've also done the Edinburgh fringe festival, Theatre Clwyd and so on, and he'll think, "Hang on, who have we got here?" My situation's similar to Sylvester's, really – his CV is even more wacky than mine! Neither of us can be put into one category. I think that's a slight disadvantage, sometimes, although it can work in your favour if someone wants an actress who can sing and play the trumpet or something!

'In an ideal world, I'd like to be doing drama or film, but you have to wait for things like that to come up. In the meantime, what I'd love to get involved with on the presenting side is a programme for older children or young adults, perhaps a live show, interviewing people and that sort of thing. I think that would be good fun. On the other hand, though, I'd really like to do a serious play at somewhere like the Royal Exchange or the Birmingham Rep, or something along those lines. So again it comes back really to the two different strands of my career.

'At the moment, though, it's actually a really bad time for the acting profession. There's very little work around and very little drama being made – it's all light entertainment and sitcoms, very much tried and tested things. The joke going around is that anybody who is actually in work is a star!'

Stephen James Walker

Interview conducted by Stephen James Walker and Mark Stammers

---

67 This accident occurred during recording of 'Battlefield'.

BONUS FEATURE: VISUAL EFFECTS OF SEASON 25

As our interview feature on the visual effects of Season 24 (reprinted a little earlier in this book) had been very well received by readers, my co-editors and I on The Frame *were keen to follow it up the next year with a similar piece on Season 25. Our three previous interviewees, Mike Tucker, Susan Moore and Stephen Mansfield, were again happy to contribute, as was Robert Allsopp, another freelancer who had worked on a number of effects for the season; and we had the blessing of series producer John Nathan-Turner. The only problem was that, at that time, the 'powers that be' in the design departments at the BBC seemed to have taken against the idea of assistants and contractors talking to the fan press – and the last thing we wanted to do was to cause our interviewees trouble with the people they worked for. We therefore decided that it would be better all round if, instead of presenting interview quotes per se, we took the information that Mike, Susan, Stephen and Robert gave us and wrote it up in the form of a series of factual articles. Even then, our attempts to cover 'Remembrance of the Daleks' ran into serious objections from that story's visual effects designer Stuart Brisdon (we later learned that he had recently been hauled over the coals for overspending his budget on it, which may help to explain why) – hence our articles, published in Issue 9 of* The Frame *in February 1989, focused on the season's other three stories, 'The Happiness Patrol', 'Silver Nemesis' and 'The Greatest Show in the Galaxy'. We also encountered a few difficulties with Dorka Nieradzik, the make-up designer on 'The Happiness Patrol'; although she was willing to talk to us, and keen to vet our text (in particular to ensure that there was not the slightest suggestion that she had been in any way influenced by the famous Bertie Bassett advertising character in her designs for the Kandyman!), she was unwilling to be quoted directly, so again we were restricted to simply reporting what she told us. Despite the rather difficult circumstances in which they were written, the resulting articles were generally agreed to give an excellent insight into the creation of some of the most memorable aspects of the twenty-fifth anniversary season.*

THE HAPPINESS PATROL

Doctor Who is rightly renowned for the incredible succession of strange and unearthly creatures it has featured over the course of its 25 year history. The anniversary season's second story, 'The Happiness Patrol', introduced a number of new additions to this alien hall of fame, including the robot Kandyman, Helen A's pet, Fifi, and the Pipe People.

THE KANDYMAN
In Graeme Curry's script, the Kandyman was described as follows:

> Humanoid but not human. He is actually composed of sweet substances and a robotic skeleton completely unseen deep inside his synthetic body. He is chubby and jolly looking but at the same time elegant and sinister. The colour of his skin, lips etc suggests sweets and sugar confections rather than human flesh. He is tall and powerful. He wears a white lab coat, a bow tie and red-framed movie-star glasses. These and his other items of apparel, the pens in his pocket etc, are all made of candy.

This description suggests an essentially man-like creature with a 'sugary' complexion, which could perhaps have been achieved by simply applying make-up to the actor's face; and indeed it was the story's make-up designer, Dorka Nieradzik, who was given the task of devising the Kandyman's distinctive appearance. When we spoke to Dorka recently, however, she told us that there was never any question of creating the effect using make-up alone – producer John Nathan-Turner and director Chris Clough had always thought in terms of a costume being constructed, as they wanted the character's robotic nature to be readily apparent to viewers.

Dorka thus conceived of the Kandyman as being, quite literally, a 'sweet' robot. In her designs, she gave him rotating eyes, three panels of flashing lights (to emphasise his mechanical origins) and metallic teeth, jaws and chin. She also decided that there should be a pipe running from his chest to his chin, with red liquid constantly pumping through it as if to lubricate the robot's joints. The idea of dressing him in a lab-coat was dropped, however, as Dorka felt that this would obscure too much of the body.

The person chosen by Dorka to build the Kandyman costume was freelance model-maker Robert Allsopp (whose previous film and TV work included contributions to *The Last Emperor*, *Max Headroom* and the BBC's latest adaptation of *The Lion, the Witch and the Wardrobe*, as well as some earlier contributions to *Doctor Who* as assistant to another freelancer, Martin Adams).

An outside effects company called Artem was contracted to put in all the electrical parts (flashing lights, rotating eyes etc), while the dental firm of Haynes and Kulp was called upon to make the metal teeth, which had to fit perfectly over actor David John Pope's own teeth so that he could speak his dialogue 'live' in the studio.

After preliminary discussions with Dorka, Robert Allsopp's first task was to put together a prototype version of the costume to establish the shapes and sizes of all the various body sections. One fact he had to bear in mind in doing this was the need to allow sufficient space inside the costume to accommodate Artem's eye mechanics and chest panel lights. He also had to leave enough room for a small pump to be fitted, as this would be needed to circulate the red liquid through the tube mentioned above.

Once Robert's prototype had been approved, he went ahead and made the final costume. This consisted of a number of separate pieces that clipped together like a suit of armour, and great care was taken to ensure that they all looked convincingly like sweets. The head section, for example, was covered with hundreds of individual pith balls, arranged in a pattern of concentric circles and sprayed various shades of blue. The balls were not all of uniform diameter but gradually decreased in size towards the centre of the face, which was cast in latex and polyurethane foam to allow for realistic movement of the mouth. One of Dorka's aims in choosing this design, she told us, was to give the face a grotesque, 'spotty' appearance that would make the Kandyman more menacing. Blue was used because it was considered to be the least 'human' colour – not many people have blue faces! – and also because it provided a good contrasting background to make the rotating eyes stand out.

It was suggested at one stage that candyfloss hair should be added on top of the head, but this idea was abandoned as it might have made the Kandyman seem too human.

Moving down the costume, the main chest section was moulded in fibreglass and given a pattern of red stripes so that it resembled a humbug or boiled sweet. It was then covered in clear plastic sheeting to make it look as if the sweet was wrapped, and the electrical panelling was added to the front and back by Artem.

The lower torso section that formed the hips was made of foam rubber, suitably textured. The intention here, Dorka told us, was to create the impression of a coconut-covered marzipan sweet with a liquorice centre, and the colour scheme was chosen accordingly. Foam rubber was used so as to give the costume a little flexibility at this point, allowing the actor to bend slightly for comfort. The Kandyman's arms and legs, on the other hand, were made from fibreglass and polypropylene pipes, jointed with flexible ducting and aluminium strip callipers (which helped the actor to achieve a convincingly 'robotic' gait). The various arm and leg sections were then treated in different ways to suggest different types and colours of confectionery: striped rocks were created by affixing a combination of coloured and clear plastic tapes under translucent fabrics; barley sugars were made out of smooth, polished fibreglass, tinted orange; and green, sugar-coated jellies were effected by covering the relevant parts of the costume with plastic granules that had been run through a coffee grinder to give them a more crystalline look and mixed with iridescent sequin dust for added sparkle.

The marshmallow feet were made in such a way that, as each one in turn bore the weight of the robot, it squashed up slightly, just as a real marshmallow would. This realistic impression was enhanced by the addition a 'sugary' coating designed to crack slightly as the foot was compressed.

Overall, it took Robert about four or five weeks to complete his work on the Kandyman, and he had several other people helping him intermittently over that period.

One aspect of the costume that subsequently underwent a modification was the hands. Robert had supplied specially-made, one-piece hands to match the rest of the body, but Dorka thought they tended to look too much like rubber gloves. She therefore decided to use only certain pieces of them, attached directly to the actor's own hands. This allowed for natural movement and bending of the fingers, and although it was more time-consuming (as the pieces had to be built up from scratch every day and needed constant repair work carried out on them during recording) the result was judged to be well worth the effort.

It took about 45 minutes to get actor David John Pope into his costume before each recording session, as the various body sections had to be linked up around him. The first section to be fitted was the hips, followed by the legs and the feet. Next came the two halves of the upper torso, which clipped together around the tops of the arms and helped to support them. Then the hand pieces were stuck on and coloured with make-up to match the rest of the body, and finally the teeth were inserted and the head put on. (There were areas of fine wire mesh just below the rotating eyes to enable the actor to see out.)

As a finishing touch, Dorka added a sugary solution to the outside of the costume to give the illusion that the Kandyman's body was constantly lubricating its own joints to keep it mobile.

FIFI

Helen A's dog-like pet Fifi was always intended to be realised as a puppet, and the job of creating this went to Perry Brahan of the Visual Effects Department, who subcontracted it to freelancers Stephen Mansfield and Susan Moore.

The design meetings to discuss Fifi were held at an early stage of production, at which point Susan was still working on the Gods for 'The Greatest Show in the Galaxy' (see below). From the outset, everyone was keen that the puppet should be as convincing as possible; it had to be able to look evil and menacing, but at the same time still loveable enough to be a pet.

After discussions with Susan, Stephen produced a number of initial design sketches, and these were approved. While Susan completed her work on the Gods, Stephen began to put together the mechanisms that would be needed inside the puppet to animate the eyes, the eyelids, the ears, the snarl, the frown and the moving spines on its back.

The requirements of Graeme Curry's script were such that Fifi needed to be quite a versatile creation; it had to be capable of running down the pipes, for example, and of showing a reasonable amount of expression in its face. For this reason, three different versions of the body were made, each with a specific purpose in mind. One had its own head, while the other two shared two interchangeable, animatronic heads. The first of these simply had moving eyes, while the second could perform all the various functions described above.

Of the three bodies, one was just a foam rubber dummy for use in the scenes where actress Sheila Hancock had to be seen carrying the creature about. The other two, however, were more complex working puppets. One had fully articulated legs (each of which was attached to a rod so that it could be moved from below) and one was fitted with a device that made the feet look as if they were walking when it was pulled along on wires. This latter version was the one that had its own head (whereas the other two used the animatronic models).

When it came to the actual recording of the story, things on occasion did not go quite as smoothly as hoped. This was due mainly to the fact that other departments involved in the production were unfamiliar with puppetry work (which is of course very rarely used in television drama). For example, the scenes where Fifi is in its cage proved challenging to shoot because the lay-out of the set was such that Stephen and Susan could not avoid being seen on camera. In the end, they were painted out in post-production; in other words, a different image of the area underneath the cage, with no-one in shot, was overlaid on the picture to conceal their presence.

A similar situation arose when it came to recording the scenes where Fifi dies on the park seat. Again there was nowhere for the operator to hide, and an added complication here was that the puppet's eyes had to be held shut (as it was designed in such a way that the eyes would spring open whenever the control was released). This was resolved by careful editing of the final scene, in order to conceal the operator's arm.

For the scenes where Fifi is in the pipes beneath the city, the original idea had been to build a special raised section of set from below which the puppet could be operated. As things transpired, however, this could not be achieved within the strict budget, so a section of the ordinary pipe set was raised up by the visual effects team in time for the second recording block to enable the puppetry work to be done.

To achieve the effect of Fifi running along the pipe, six people knelt down in the confined space beneath the set, holding on to the puppet's controls. Initially they all leant as far back as they could; then, on cue, they pushed the puppet as far forward as they could, thus giving it the maximum possible range of movement.

It took three people to control the operation of Fifi's head and face during all the close-up sections, although director Chris Clough decided to keep the puppet's movements to a minimum in longer shots as he felt that it might otherwise be distracting. In the final analysis, with all the attention to detail lavished on Fifi, and despite the occasional difficulties that arose during recording, Stephen Mansfield and Susan Moore managed to make not only the most sophisticated puppet ever used for *Doctor Who*, but also the most successful.

THE PIPE PEOPLE

Like the Kandyman, the Pipe People in 'The Happiness Patrol' were the responsibility of make-up designer Dorka Nieradzik, These characters were played by child actors (although earlier it had been thought that they might be achieved as puppets, or played by midgets), and the masks were made, under Dorka's supervision, by Susan Moore.

Mark Stammers

SILVER NEMESIS

It has often struck me that designing visual effects must be a rather thankless task. After all, the ultimate aim of any effect is to create an illusion – to convince the audience that what they are witnessing on screen is actually taking place in reality – so the better the effect, the more complete the illusion ... and the less likely anyone is to realise that they have even seen an effect.

To understand the point I'm trying to make, just consider the opening shot of de Flores' South American villa in 'Silver Nemesis'. Did you realise, when you saw this, that the trees behind the villa were not real ones on location but were in fact added to the picture during post-production, using the paint-box technique? I certainly didn't, until it was pointed out to me. Even more surprising is the fact that the blinds over two of the villa's windows were created in a similar way – complete with shadows – by storing the image of one of the real blinds in the paint-box (the electronic image-processing device that had previously been used on *Doctor Who* to produce, for example, Thoros Beta's strangely coloured sky in 'The Trial of a Time Lord' and the Rani's bubble traps in 'Time and the Rani') and copying it onto the picture in the appropriate places.

These are not the sort of spectacular scenes that most people think of when they hear the word 'effects'; but that doesn't make them any less impressive. And it is precisely because they were so convincing that, sadly, very few people will even have noticed them; still less will they have appreciated the artistry of the designers responsible. The credit for achieving such convincing results in fact belongs primarily to the series' regular paint-box artist, Jim McCarthy, who collaborated with set designer John Asbridge on 'Silver Nemesis' to work out what exactly was required. For another illustration of the excellence of their work, take a look at the scenes showing the exterior of Lady Peinforte's house in the 17th Century. In reality, this house had modern dormer windows in the roof, but these were completely covered up in the finished programme by a pattern of tiles overlaid onto the picture using the paint-box.

The more 'traditional' video effects for 'Silver Nemesis' were handled, as usual, by Dave Chapman (who had been responsible, earlier in the season, for such brilliant innovations as the extermination visuals[68] in the first episode of 'Remembrance of the Daleks' and the various Dalek materialisations seen during the course of that story). One of his tasks on this occasion was to tackle the CSO work required for shots of the meteor in flight, including its crash-landing on Earth in episode one and its take-off outside the hangar in episode three. He even managed to mix the image of the meteor into the smoke from the 'real' explosions detonated on location for these scenes (which was in fact cement dust shot out of a compressed air device known as a 'woofer'), making the effect that much more believable.

CSO was also used for the noteworthy sequence in episode two where the Cyberman spaceship hovers over some trees and eventually touches down on the grass beside them. In this case, director Chris Clough arranged for a helicopter to be flown over the location, following the course that the spaceship was supposedly taking, so that the trees would be blown about in a realistic manner. Then, in post-production, Dave Chapman laid the CSO spaceship image directly over the recorded picture of the helicopter, so that the latter would be invisible to the viewer (although in fact the very tip of its rotor blades can still just be seen

---

68 The impressive extermination effect was unfortunately omitted by mistake from the BBC's DVD release of 'Remembrance of the Daleks'; it can however be seen on the VHS release of the story, which although now deleted can still occasionally be obtained via collectors' outlets, internet auction sites etc.

at one point – if one knows what to look for!)

The Visual Effects Department was likewise kept very busy on 'Silver Nemesis' – particularly as preparations for 'The Happiness Patrol' were in progress at the same time. Perry Brahan was the designer assigned to the project, and supporting him he had a team of four assistants, namely Mike Tucker, Paul McGuiness, Alan Marshall and Russell Pritchett.

One point Brahan had to bear in mind right from the outset was that this production was to be shot entirely on OB. He and Paul McGuiness visited the chosen locations some time in advance, to do an initial reconnaissance and map out exactly where all of the effects would need to be shot. Then, as the recording date approached, the whole effects team set off a full three days in advance of the rest of the crew to rig up the explosions and firing lines. (Explosions are, in fact, one of Brahan's specialities, so it is no surprise that the battle scenes in 'Silver Nemesis' are particularly spectacular. A stuntman was also on hand to help create the shots of bodies flying through the air, etc.)

As for the special props required, these came from a variety of different sources. The Nemesis statue, for example, was a collaboration between the Costume and Make-up Departments. Make-up was primarily responsible for the face, which consisted of a latex mask taken from actress Fiona Walker's own face, while Costume basically produced the rest of the body. With the exception of the eyes and the mouth, which were tinted jet black, the whole thing was covered with Front Axial Projection (FAP) material – a highly reflective substance, similar to that used on fire extinguishers and road signs, which can be made to 'glow' by shining a bright light onto it. FAP is a technique that has been used many times on *Doctor Who*, going right back to the Pertwee era. Examples include the glowing 'rash' produced by 'The Green Death', the skull in 'Image of the Fendahl' and the Rani's tripwires in 'Time and the Rani'. In some instances the effect is achieved using a special type of reflective paint rather than FAP material – as indeed was the case with the statue's bow and arrow in Silver Nemesis.

Visual Effects produced a polystyrene mock-up of the statue for the scenes where it had to be shown lying inside the meteor, while the meteor itself (in its full-sized version) was a prop constructed by an outside contractor working to Perry Brahan's designs.

Amongst the other props made in-house by Visual Effects were the Cybership models, Ace's new tape player and the Doctor's pocket watch. The latter of these came about fairly late in the day when producer John Nathan-Turner suggested on location that something more should be done than simply having the Doctor hearing an alarm sound from his watch (which had been the original intention). Mike Tucker put the prop together in between location sessions, and it was approved for use by Perry Brahan.

Of course, one very important aspect of 'Silver Nemesis' was the Cybermen. Costume designer Richard Croft decided that their appearance should again be altered slightly for this story, and the idea of giving their helmets a silver chrome effect was hit upon at an early stage of production. Visual Effects constructed a special chest unit for the sequences involving explosions, with a foam insert for Lady Peinforte's arrow to stick into. Chris Clough specifically asked that the Cybermen's weapons should be working props, firing pyrotechnics, and this was again handled by Visual Effects.

There were quite a number of differences between the original scripts of 'Silver Nemesis' and the version that eventually reached the screen. This was partly because Chris Clough decided to set more of the action in the hangar location than had at first been intended; a more important reason, however, was that the episodes all over-ran, which led to a certain amount of recorded material being edited out. One consequence of the editing was that viewers never got to see any of the scenes featuring the new TARDIS key, which had been made by Mike Tucker. In fact, this key had been available during the latter stages of production on 'The Greatest Show in the Galaxy' (which was recorded before 'Silver Nemesis'), but as all the TARDIS scenes had already been shot, it was not seen in that story either!

Which brings me back to my original point about the work of effects designers not always being fully appreciated. This is never more true than when an effect doesn't even reach the screen in the first place! And that's one of the good things about being able to write an article like this, because it hopefully results in the behind-the-scenes team getting a little more of the recognition they so richly deserve for helping to make *Doctor Who* the highly polished production that it is.

Stephen James Walker

THE GREATEST SHOW IN THE GALAXY

THE GODS

The Gods of Ragnarok as seen in episode four of 'The Greatest Show in the Galaxy' were the responsibility of costume designer Rosalind Ebbutt (whose previous *Doctor Who* work was on the Peter Davison story 'Black Orchid').[69]

The concept of the Gods was rooted in a sort of 'classical' look, although from no particular period or geographical area. They appeared in the ancient circus and so had to look at home in that environment. They also had to look as if they had been roughly carved from the same stone as the rest of the set, so a lot of discussion took place between Rosalind and the set designer, David Laskey. For the look of the helmets, inspiration was gained both from a book of African masks and from a type of Grecian helmet that covered the whole head.

Having agreed this concept with director Alan Wareing, Rosalind then produced some fairly detailed design paintings showing exactly what she had in mind. As in most cases, it was the responsibility of the people who actually made the costumes to ensure that their final appearance was as close to these designs as possible; and here the job went to freelancers Susan Moore and Robert Allsopp.

The costumes had to be made to fit the three artistes chosen to play the Gods, so initial measurements were taken in order to produce mannequins around which they could be constructed. A potential problem with making 'monster' costumes is that there is always some degree of doubt as to how much the characters will be required to do – will they have to walk, climb stairs, run etc? – and so the costume makers need precise directions from the designer based on the requirements of the script. In this case, all that the Gods had to do, it seemed, was to sit and move their arms. Susan and Robert therefore decided to make the costumes from slabs of foam rubber carved into the appropriate shapes and covered in latex mixed with Cabasil (a latex thickener). The helmets were sculpted and cast in latex backed with Samco (a stiff material to hold the flexible latex). Their eyes and the eye motif on the helmet were painted with FAP paint, so that they could be made to glow when the script called for it.

As is normally the case, small alterations had to be made to the costumes when they actually

---

69 See the interview with Rosalind Ebbutt presented earlier in this book, which discusses the costume requirements of 'The Greatest Show in the Galaxy' in more detail.

came to be fitted to the actors – some sections had to be built up and others cut down – so that they hung correctly and were relatively comfortable to wear.

An example of the way requirements can sometimes change came when Alan Wareing decided to do some shots from behind the Gods, looking down into the circus ring. Because it had originally been intended that the costumes would be seen from the front only, all the fastenings were visible at the back. After this had been explained to the director, he was able to edit the shots carefully to avoid showing the joins in the costumes.

THE MEDALLION

Another small prop constructed by Susan and Robert from Rosalind's design drawings was the medallion worn by Deadbeat. Three different versions of this were made: one out of fibreglass for the 'stunt' scenes where it gets thrown down the well, the other two out of beaten copper with a mirror and magnetic central eye attached.

The inspiration for the eye logo on the medallion came from a Grecian lucky charm that contains concentric circles in an eye pattern; the idea being that the 'all seeing' eye wards off evil.

The medallion was supposed to look like a piece of 1960s junk jewellery so that when first seen it would blend in with the rest of the jewellery around Deadbeat's neck and not appear to be anything special.

David J Howe

INTERVIEW: JOHN NATHAN-TURNER—PRODUCER

John Nathan-Turner was born on 12 August 1947 and brought up in the Midlands. As a boy, he acted in numerous school plays and revues and appeared as an extra in several TV series, including The Newcomers and United! for the BBC and Crossroads for ATV. By the time he reached the sixth form, his interests had widened to encompass producing, directing and writing. On leaving school, he turned down the offer of a university place in order to pursue a theatrical career. A short spell as stage manager of a nightclub led to a post as assistant stage manager at Birmingham's Alexandra Theatre. Later, during a period of unemployment as an actor, he filled in for a couple of months with a job in the Costume Department at the BBC's Gosta Green studios, where he gained an interest in television production. He was working as a senior stage manager and actor at the Everyman Theatre in Chelmsford when an acquaintance suggested that he apply to the BBC in London for a general exploratory interview. He did so, and shortly afterwards was taken on as a floor assistant. It was in this capacity that he first worked on Doctor Who, being assigned to 'The Space Pirates' in the sixth season, 'The Ambassadors of Death' in the seventh and 'Colony in Space' in the eighth. He remained at the BBC throughout the 1970s, gaining successive promotions to assistant floor manager, production assistant and production unit manager. It was in the latter capacity that he was again assigned to Doctor Who, handling the series' budget during the fifteenth, sixteenth and seventeenth seasons. He took over from Graham Williams as producer as of Season 18 in 1979, and remained in that post until the series was discontinued a decade later, at which point he left the BBC. Over the years that followed, he maintained contact with the Doctor Who world by, amongst other things, producing some special releases for BBC Video in 1991 and 1992 and the Dimensions in Time skit for the BBC's Children in Need telethon in 1993. He also pursued a number of projects unrelated to Doctor Who from his home base in Brighton, although few of these ultimately came to fruition. He died of liver failure, after a short illness, on 1 May 2002. He was survived by his long-time partner Gary Downie – a former choreographer and production manager on Doctor Who – who died on 19 January 2006 after a lengthy battle against cancer.

John was without question the most controversial behind-the-scenes figure in Doctor Who's long history. He gained, and appeared to relish having, an unusually high public profile for a BBC producer, granting numerous interviews, making many TV appearances and attending literally dozens of conventions over the years. However, this exposure was arguably something of a double-edged sword, as – particularly during the mid-1980s – he was subjected to a great deal of criticism, some of it very scathing, over what many perceived as a downturn in the series' quality and popularity. This criticism did not come solely from the series' fans, either: a number of those who had been involved in the series' production in the past or who had worked with John, including most notably script editor Eric Saward, subsequently made damning remarks about him in the genre press. On the other hand, some fans greatly admired and appreciated what John brought to the series, and many of those who had worked with him remained staunch friends and supporters.

For my own part, while I had serious reservations about the direction in which John took Doctor Who during his time as producer and felt that he sometimes made highly questionable artistic decisions, I never found him to be anything less than approachable, courteous and helpful in person. I met him on numerous occasions over the years and had several opportunities to interview him more formally, and although he was always rather guarded in the answers he gave, he seemed to me to have a great deal of humility and modesty about his achievements, a good *sense of humour, and – particularly toward the end of his run on the series – a willingness to acknowledge his mistakes. In one conversation, for instance, he conceded that it had been an error on his part to insist on giving the sixth Doctor such a garish, intentionally 'tasteless' costume – a decision that had drawn a great deal of criticism earlier in the decade.*

In the summer of 1989, I was asked by Doctor Who Magazine *to interview John for them about the then forthcoming twenty-sixth season – although, as it seemed almost certain that he would not be continuing as producer after that season (which would eventually turn out to be the last of the classic series anyway), I also took the chance to ask him some questions looking back over his whole tenure in the post. The interview was conducted at John's office in Union House, on Shepherd's Bush Green in west London. Strangely enough, although I had been writing about* Doctor Who *and been involved in its fandom for many years, this was the first and only time that I ever visited the series' production offices. As I was very busy on other projects at the time, I subsequently enlisted the help of my friend Dave Auger in transcribing and writing up the interview, although he hadn't been present when it was conducted. The finished piece appeared in Issue 153 of* Doctor Who Magazine *in October 1989, and is reprinted in full below.*

John Nathan-Turner, *Doctor Who*'s longest-serving producer by far, tends to choose his words carefully when he speaks about the programme – understandably so, bearing in mind the way he has sometimes been misinterpreted in the past. Never before has anyone connected with the series been subject to such vitriolic attacks from fans (albeit a small, highly vocal minority). On the other hand, almost paradoxically, neither has any other producer been so highly praised or lauded for his or her contribution to the series. Often, fans' opinions seem to fluctuate according more to whim than to reason.

In person, John comes across as a dedicated television professional who genuinely cares about the series. His conversation is punctuated with dry humour, even though it seems, at times, that he is left with a slight bewilderment, perhaps even bitterness, at the more extreme fan criticism he has had to endure.

At the moment, though, John's popularity is at a high-point, due largely to the great success of Sylvester McCoy's second season as the Doctor. Had he foreseen, when the season was in production, that it would be so well-received by the fans and, indeed, the general public?

'I think it's very difficult to predict how people are going to react. We did feel more confident about that season. As Sylv has often said, for his first season, he was cast very late, and the scripts were already in the pipeline before he got the part. I felt that last season was much more tailored to him, so we felt confident about it to a certain extent. But we didn't feel that it was necessarily special.'

The scripts for Sylvester's first season had bubbled with a surfeit of humour, but in the second season, a darker quality had emerged through the writing, with the Doctor being portrayed as a more mysterious character.

'When you've got a season in the can, you can look back at it and say, "We went a little bit too far in that story, and a bit too far in that story." The strategy for the twenty-fifth season evolved out of a very lengthy chat that Andrew Cartmel and I had with Sylvester. And I think it was a move in the right direction. I distinctly feel that there is a place for humour, but because we were "running on the spot" in Sylvester's first season, it all went a bit too far.

'The darker theme will be continuing in *some* of the new stories, whereas in others, whilst the mystery remains, there's a lighter side to it as well. It's certainly not a bleak, ultra-moody season. With the times of year we shoot, it would be impossible to achieve that anyway.'

At the time of the interview, no transmission details for the new series had been announced. John hoped the show would stay in the same slot as last year, when it competed quite favourably against Britain's longest running soap opera. 'Now that *Coronation Street* has its built-in repeat, I think our potential is even greater. I think split households tended to tape our show – which meant it didn't register in the ratings – and watched *Coronation Street* on transmission. Now we stand a lot more chance that they will watch *Doctor Who* "live", because they can see *Coronation Street* on the Sunday. Personally, I think it's very flattering that we have been placed in that slot for the last two years, against a show that has now been proved as being the top rated programme in the country.'

If John professes surprise at the series' runaway success last year, he is in no doubt about the quality of the forthcoming season. 'I think the show is going through a good period at the moment. Sylvester and Sophie are working absolutely brilliantly together, everyone is pulling together and doing very good work. It is a dangerous thing to say, I know, but I honestly feel that, of Sylvester's three years, this one we're doing now is the most right.

'The first story, "Battlefield", is written by Ben Aaronovitch, and is a very traditional *Doctor Who* with some exciting new elements. And of course, there's the return of the Brigadier. I'm very pleased with the way it's going, as it's looking very good.

'We then have "Ghost Light", which we have yet to record. Moving the story to second in order of transmission makes it quite tight to get it ready. We were asked to get the series ready by week 36, which is the beginning of September.

'"Ghost Light" will be a very spooky story, with a very interesting, smashing first script from Marc Platt. I'm absolutely delighted with it. We have a very strong cast; nearly everyone in it is a well-known face, if not name, on television. Sylvia Syms is playing Mrs Pritchard, Frank Windsor is Inspector MacKenzie, Sharon Duce is playing Control, John Hallam is playing Light, Katharine Schlesinger is Gwendoline and Michael Cochrane is playing Redvers.

'Then we've got "The Curse of Fenric", which I'm also delighted with. It's the darkest story, very black, very moody, a very good story. Once again a good cast, including Dinsdale Landen, Alfie Lynch and Nicholas Parsons.'

There has been much talk that some of the episodes of 'The Curse of Fenric' overran, but John stresses that this has been wildly exaggerated. 'They *were* all over length, but not as substantially as some fanzines are leading people to believe. There was never enough material to make a fifth episode.

'It is very difficult to time a *Doctor Who* episode. You can read a script from front to back endlessly and get 53 *different* timings. For example, it might depend on how long you are going to hold on a battle: are you going to hold on it forever, or are you going to make it very tight? Because of the way we shoot the programme, those sort of things are quite often not decided until it's on the bench and we're cutting it. Then you suddenly realise that, even though you conceived it as a two-minute battle, all you want are the first two gun shots. Also, because so many scenes in *Doctor Who* don't have any dialogue, it's very difficult to time how long they are going to take, even in the rehearsal room. When we do cut it together, it is simply with regard to pace and not time. Then we try to detach ourselves from it and make the trims afterwards.

'The last story this season is "Survival", another OB[70] story like "The Curse of Fenric", which makes seven OB episodes out of the 14. June Collins, a marvellous production associate[71], has

---

70 Outside broadcast – i.e. recorded with video cameras on location.

71 The person responsible for managing the series' budget.

shunted the money around in such a way that it has enabled us to up the OB content. Guesting in this one is Julian Holloway, Stanley Holloway's son, and – in cameo roles – Hale and Pace.

'"Survival" is not necessarily a traditional *Doctor Who* story, but I would hesitate to describe it as oddball. Usually, the minute I say something like that, it prejudices people to say, "We're not going to like that one!" I wouldn't say it is as oddball as "The Happiness Patrol", but there are certain oddball elements in it.'

As viewers of *Wogan* and other live programmes will be aware, the BBC is currently involved in industrial action with members of the BETA union. Has this affected production of the new series?

'It's been a bit of a problem, but we're more or less on keel. For "Battlefield", we were hit once in rehearsal and on two days on location, which meant we had to stay up there. This meant that for "Survival"'s rehearsal period, the regulars arrived exhausted. We've lost the odd dub, but we will still be ready for transmission in September if we're required to be. We've got off lightly. During the shoot for "Survival", we always knew it was extremely tight, with very little manoeuvrability at all, because when we finished, our unit was due to go to the Wimbledon tennis tournament at three o'clock in the afternoon. A strike was called for that three o'clock, so we literally just managed to get it all in in time!'

Despite the popularity of Sylvester McCoy in the United Kingdom, most fans in the United States have not yet had the opportunity to see the new Doctor. 'We've had terrific success in the States, but we've never been able to supply them with enough shows quickly enough, especially when many stations transmit them five days a week. To keep the stations and the fans happy, we've sold them various packages in the interim – like *The Pertwee Years, The Hartnell Years* – while we're building up a small stockpile of, say, Peter Davison or Colin Baker episodes.

'At this moment in time, the States have had every single thing that we've got, and they're literally waiting for us to make a new season – which, when they strip it five times a week, will be all over in three weeks. So there is a slight impasse, in that we don't have anything more to sell other than each new 14. Similarly, because 14 is an unattractive number to buy – they'd much rather buy 39 – some stations are holding off buying it until they've got 42, which is nine weeks stripped.

'I think, to a certain degree, we are not as high-profile in the States as we were, but by the same token the real reason is that we don't give them nearly enough shows per year for the American audience.'

The latest news is that Sylvester's first three series have just been sold to Germany, even though the third is still to be completed. 'Sophie, Sylvester and I are going out in August to promote it. Someone was saying that they'll probably be transmitted in English, as there is a huge English speaking audience in that country.[72] We've not traditionally done very well on the continent, so it's very nice that they've made a relatively large commitment by buying three series. Not surprisingly, we're pretty keen on Germany at the moment!'

Doctor Who is unusual when compared to other BBC programmes, because of the sheer scale of merchandising associated with it.

'The merchandising interest in *Doctor Who* is unusual, but that is mainly because on most shows there is a limit to what you can produce. A phenomenal success is *All Creatures Great and Small*, but apart from the occasional tea towel and a few books, there is no other

72 In the event, the episodes were dubbed into German.

merchandising – they can't really do inflatable cows that you can put your arm up! On this show, because of its wide audience, and the fact that some of its audience is young, there's an ability to provide a platform for all sorts of merchandising.'

Other producers seldom seem to become to involved with the merchandising aspects of their programmes, or indeed with their promotion abroad.

'Quite often, what happens is that a hugely successful show in the home market, which may run for three series, later on becomes a highly successful show abroad. By that time, the producer of the original three series may have left the Corporation, in which case it falls to Enterprises to capitalise as much as possible on that product. Because I've been here a long time, it has enabled a kind of continuity to be maintained with Enterprises, whereas on other shows the people have disappeared.'

A recent and popular branch of merchandising is the release of past *Doctor Who* stories on the BBC Video label. Does John liaise with BBC Enterprises when they decide the serials that are to be released?

'I used to have occasional working lunches with them, but of late they've been doing their own selections. I remember advising them not to release "The Five Doctors" in 1985. I felt sure that it wouldn't sell, because it had only been transmitted in 1983, and had a repeat in 1984, but it sold equally well! That proved how well they understood the home video market. It's fascinating to me that it doesn't matter how old a story is, or how recent it is, or how many repeats it's had, it still sells roughly the same.'

When asked what Peter Davison story he thought would be successful if released, John had no hesitation in replying:

'"Earthshock". It has Cybermen, which is good for marketing, a good script by Eric Saward, and it was well directed by Peter Grimwade. That would be a good one.'

Considering John's past associations with the theatre (he has written and directed several pantomimes), it comes as no surprise to learn that he was originally due to direct the latest *Doctor Who* stage play, *The Ultimate Adventure*.

'I would have dearly liked to direct it, as I do love the theatre, but they put the dates back to when we were just about to begin rehearsals for the new television series. For me, the chance to work in the theatre is like my annual fix, because the demands and techniques of the medium are so different. So when I return to *Doctor Who*, I feel doubly refreshed!

'Mark Furness, the producer of the play, then asked me if I would be creative consultant for it, which I thoroughly enjoyed. It was rather marvellous *not* to direct it, and just to be consulted. Basically this meant I made comments on the script, helped with the casting and went to most of the rehearsals at the Wimbledon Theatre – the play's first venue. It's a rather ambitious project and I'm very pleased at its success. I saw it again last Friday with Colin Baker. All the actors who've played the Doctor have done it differently and put in something of their own, and it's a very different show with Colin. I enjoyed both actors' portrayals[73] very much indeed.'

After a decade as producer of *Doctor Who*, John now intends to leave. 'It is time that somebody else came in and took it into the '90s. I don't feel stale, but after ten years, you learn an awful lot of short cuts and how to cope with things. In some ways, the challenge goes out of it and, on a purely selfish level, I need something that gives me a tremendous challenge – something brand new, something very, very different. After all, ten years is a large chunk out

73 Jon Pertwee had previously played the Doctor in this stage production.

of your life. It's way past time that somebody fresh came in and took it off in a different direction.'

Looking back over that past decade, what aims had John had when he took *Doctor Who* into the '80s?

'I think you really have to look at the expectations of an audience. The late '70s and early '80s, and indeed the late '80s, have seen a level of sophistication in television and the movies that no one could have foreseen. Children particularly now, possibly due to the advent of computer games and so on, have very high expectations of television programmes in our genre. My idea was simply not to attempt to compete with the likes of *Star Wars*, but to use the resources that were available to us to the best possible effect. In that way, we would appear to be moving with the times.'

John also has strong feelings about the pacing of the shows he has produced. 'I hesitate to say this, because I know what some people say about my opinions, but what happened in some – and I would emphasise not *all* – of the older episodes was very minimal. There were a lot of very long scenes, a lot of exposition, and not a lot of action or plot development. I like episodes sharply cut, with a strong narrative drive. The optimum length for a *Doctor Who* episode is now 24 minutes and 15 seconds, and once you take away the titles, you have about 22 minutes to play with. So you really want to get on with a whole lot of story development – not just to hold the attention of the audience, but to make what you are handing them more substantial.'

John leaves *Doctor Who* with no regrets, but he would not like to lose all connection with the programme. 'For me, it has been a hugely enjoyable experience. It sounds rather corny when you say it's like a huge great family, but it really is – Colin Baker came to stay with me last Friday whilst he was in Brighton. It's a very closely-linked thing, and I wouldn't want to sever those links completely, because through the working environment of *Doctor Who*, I've made some very good friends, and in the fan world as well.

'Also, I feel very privileged in a way, because this show deals with virtually every department of BBC Enterprises. I found my way around the industry all in one fell swoop. There are some producers who've been in the BBC for 20 years and have never really sussed out that whole Enterprises setup. Because of *Doctor Who*'s involvement with records, books, merchandising, exhibitions, foreign sales and so on, I've learnt a great deal, and I feel I'm in a very strong position with regard to what I do next. I shall miss it most dreadfully, but it's time to move on to something new.'

When questioned about these new projects, John is naturally cautious, as they are still in the planning stages. However, after a long association with *Doctor Who*, he has developed a keen understanding of the importance of promotion. 'The minute any of these projects *is* definite, I'll be singing about it from the hill tops!'

Stephen James Walker and David Auger

Interview conducted by Stephen James Walker

BONUS FEATURE: RISING FROM THE DEPTHS

For another in The Frame's *series of in-depth interview features on the making of the stories of the seventh Doctor's era, David Howe, Mark Stammers and I spoke to some of those involved in the realisation of key aspects of 'The Curse of Fenric' – the first story of the twenty-sixth season to go before the cameras, although it would be the third to be transmitted. These were costume designer Ken Trew – who had first worked on* Doctor Who *as an assistant during the William Hartnell years and later, after his promotion to designer, been responsible for the Master's original costume on 'Terror of the Autons' – and four of our previous interviewees: make-up designer Dee Baron and the three freelancers commissioned to work on the Haemovores, costumier Robert Allsopp and effects contractors Susan Moore and Stephen Mansfield. The following text first appeared in Issue 13 of* The Frame, *dated February 1990.*

THE HAEMOVORES

Our first thought was to ask if any problems had arisen from the fact that the Haemovores had to be seen underwater and emerging from the sea. Dee told us she had known from the start that this requirement would cause difficulties. 'The Ancient One wasn't so much of a problem, as the actor's head was going to be completely encased and the mask was going to be quite heavy. With the other Haemovores, though, the problem was going to be keeping the prosthetics on in the water. What we decided to do was to make all the masks extend around the back of the head. If we'd put on a section covering only the face and not the back of the head, the likelihood of it coming off in the water would have been very great.'

'It was the same thing with the costumes,' explained Ken. 'Most of the necks came up really high, because the prosthetic pieces could actually be anchored under them.'

'That's where we worked very closely together to make sure that we didn't cause any difficulties for each other,' confirmed Dee. 'We helped each other solve problems.'

Talking about the prosthetics that were required, Dee explained one of the differences between television and film work. 'On screen, the Haemovores don't appear for very long, but we were using the masks over at least ten different days. To apply prosthetics properly you really need a new piece every time the make-up is re-done, but we didn't have the budget for that. As a result, the pieces had to be strong and substantial so that they would last for the duration of our recording.'

'What we worked out,' clarified Sue, 'was that we would use over-head masks, half-masks and quarter-masks. There were four stages of Haemovore. We made two of the first stage, three of the second, three of the third, and two of the fourth. We decided to hold the masks on with elastic, which if you disguise it works fabulously. Dee used latex-covered wigs to do that.'

During the modelling of the masks, an unusual effect had been achieved quite inadvertently, as Steve told us. 'We used little seeds like lentils in the clay to give texture, and they started to sprout! This wasn't deliberate at all. The seeds thought, "Ooh look, it's dark and wet, let's start growing," and so the masks sort of modelled themselves, giving a rather interesting effect. We kept them all on because it looked good – like little tentacles.'

The half and quarter-masks for the first three stages were made in latex and 'foamit' foam (a two part chemical foam that expands when the chemicals are mixed together), while those for the fourth stage were simply latex pull-over head masks.

Sue explained that after the colour schemes had been worked out, these were applied to the masks with leather shoe sprays. 'If we were doing it again and we had more time, I think we would air brush them using acrylic paint. But as it was, we used leather sprays with washes of acrylic added over them. Another reason for doing this was that it would be easier for Dee to retouch the colours on location if we used standard tints. Dee ordered a set of the same colours that we had, and I know she used them at one location, as there were little Haemovore-shaped patches on the pavement! There were four colours that we used: an olive green, a dark blue, a light blue and a pink. The acrylic wash was dark blue and I rubbed that in all over to give the masks a pallid look.

'It was a very straightforward job in many ways, because it used tried-and-tested techniques. There was nothing new involved – but there was an awful lot of work. For example, we had 15 pairs of arms to prepare.'

'That again was a combined effort,' Ken added. 'We worked out these long gloves, and Dee arranged for the nails to be made, to be added to them.'

Dee commented that initially the idea had been to have metal nails, but John Nathan-Turner had thought this would be too like Freddy in the *Nightmare on Elm Street* films, so they were changed to ordinary nails.

Going back to the four stages of Haemovore, we wondered how these had been worked out. 'We worked them out according to time periods,' Ken told us. 'By the time we got to the Lulworth Cove location, we had christened every one of them – they all had names! There were two Vikings (the Grace Brothers), a Victorian lady with a mob-cap (Mrs Bridges), a '20s lady (Mary Quant), two Edwardian fishermen (I forget what their names were), and a First World War sailor (Popeye). All the costumes were taken from BBC stock and then "dirtied down."'

'Once the actors and actresses were in these costumes,' Dee added, 'there was no way of identifying them, so we used to talk to each other about Popeye and Mrs Bridges. It was terribly helpful when we filmed them emerging from the water. For instance, they were using stones to weigh themselves down, so you would hear, "Give Mrs Bridges another brick!"'

THE ANCIENT HAEMOVORE

The Ancient Haemovore – the oldest and most fearsome of the race – posed its own specific challenges. In a sense, this is really where the story begins, as the Ancient One was actually the first to be designed. This task eventually fell to Ken Trew, although the BBC Visual Effects Department had earlier come up with a concept based around a white leech-like creature that was to have been operated as a puppet.

Ken completed some design sketches of the Ancient Haemovore's head and contacted Sue Moore to talk about building it. At that time, it was assumed that Dee Baron would be handling the rest of the Haemovores, and Ken realised that it would be sensible if the people who were building the Ancient One were also involved in the others to get consistency in the way they were made. Therefore Ken and Dee, together with Sue, Steve and Robert (who had been asked by Ken to make the Ancient Haemovore costume) got together for the first of their many meetings and discussions to work out how best to realise this race of creatures.

Ken explained the background to the design of the Ancient Haemovore. 'I had meetings with John Nathan-Turner and the director, Nick Mallett, to work out what he, she or it should look like. As there were a lot of Viking influences in the story, I initially tried doing something like the prow of a dragonship; then I started looking at Viking armour. Neither of these ideas seemed to work. Finally, I thought about vampires and blood. There was a line in the script about sucking blood and, without being obvious and using the Hammer vampire fangs, I wondered how you could get blood out of a person. I immediately thought of something along the lines of a leech. Then I considered that a leech has only one sucker: so what about using something like an octopus arm? The concept developed from there.

'I drew the head, working out how big it should be and what parts ought to be moveable. I put in the gills and the suckers around the mouth and, because the Ancient One was more developed than all the other Haemovores, I put suckers all over the place. Then I considered how this mutated human figure would support its head and came up with the idea of the spine coming up out through the back of it.

'The basic idea for the costume was of all the old rubbish he'd collected from the bottom of the sea, all encrusted on him with barnacles. There were pieces that went over the shoulders and came out of the chest, like extensions of the lungs, which actually went into a man-made bit at the back. There was a tube at the back and the rib-cage was built out. The effect I hope we achieved was that this creature had almost built itself a breathing apparatus, which was incorporated into its own flesh, and that the body had actually been stripped of skin. By the time I'd finished it, I thought, "You've got a very nasty mind, Ken Trew!"'

Once Ken had come up with the design drawings for the Ancient Haemovore, these were then passed on to Sue, Steve and Robert so that they could start making the creature. Sue takes up the story:

'I roughly assembled the head in clay over a building site helmet, because the mask was worn like a helmet – the actor looked out through the neck, and the creature's eyes were actually above his head. With the ordinary Haemovores, we were using actual face casts to work from, so the final masks naturally had some character and expression, but with the Ancient Haemovore, although we did have a face cast of the actor, we just started from a shapeless lump of clay. Steve and I therefore worked it out between us to give it some character. It was a bit of a struggle, but I think it worked.

'Assuming that this conversion from human to Haemovore was some sort of an infection, we also worked out how it would spread. We decided it would go through the blood system, which is why all the veins on the head became swollen, started bursting out and became tentacles. These then finally became the main ridges down his back and also the tentacles that burst out of the side and joined up round the back. All the Haemovores were worked out according to this idea, and the two that were closest to the Ancient Haemovore had embryonic bits of tentacle coming through their skin.'

'The skin was all sort of pushed away,' Steve elaborated. 'It had become unimportant but it was still there. Something similar to the Elephant Man – that was the sort of thing we were aiming for. We didn't want it to look like an alien creature; it had to look as human as possible. Ken had got a lot of that idea in his drawing, which was of great help.'

To operate the head, a simple air-controlled system was installed. One air line worked the eye blink and the other the gill movement. The controls were operated during recording of the story by Ken's assistant, Andrew Duckett, who followed the script so that the eyes would blink normally in time with the dialogue. The mouth was attached separately via a harness to the actor's jaw, so that it would move when the actor spoke his lines.

Colour is always an important consideration, and Sue explained how the colour scheme had been worked out for the Haemovores.

'We chose blue around the mouth basically because we didn't want to use green. Everything that comes out of the sea is green these days, and blue is the nearest you can get to a deathlike pallor, tying in with the vampire idea. As in the past, we couldn't use oranges or reds because they might suggest blood, which is taboo in *Doctor Who* at the moment, so it really only left blues, greys and whites. I would have liked to have used greys and whites, the colours of a shark, but that wouldn't have been very effective on screen and, taking into account the fact that the masks had bone elements in them, they could have ended up looking like polar bears walking up from the sea! Blue is an unusual colour and it registers well against flesh. It gave a drowned, *The Evil Dead* sort of effect, which I quite liked.'

As well as the head containing the air controls described above, a second head was built for the Ancient Haemovore, for the scene where it emerges from the sea. Steve explained the differences: 'The second head looked the same as the first but it didn't have the mechanics and it was made out of solid "foamit" foam rather than fibreglass, which would have had a large air pocket inside it. The mechanical head wouldn't actually have sunk, but the water soaked into the "foamit" foam one and made it easier to keep underwater.'

Despite these precautions, a few problems still arose in keeping the head underwater when the scene actually came to be recorded, as Ken remembered. 'The only thing that operated on the second head was the jaw – that was the way it was built – but the jaw didn't have any drainage holes in it, so it sort of floated off! We had a bit of panic on the morning when we used that, drilling holes under the jaw and through the top of the head so that the water would flow in and out easily. When he rose up out of the water on the screen, I thought it looked wonderful.'

The construction of the head was only one part of the process of creating the Ancient Haemovore. The costume had to be made to match in with the concepts and designs worked out for the creature as a whole. Robert Allsopp told us how he had approached this.

'Ken had done some superb drawings, with a back view and everything, and he and I then had a look round the costume store to see what we could use from it. This was partly to save time, but also because the costume was meant to look as if it had been put together from other bits and pieces over the centuries.

'Using Sue and Steve's work on the other heads as a guide to texture and colour, I worked out the skin pieces that would show through the costume. I started by making a kind of vest in a stretch fabric for the body, then applied cast sections of latex that had rib shapes and suckers moulded in. I moulded one set of ribs and a sheet of suckers about a foot square, then combined them to give the required effect. I interpreted the strange, fleshy tubes that ran over the shoulders and went into the mechanical bit at the back as being probably the results of the Ancient One altering his body to enable him to be an amphibian. I assumed that he had constructed a kind of breathing apparatus that was part organic and part mechanical, and that what had originally been his lungs had grown into this external filter.

'The vest piece stopped just below the waist, and under that he wore very full, baggy cotton trousers. These tucked into the tops of boots, which came up to just below the knee. To convey the idea of the creature growing and evolving over the centuries, I made his toes burst through the ends of the boots and also gave him fins growing from the backs of the boots.

'He had an adjustable belt from which a variety of things hung. For these I tried to use as many different textures as possible: chain mail, scale armour and various bones, shells and bits of seaweed. There was also a kind of Viking belt buckle that was made from some small reproduction Celtic brooches that I cut up and re-worked.

'On the chest, part of an Air Force breathing mask was used. Various tubes were heated and then twisted, distorted and burnt, with plastic mesh tubing added over the top to give a layered look to the rib-cage.

'Moving up to the shoulders, the left pauldron piece was a fibreglass cast of a horseshoe crab shell, which was then combined with some bits of metal armour from the stores and also some real chain mail. Again, this was to give the organic/metallic combination. The sleeves of the costume also had latex pieces where the body showed through, and I made some wrist bands to cover the joins at the ends of the arms.

'I wanted the back part of the breathing apparatus to look like ship fittings, so I put a little plaque on it saying "HMS Hercules" or something, as well as various bits of tubing and taps and so on.

'Having got all the components together and worked out where all the fittings and clasps would be and how the actor would get into and out of it, I used the same paint techniques for the body as had been used for the head. Once the costume had been painted, I modelled up some barnacles in plastic filler and added lots of these all over it so that it was quite encrusted, as though it had been in the sea for centuries. Finally the whole costume was worked with sprays and coloured lacquers to simulate rust and the effect of time on all the materials.

'It took about two weeks solid to get the thing together, with two fittings during that time to check that it would all fit together and match with the head and hands.'

As the costume was relatively complex for the actor to wear, Robert went down to the location to be on hand for the shooting of the scene where the Ancient Haemovore emerges from the sea. As a last minute addition, he and Andrew Duckett used seaweed collected from the beach to adorn the creature as it made its impressive entrance into our world.

HAIR

Much of the detailed work that goes into designing costumes and make-up can be lost on the general viewing public. For example, in 'The Curse of Fenric', many people failed to notice that Commander Millington should really have had a full beard and moustache rather than just a moustache. Dee Baron explains:

'This whole aspect of Navy life was governed by a decree of Queen Victoria. It was sometime after 1880 when she decreed that her Naval personnel would have a beard and moustache or nothing, to differentiate them from her Army. Millington had a moustache and no beard but he should really, in fact, have had a full beard or nothing at all.

'The reason he didn't have a beard was that when he was sitting underneath the portrait of Hitler, trying to think in the way of the Nazis, we wanted him to have just the moustache to provide the similarity.'

UNDERWATER BODIES

'The Curse of Fenric' featured a number of underwater sequences, and Dee Baron told us of an amusing incident that had occurred when the crew came to record the shots of the dead Russian floating by the dragonship:

'One of the Visual Effects guys – I think it was Graham Brown, the effects designer on "The Curse of Fenric" – is a diver, as are several of his assistants, and he was going to be the dead Russian body floating around the bows of the ship. Come the day, all hell is breaking loose. We're shooting one thing on the shore, something else out at sea and something else again underwater. So the Department's personnel were split between all three. Ken and I were with the main party on the shore, and I turned around to see two of my assistants heading out to sea with John van der Pool, a visual effects assistant, who is black. He was going to be the dead Russian. Now, there weren't any black Russians in the 1940s, so we had to make him up as a dead Caucasian!'

TAKE TWO

On one of the location days for 'The Curse of Fenric', a camera team from the BBC's *Take Two* – a children's magazine programme – was present to catch the cast and crew in action. Dee Baron recalled the situation when they came to record the disintegration of the two girl vampires:

'We had worked out two different make-ups for the effect of the girls' disintegration: one we could use if we had a lot of time, which my assistants were terribly keen on, and another that was very quick. I suspected we would use this latter method on the day: however, I didn't realise we would have to work quite so quickly as we did!

'We had about 15 minutes to get the girls' nails on and to get half their cracked-up faces on. We had wanted to do it in about five stages, but we had compromised and were going for three stages – I think what actually went out on television was one stage!

'What happened was that my assistants, Helen and Wendy, raced back to the make-up room to apply the cracked-up faces on the girls, and they had literally ten minutes to do it in. At this point, the *Take Two* team walked in to interview the actresses and the make-up assistants! Of course, my assistants were frantically working on each of the girls to get the make-up on and latex applied over the top. (The latex was to protect the make-up from the rain that would be used in that shot – otherwise, it would just have pulled off their faces.) So the *Take Two* team arrived and Helen said "Never mind that microphone, put it away and grab a hairdryer!" The crew ended up holding hairdryers so that my assistants could carry on working!

'Then the dressers, my make-up assistants and the two actresses ran out into the mud and raced across to get this shot in. The two girls lay in their positions, and I remember Helen shouting at the visual effects guys to keep the rain off them as they hadn't had time to get the latex on their faces! It was very fraught, and yet very funny.'

David J Howe

Interviews conducted by David J Howe, Stephen James Walker and Mark Stammers

BONUS FEATURE: CREATING THE DESTROYER

Following on from the preceding feature on 'The Curse of Fenric', The Frame *spoke to regular interviewees Susan Moore, Stephen Mansfield and Robert Allsopp about how they realised the Destroyer for the next Season 26 story to go into production, Ben Aaronovitch's 'Battlefield'. This piece was originally published in Issue 12 of the fanzine, dated November 1989.*

Over the last couple of seasons, the names Susan Moore and Stephen Mansfield have become synonymous with the creation of *Doctor Who* creatures of high quality, in terms both of their technical sophistication and of the effectiveness of their appearance. Season 26 is no exception. Susan and Stephen worked on two of the four stories, 'The Curse of Fenric' and 'Battlefield'. For the latter, the season opener on transmission, they were heavily involved in the realisation of that story's only monstrous element – the brooding demon known as the Destroyer.

Normally, the creation of a creature or a prop is under the jurisdiction of the appropriate designer or designers – for example, the costume and visual effects designers for the Tetraps ('Time and the Rani') and the Haemovores ('The Curse of Fenric'), and the make-up designer for the Kandyman ('The Happiness Patrol') – but, for the Destroyer, Susan and Stephen were contracted direct by the director of 'Battlefield', Michael Kerrigan. However, the concept actually originated some time before that, as Stephen explained.

'We had contacted the *Doctor Who* office and arranged to discuss several ideas that we'd had with regard to special make-ups and creatures. We took with us a number of maquettes, masks and photographs to illustrate the concepts that we had in mind. For example, one of the masks had a jaw that was built out from the face, showing that you don't have to use the actor's own jaw all the time. Eventually that concept was used on the Haemovores as well as on the Destroyer.

'One of the maquettes was of a demon-like creature and suggested the scope that they could have with such a character, should they require it. It was a happy coincidence that "Battlefield" featured a demonic entity.

'We sat and talked with John Nathan-Turner for about an hour and a half, and he obviously had a great deal of interest in the way things were done and what could be achieved. For example, one of the things we discussed was the problem of not being able to hold a long close-up shot of a monster, simply because it wouldn't stand up to that kind of close scrutiny. This is of course quite true. He was also very keen on getting a lot more movement into the faces of the monsters.'

Stephen and Susan left some of the maquettes and polaroids with John, and over the next couple of weeks began really to get to grips with creating the Haemovores. Susan takes up the story:

'It was when we were completing the Haemovores that we next heard anything about the Destroyer. The director's secretary phoned us up! This was quite unusual – usually it's one of the designers. She explained that Michael Kerrigan wanted to talk to us about doing the Destroyer, so we went up to see Michael and, together with the designers from Visual Effects, Costume and Make-Up, who would also be involved, we discussed how the Destroyer might be realised.'

It was at this point, as with any complex effects work, that the script was adapted to fit in with what time, money and facilities would allow. Stephen explained what happened in this case: 'In the original script, the Destroyer started out as an ordinary guy who transformed into a demon. They had already cast Marek Anton in the part, because he had the ability to sort of scrunch himself up and then expand himself again as he transformed – that was the original idea.

'About half-way through the meeting, they decided to lose the idea of the transformation and make him appear as a demon from the outset. The only remaining nod to the original transformation concept is that he pulls a section of his chest armour off at one point.'

Having arrived at an agreed position of what the Destroyer would do and how he should appear, it was down to Stephen actually to take the original maquette and turn it into a realistic and believable demon.

'What they essentially wanted was a mask,' he explained, 'and they were very keen on keeping the image of the maquette – the traditional idea of a demon. We had to change the mouth, because the Destroyer has dialogue and you wouldn't be able to talk if the teeth were as they are on the maquette.

'What we tried to do was to give it a bit more character than most run-of-the-mill monsters. The Destroyer is supposed to be a very distinguished, proud-looking creature, which is one of the things they asked for.

'One of the problems with modelling a mask away from the face is that as you move away, the eyes become smaller, until you end up with this Marx-brothers-type gorilla thing with little tiny eyes in a massive great head, which I think makes it look a little stupid. You have to get the balance right.

'The head was modelled in clay, to get the proportions correct, then split up into sections – the horns, the ears and so on – for moulding. The mould was made by a chap called Mick Hockney. Then foam latex was pumped into it to make the mask.

'Because the mask was quite a way from the actor's head, we had to work out a method to get a proper alignment of the eyes and the jaw, which are probably the most important areas. We used a fibreglass underskull for the mask and then another underskull to fit on the actor's head. These were put one on top of the other, aligned and then stuck together with a fibreglass paste. This made it comfortable to wear as well as providing a strong base for the two main horns.'

Because of the pressure of time to complete the Destroyer, Stephen called upon the services of Robert Allsopp (who built the previous season's Kandyman) to construct the two large, curling horns that crown the Destroyer's head. Robert explained how he constructed them:

'As the horns had to be very light, I decided against using fibreglass on them. I eventually decided to use a kind of orthopaedic bandage that comes from Belgium. It's very lightweight, durable and doesn't need a negative mould.

'The horns were worked directly over the clay, just by wrapping the bandages around it. The bandages are hard to start with, but you soften them by applying heat, for example from a hairdryer. Once you've finished modelling, they cool down and harden again in the desired shape.

'Once they had been modelled and hardened, I split the horns to remove the clay and then re-sealed them before painting them black.'

To give the Destroyer more character and to provide the facial movements, Stephen installed a cable-control system for the face. This was similar in principle to that employed on the Tetraps and on Fifi ('The Happiness Patrol').

'The cable system operated his snarling top and bottom lips and a raising brow, which we tended to work backwards – in other words, we kept it raised and then lowered it when he frowned. We made sure that every time he talked, we kept a rippling motion going on the mouth to give the impression of speech.

'All the cabling was hidden behind the cloak, which is why the Destroyer wears a cloak!'

The Destroyer appears for only a fairly brief time before he is destroyed, exploding in a climactic battle with the Brigadier. Specially built heads were made for this scene, which were only just visible in the transmitted story. This explosion was another reason for wanting the horns to be as light and yet as strong as possible; if they had been brittle, they would have shattered upon impact with the ground. However, the bandage horns just bounced around.

As with the melting of Kane in 'Dragonfire', the Destroyer's destructing head was made from wax, and several duplicates were produced to allow for re-takes. Susan explained how these wax heads were made:

'We had to take a latex cast from the mould that produced the actual head. Then, from that latex version, we took a silicone multi-piece mould. That was next used to lay up four wax duplicates – a process painstakingly carried out by Tony Clark. The completed heads were assembled and then reinforced with fibreglass around the neck and in some other places that we wanted the head to hold together. Finally, they were painted to match the real Destroyer's head.'

In the event, the actual destruction was recorded twice – once in the studio and then again at the Visual Effects Department's workshops.

The final compliment that Stephen and Susan paid was to the skill and professionalism of the actor inside the mask. Marek Anton had also appeared as a Russian marine in 'The Curse of Fenric', and it was as a result of that part that he was cast as the Destroyer.

'Marek was in the costume for up to two and a half hours at a time,' Susan told us, 'and he didn't complain at all. He would stand in front of a mirror and really get into the character before going in front of the cameras. He also discussed with us, as we were operating the mask, what he would be doing, so that the facial expressions could be made to match. He was great.'

The Destroyer is only the fourth walking, talking animatronic creature to have appeared in *Doctor Who*. Previously we have seen the Terileptils ('The Visitation'), the Androzani Dragon ('The Caves of Androzani', although ultimately the animatronic movement was not used in the finished production) and the Tetraps. Each time, the process has been refined and improved upon, and Susan and Stephen are very pleased with this latest addition to the ranks of the Doctor's adversaries.

David J Howe

Interview conducted by David J Howe, Mark Stammers and Stephen James Walker

BONUS FEATURE: ON LOCATION WITH 'SURVIVAL'

To research the latest in The Frame's *series of interview features on the production of the Sylvester McCoy stories, David Howe, Mark Stammers and I arranged to attend a day of location recording for 'Survival' – which, although we did not know it at the time, would turn out to be the last classic* Doctor Who *story to be transmitted. Our impressive line-up of interviewees on this occasion comprised actors Sylvester McCoy (the Doctor), Sophie Aldred (Ace), Anthony Ainley (the Master) and Will Barton (Midge), producer John Nathan-Turner, director Alan Wareing, designer Nick Somerville, make-up designer Joan Stribling and visual effects designer Malcolm James. The piece was written up by David and published in two parts: the first, in advance of the story being transmitted, in Issue 11 in August 1989, and the second, after the story had gone out (to avoid giving away any 'spoilers') in Issue 15 in August 1990. The two parts are both reprinted below.*

A DAY IN PERIVALE

'Survival' was the third story of the twenty-sixth season to go before the cameras. Written by Rona Munro, a newcomer to *Doctor Who*, it involves the Master, some strange happenings in Perivale, a race of Cheetah people on a distant planet, and a survival course being run by a man named Sergeant Patterson (played by Julian Holloway, a character actor who has appeared in many films, including a number in the *Carry On ...* series). Just how all these elements tie up will become apparent only when the finished story is transmitted, but you can rest assured that it will be a fitting return for the Master. We can also reveal that it will play on people's innate suspicion of our feline friend, the household cat, which explains its original working title, 'Cat-Flap'. After this one, you may never trust another cat again!

'Survival' was shot entirely on outside broadcast, with no studio time allocated. The locations used reflect the difference between Perivale in the 1980s (for which, reasonably enough, Perivale was the location) and the alien planet of the Cheetah people. For the latter, the crew returned to the same quarry used in director Alan Wareing's debut story, 'The Greatest Show in the Galaxy'.

The day that we joined the crew, they were using a martial arts centre just outside of Perivale to represent the youth club where Patterson's survival classes are held. All the scenes in and around that location were due to be recorded, and these will be seen mainly in the opening episode of the three-part story. We were lucky that on this particular day, most of the main characters appearing in 'Survival' were present, the only significant exception being that none of the Cheetah people were required. We arrived at about 10.00 in the morning, when Alan Wareing and his team were recording some material with the Master himself, Anthony Ainley. Once these sequences were in the can, Tony was free to talk to us.

Since making his debut in the programme back in 1981, in the penultimate Tom Baker story 'The Keeper of Traken', Tony has had the good fortune to appear with all seven Doctors (Patrick Troughton and Jon Pertwee in 'The Five Doctors', with Richard Hurndall taking the part of the first Doctor, and Tom Baker, Peter Davison, Colin Baker and Sylvester McCoy within their own respective eras). Although he never worked with William Hartnell, which he regrets, he told us that he had in fact met him.

We wondered if he had been aware of the history of the Master when he first took the part in 'The Keeper of Traken'. 'Yes, I was aware of the Master before I took the part,' he confirmed. 'But I wasn't aware of how deeply probed, analysed and scrutinised these episodes were. That is the thing that has surprised me – how much in the searchlight they are for so many years after they have been transmitted. Matthew Waterhouse had told me that there were fan clubs, but I was rather surprised by it all, by how much it was loved around the world.'

Since then, Tony has had the opportunity to meet the fans at conventions, including many in America, and among his memories of those events is the sad occasion when Patrick Troughton died. 'I was with Patrick at that convention, and one of the last things he said to me was, "Do you think these *Star Trek* actors will mind if I ask them for their autographs for one of my grandchildren?", which was rather sweet. His death was a terrible shock. I had dined with him on the Thursday night and the Friday night, and on the Saturday morning at breakfast I was told he was dead. We had two days to go at the convention. The people there were visibly moved, and some were weeping. We had to work through two days, and there was a very strange atmosphere. One felt that he was still there. I'd never known anything like it. It hit us for six.

'Patrick was wonderful and very, very well. I mean, on the Friday night at dinner, he was well and fit and happy and joking around. It was a big shock.'

We next moved on to talk about 'Survival'. In keeping with the theme of change this season, the Master – like the Doctor – has a new costume, courtesy of costume designer Ken Trew. What did Tony think of his new look? 'It's stylish. I like the idea of the silver collar of the waistcoat coming out over the collarless black jacket. I've never seen that before.'

The entire costume is made of silk, a fact that Tony is quite pleased about. His original costume had used rather heavier fabrics like velvet, and he had wanted something cooler and less restricting. In addition, John Nathan-Turner had suggested that a new look would be in order.

Quite rightly, Tony did not want to give away too much about the plot of 'Survival', but he did comment with a smile that he had never done anything quite like it before. Apart from some of the special make-up being a new experience for him, he suggested that we would find this very different from his past appearances in the series.

We mentioned a rumour we had heard that this would be Tony's last appearance in *Doctor Who*. His reaction was one of genuine surprise, but he went on to explain that acting is a precarious business. 'You don't know what you are going to play in the future. It's possible I may never play the Master again; it's possible that I may never work again. You just don't know. On the other hand, I was and am very willing to play the Master until I drop, because it is a part I like.

'I do think that sometimes in fandom, all kinds of unsubstantiated rumours circulate. I don't know who creates all these stories, but I suppose they're quite good from a magazine selling point of view. But what you have to realise, and some journalists do not, is that actors know very little and are told very little about the internal politics of a show.'

Tony himself has been the subject of many an idle gossip-monger in the past, which has understandably made him rather wary about approaches from journalists. 'There was a lady in America, a journalist, who pulled the trick of taking everything I said out of context and changing it. She wanted to imply that I was in some way siding with Eric Saward against John Nathan-Turner, which I would never do. I like Eric very much, but John has done far more for me personally than Eric has. Actors don't know the full story and I don't know the circumstances of why Eric left *Doctor Who*.'

Moving back to the subject of the Master, Tony had said that he enjoyed playing the part, and we wondered if he could put his finger on what it was that appealed to him.

'It's stretched me a lot as an actor,' he decided. 'It is very difficult to do voices and wear disguises and the like, and I've had to do more of them in this role than in any other. In that sense, it's been good for me.

'The actual business of playing someone like Kalid in "Time-Flight" and having a lot of make-up on and carrying a lot of weight is very difficult, and to try to maintain that character's truth throughout is also very difficult. In 'The King's Demons', I had to ride a horse and speak with a French accent. That was difficult too, because I don't do either very well. I had some horse riding lessons, but no help with the accent.

'I think it's worth doing these things in one's career, because otherwise one is just playing safe, and just being a personality actor. There is nothing wrong with being a personality actor, but I admire actors who can do the protean work and change their personalities in the way that Sellers or Olivier did. I like versatile actors and bold acting.'

Watching Tony at work later in the day, we could certainly see that he has the character of the Master down to a fine art. It is very difficult to relate the genial, friendly and helpful person of Tony Ainley to the cold-eyed and electric presence that he brings to the Master – a tribute to his skill as an actor.

While we had been talking, the visual effects team, headed by designer Malcolm James, had been setting up a sequence involving, believe it or not, an animatronic cat.

By mid-morning, the scenes showing the outside of the hall had all been completed, and the crew moved inside to continue with the rest of the day's recording. If it had been warm outside – and it had! – it was even hotter in here. A camera track had been set up down one side of the hall, so that a tracking shot could be taken later in the day, and huge white reflector boards had been mounted at the far end with strong arc-lamps directed at them to provide ideal lighting conditions. Props, meanwhile, had set out a variety of gymnastic training equipment in the main body of the hall, including punchbags suspended from a metal bar, a couple of floor-mounted punch-balls and some weights.

The scene being rehearsed and recorded was of a fight between two of the boys attending the survival class run by Sergeant Patterson. They grapple with each other on mats on the floor, ringed by Patterson and the rest of the boys, and eventually one gains the upper hand. Patterson then congratulates the class and dismisses them for the day. One of the boys involved in the fight is upset at Patterson's treatment of him, but the Sergeant uses this to make a point about survival of the fittest. At the end of the action, the Doctor and Ace arrive to ask Patterson some questions.

Despite its simplicity, this scene had to be gone through a surprising number of times, not because mistakes were made – although Alan Wareing quickly spotted that one of the boys was wearing a chain, which would never be allowed in this sort of physical training! – but simply because of the variety of different camera angles required. A couple of takes were needed just to record the sounds. However, despite the intense heat, the crew remained patient, helpful and unflustered throughout, and Alan Wareing certainly proved himself a very capable director, extracting superb performances from all the cast and keeping his eagle eye peeled for anything that might detract from a shot.

We had noticed that the walls of the hall were decorated with numerous boxing and fight posters, and at first glance this had seemed perfectly normal. However, when we went outside again to get some fresh air we noticed something rather strange – while from the inside the hall did not appear to have any windows, from the outside it clearly did! We deduced that the windows had been panelled over, and this prompted us to seek out the man responsible for preparing the hall for recording – the story's designer, Nick Somerville.

This was Nick's first *Doctor Who* as a designer, although he had previously worked on 'Mawdryn Undead' as assistant to Stephen Scott. We were interested to learn that he had also been, for several years, assistant to one of the series' most celebrated former designers, Raymond Cusick (who has now retired).

Like the rest of the crew, Nick was working on 'Survival' back to back with the following story into production, 'Ghost Light'. We asked him if this had caused any difficulties. 'Well, it is tricky, but I'm reasonably relaxed about it at the moment. It is a little unfortunate that Alan is the director on both, as I can't really discuss any of the finer details of the next story until he has finished with this one.'

As already mentioned, Nick had arranged for the hall to be prepared prior to its use. 'We had to come in here early and panel over those windows in the hall. We did that basically to make it look more sinister and dark. The hall is in reality a judo and martial arts place and it had drawings all over the walls, which weren't quite what we wanted. So we re-panelled it, but in a way that could be done really quickly. If we had gone any further than that, we might as well have built a complete set in a warehouse or something.

'To finish off the hall I got hold of those boxing posters. They were quite difficult to come by – the promoters don't tend to keep the posters. If you look at the bottom of them, you'll see that they all come from the same printers. For some unknown reason, these printers had drawers full of them. It's amazing, but some things that you'd think would be easy to come by are not.'

We asked Nick what his other contributions to the story had been. 'It's split down the middle really. Because one half is set in contemporary Perivale, that is light for me – for the most part, you just see things as they are. It is really the things you don't see that are my responsibility. We hide things or remove things because in the director's eyes they just don't feel right. There has been a little bit of that going on.

'For the other half of the story, we have got some work in the quarry, where the Cheetah camp has to be made, but that again is pretty straightforward. Because we are relatively in control of the location, we can get in there a couple of days early and make it ready for the recording.'

Nick's other major task was to obtain, of all things, a large number of animal bones to be scattered around the landscape of the alien planet. 'I've ordered a ton of bones, and it's a bit difficult to know what a ton of bones actually looks like. It's very hard to get the scale right, because when you place something on a landscape it can get lost very easily. Hopefully careful positioning will remove any problems there. I've had an abattoir boiling them up and cleaning them, because otherwise there would be a health hazard as well as the smell.

'Even the bones were not easy to find. Abattoirs don't advertise nowadays. Luckily this abattoir is bringing stuff halfway across the country anyway, and they can easily divert a lorry to drop our bones off. That's the sort of thing *Doctor Who* gives you the opportunity to deal with. It's great fun.'

During the lunch break, which came part way through recording of the numerous set-ups for the scene described above, we were able to corner the director, Alan Wareing, for the first time.

Alan was obviously working very hard and yet, when we spoke, he seemed calm and collected as if he was doing nothing more strenuous than spending an afternoon out in the sunshine. We asked him first how shooting had been progressing on 'Survival'.

'It's been going very well indeed. We're up to schedule, after a few difficulties with cats and horses – which is going to be the main problem throughout the shoot really.

'We're using three real cats, but there are no definite number in the story. In the script, they are called Kitlings and are described as having red eyes, but we couldn't quite achieve that. What we decided to do was to make them all black and give them a ruff of hair up their backs, which sort of matches the ruff on the Cheetahs.'

We had noticed that for one sequence involving a cat peering through the youth club window, Alan had taken a very low camera angle. Was this a technique he would be using a lot on 'Survival'?

'It's interesting that when we went on the camera recce, the cameraman said that he would get the lowest pair of tripod legs he could find, because he could see that most of the shots would be low angle. As a style, I find it dramatic to shoot low angles anyway. I always like to get below the eyeline as a technique, and particularly on this story, because it features a lot of cats.'

One aspect of the story that Alan knew a bit about from first hand experience was the Master – his first job on *Doctor Who* had been as assistant floor manager on 'The Keeper of Traken', Anthony Ainley's debut story. How did he see the character of the Master, now that he was directing a story with him?

'Well, in Sherlock Holmes terms, he's the Doctor's Moriarty. But I also think that he's a very different character, and I don't think he'd thank me for making that comparison so readily. But he's certainly of that type. He's also as indestructible as the Doctor. I like the idea that everything is under his control with just a glance of the eye. He's a very sinister character, and I think Tony plays him brilliantly.'

Turning to the subject of locations, we were interested to know why Alan had chosen to return to the same quarry he had used for 'The Greatest Show in the Galaxy' to shoot the scenes set on the Cheetah planet.

'It's simply because I know you can get another planet's surface there. It's a vast quarry – you can drive round it for hours. For the most part, we will be using different sections of it, including some wooded areas. In fact, we are going to just one of the same places again – it's where the hippie bus was, and this year its going to be the Cheetah encampment.'

When they had recorded there the previous year, the temperature in the quarry had regularly hit 100 degrees. This time, Alan was hoping the good weather would break. 'To be honest, when we get to the planet, I want grey, overcast skies, because shadows and sunlight are a problem. I'm going to paint a lot of heavy skies in anyway on locked-off shots, because the planet itself is supposed to be very stormy, with volcanoes and the like. We will be painting on volcanoes and lava flows, so I'll be looking for clean skylines and piles of sand to use for those purposes.'

Before Alan dashed off to grab a bite to eat in preparation for the gruelling afternoon session, we asked if he enjoyed working on *Doctor Who*.

'It's absolutely fascinating. One of the real attractions is that as a director you get a free hand. It's pure imagination. There are only certain rules laid down by the production office, and those concern the Doctor and his companion and what they are or are not allowed to do. Basically the Doctor is free to do almost anything within the bounds of moral responsibility, and all the other characters are of your own invention and those around you. I've been really lucky to have so many creative people around me.'

With that, Alan left us, and it wasn't long before he was back in action overseeing the afternoon's recording. As well as the end of the scene with the Doctor and Ace encountering Patterson, several other sequences were shot. One of the last ones to be done involved a character called Midge, a young man of about 18, who is somehow involved in those strange happenings in Perivale. During the afternoon tea break, we chatted to the actor who has landed the part of Midge. He is Will Barton, and this is the first television he has done – his previous experience has been in the theatre. How was he finding it?

'Really enjoyable. I was a bit green to begin with, with regard to the rehearsals, but I've learnt an awful lot from the experience, and particularly from Alan Wareing, who is a very good director.

'The pace of work is very different, but I suppose the essence is still getting a kind of truth within the type of acting that you're doing. Obviously it is a different style, and you've got to be aware of that, but a lot of the theatre that I do is studio theatre, which is very truthful and close to the audience, which in a sense is very like television.'

Will confirmed that Alan had cast him in the role but said that he wasn't sure if this was on the basis of any of his previous work in particular. 'He gave me an interview once for a part in *Casualty*, and he met me then. For this *Doctor Who* part, they needed someone who could ride a motorcycle, which I do. Apparently Eddie Kidd is my stunt double!'

Moving onto the actual character of Midge, could Will explain a little about him?

'He is in all three episodes, so it's a very nice part. Midge is originally a cynical kid who comes from Perivale. He becomes involved with the Cheetah people and then becomes totally evil, deciding that the secret of success in survival is basically survival of the fittest. It's a very good part, and I'm very pleased to be playing it.'

On that note, we left Will to grab some refreshment before his next ordeal in the, by now, oven-hot hall.

We decided to stay outside for the moment, as both Sylvester McCoy and Sophie Aldred were there too, taking a well deserved break. We cornered Sophie for a photo session and she cheerily obliged, while Sylvester heckled us from behind. However, his turn was next, and after we had snapped away at him, we settled down for a brief chat about his interpretation of the Doctor.

'The first season I did was just written for any old Doctor and I happened to come along. In between the first and second seasons, I suddenly realised how it should be played, because I hadn't seen it for years – I didn't really know. John, Andrew Cartmel and I then sat down and chatted about how we saw the Doctor. We were all agreed that we wanted to make him darker, harder, bringing in more anger, but at the same time keeping the humour.'

We noted that in both the twenty-fifth season and, it appeared, the twenty-sixth, the stories themselves seemed to have a darker, more spectral tone to them. 'Yes, they're all very sinister. The Doctor is even darker this time. There are one or two moments of humour though – they make me laugh, anyway!'

One of the notable things about the current TARDIS crew is that they really seem to be hitting it off together.

'That's another thing I thought was important. The companion shouldn't be someone who screams all the time, and shouldn't be the token woman. She should be a fully fledged character in her own right. I'm sure that others have been; I'm just going by my own prejudice of what I thought. Sophie is great, and we're great mates. We've actually got the same birth date, and Tony Ainley has the same birthday too, so I don't know if that means anything.

Sophie and I do have the same sense of humour.'

We then asked the million dollar question – would Sylvester be staying on for another season after this one? We were delighted to receive a positive answer.

'Yes. They've asked me if I'll do another season, and I've said yes. I'll go for one more and see what happens.'

Presumably, then, Sylvester still saw scope in the character?

'Yes. I think partly because it is only 14 episodes a year and it's my summer job. I could imagine doing this as my only job, and it would be very wearing – just time for a holiday and then back. It would be a bit much. I have only a short period of time, and then I go off and do other things. That keeps me fresh.

'This summer, after I finish on *Doctor Who*, I'm having a holiday really, and then after that, I'm doing another run of *What's Your Story*? I'm looking forward to that. Last time we did it, everyone was learning, and we didn't know how it was going to go until the very end – you couldn't relax on it. But this time, having done it once, I think I can relax, hopefully. It'll probably be the opposite on the week!'

Recording was drawing to a close now, and after the last few scenes had been completed, the crew started striking everything ready for transportation to the next location the following day. While this was going on, we had a final word with producer John Nathan-Turner, who had kept an eye on everything throughout the day, making helpful suggestions, discussing elements of the script with Alan Wareing and ensuring that the whole thing ran smoothly. With a number of BBC programmes being hit by strikes, our first question was naturally about how the season had been progressing so far.

'Very well. We've had terrific weather so far on this one, and we're up to schedule, which is marvellous.

'As far as the rest of the season goes, the first one[74] was murder to shoot, because we had terrible weather. We had everything: snow, hail, wind, rain – it was really dreadful. I think they were the worst conditions I've worked under; but the show looks good and in many ways the bad weather helped it.

'"Battlefield" is looking good as well, although there were a few strike hiccups. What the strikes have meant is that the regular artists and crew are very tired – after "Battlefield", we went straight into rehearsals for "Survival". We do get a breather at the end of this, though. Another impact the strike had on "Battlefield" was that all the props couldn't get in on the right days, and the sypher dubs and editing were affected. Those problems have been resolved now, though.'

Did John think that 'Ghost Light', being an all-studio story, would be affected?

'I doubt it. I hope that the strike will be resolved by then. At the moment, I'd just like to get this one finished, because our OB unit is going on to cover the tennis at Wimbledon and we've got very little leeway in terms of running over.'

We commented to John how happy and relaxed everyone seemed to be, despite the heat and the hard work that was being done.

'Yes, it's a very good OB unit. It's been more or less the same cameramen and engineering managers that have been doing it since we upped our OB content, so there's a nice family feeling about it. But it is very hard work; you shouldn't underestimate it. Everyone works very long hours. To be going from an 8.30 am on site to a 6.00 pm finish every day is very, very

---

74 'The Curse of Fenric'.

long. As you can see, it's gone 6.00 now, and the crew is still de-rigging.'

Although the rest of the unit will be having a short break in between 'Survival' and 'Ghost Light', John will not. 'I'll be working through. While we're away here, they're editing "Battlefield", so there'll be rough cuts waiting for me to see.'

With that, we said our final goodbyes and made our way back to reality. The day seemed to have sped by, and yet there had been no sense of urgency or hurry about the location. Everyone had gone about their jobs professionally and efficiently; all the people we had spoken to had been open and friendly; and there had been a strong sense of camaraderie.

CAT TALES

The creation of a race of aliens is always a challenging prospect to the dedicated people who work behind the scenes on *Doctor Who*. A number of different BBC departments will often collaborate on the realisation of the creatures. For 'Survival', the Cheetah people were brought to the screen by the Make-Up and Costume Departments, with Visual Effects providing special props as required.

In charge of make-up was Joan Stribling, who had previously worked on 'Nightmare of Eden', 'Earthshock' and 'Terminus' for the series. This time, however, the problems were slightly different.

'There are eight Cheetah people, and we had to take face casts of each of the eight actors and actresses that were playing them,' Joan explained. 'The Cheetah faces were then sculpted and casts made of them. The main part of the prosthetic is made out of airbrushed cold-foam with hair attached. From the nose back, they are overhead masks, but for the part above the lip, we used a hot-foam prosthetic piece to enable them to open their mouths and snarl.'

Joan went on to explain how hair was stuck onto the actors' cheek bones to give their faces a triangular Cheetah shape; contact lenses and teeth then completed the transformation. As well as the Cheetahs themselves, Anthony Ainley, Sophie Aldred and Will Barton all required lenses and teeth as they were partially transformed into Cheetahs during the course of the story.

Handling the visual effects for 'Survival' was Malcolm James. When asked what the most challenging aspect of the story was, he quickly singled out the animatronic, cable-operated cat that his effects team created for it. 'I think, by the time we actually started work, we had about five weeks to do it all in,' he revealed. 'With the cat, though, we had a slight delay at the start, because we weren't sure which breed of real cats were going to be used for the live work. We had to build our cat to the same size and shape to match, and cats can vary on these.' He commented that ultimately his team were working around the clock to get all the effects ready in time.

As well as the cat, there were some other effects that required the use of cable mechanisms. One example was a Cheetah paw with retractable claws. 'One of the shots is of a rope pulled across a pathway, and one of the Cheetahs comes along the path on horseback and sees it. The Cheetah then stretches out its paw and cuts the rope with its claws. We want the claws to spring out and snip the rope, so obviously we will have to have some form of mechanism in there. You probably won't see any further up than the elbow for that shot, so that's all we're building. There is another shot with a Cheetah's claws raised up in front of its head and body in a fairly threatening, aggressive pose. We'll use the same prop for that sequence as well.'

Of course, Visual Effects also provide other, more mundane props that help to enhance the feel and imagery of an alien planet, as Malcolm explained. 'We made a lot of soft bones to be used in fight sequences. Also, there's a shot of a sabre-tooth skull, and one of the actors pulls a tooth from it to use as a weapon. We made that too. Just generally run of the mill stuff.'

Another task was to create the illusion of two motorbikes being involved in a head-on collision. For this sequence, it was only the explosion that Malcolm and his team had to generate, as he told us. 'They're going to split the shot and have one motorbike coming from one direction, another motorbike corning from the opposite direction, and then we'll put our explosion in the middle. So there'll be three pieces of video. One, the motorbike from the left; two, the motorbike from the right; and three, the explosion. They'll then mix the whole shot together to make it look like a real crash.'

Malcolm finally told us about another scene that had posed a bit of a challenge for his team. This was the one where Ace scoops up some water from a lake to give to a Cheetah, and the water glows in her hands. 'For that we're using a small, 20-50 Watt quartz bulb, which will be cupped in her hands. We'll obviously have to protect her, because quartz bulbs get very hot. She can scoop in the water with that and it will still operate, and in fact the water will help to keep the bulb cool. What we want is for the water, when she holds it up, to light up her face, so if the light from the bulb is not strong enough, we'll get some help from the lighting people to set up the shot. If the water itself is not glowing enough, we can use some front-axial projection material, shine a light down the front of the camera and make it glow.'

We commented that perhaps Dave Chapman, the video effects designer, could add the glow in post production, but Malcolm explained that because the shot would be a long shot, and because it would be moving, it would be very tricky and time-consuming using electronic effects to match a glow, frame by frame, where it was required.

Now that the finished episodes have been transmitted, the effort that everyone concerned put in over a hot and uncomfortable location recording – particularly in the work with the animatronic cat and the Cheetahs – really shows, and 'Survival' is a standing testament to the effectiveness of make-up, costumes, visual and video effects combined to create a believable alien world populated by unearthly creatures.

David J Howe

BONUS FEATURE: BEHIND THE SCENES ON 'GHOST LIGHT'

The Frame's *coverage of the making of 'Ghost Light' – the last story of the classic* Doctor Who *to go before the cameras – was divided into two main parts. The first of these – published in Issue 11 in August 1989, while the production was still in the planning stages – incorporated interviews conducted during our location visit for 'Survival'. (Following the usual pattern at that time, the twenty-sixth season's last two stories – 'Survival' and 'Ghost Light' – were made back-to-back by the same team.) The interviewees were director Alan Wareing, visual effects designer Malcolm James, make-up designer Joan Stribling, costume designer Ken Trew and designer Nick Somerville. The second part – published in Issue 14 in May 1990, after the story had been completed and transmitted – was written up by David in the manner of a short story (just to ring the changes), and focused on the realisation of the character of Light, drawing on newly conducted interviews with scriptwriter Marc Platt, Alan Wareing, Ken Trew and freelance costumier Robert Allsopp. The two features are collected together below, and give a unique insight into the work that went on behind the scenes to bring this landmark story to the screen.*

PRE-PRODUCTION

'Ghost Light' (originally titled 'Life Cycle' and then 'The Bestiary') has been written by Marc Platt, another newcomer to the team of writers that script editor Andrew Cartmel is building up. It is a three-parter, and this year's all-studio story. The tone of the piece is moody and atmospheric, and the action takes place entirely within the confines of a large Victorian house – a house that has a mysterious significance for the Doctor's companion Ace.

As the realisation of the house is such an important part of the production, we asked the designer, Nick Somerville, how he was approaching that task.

'We will be having an establishing shot of an actual house, and I'm hoping to use some paintbox video effects to tie an observatory to the roof to make it look a bit creepier.

'The interior is not really standard either. The requirements are quite expensive.'

Nick went on to explain that the house is owned by a strange character who is an entomologist-cum-anthropologist, which means that it has to be filled with the fruits of his work. How does a designer go about obtaining those sort of items?

'We get them through prop houses. But the thing about a large Victorian house full of trophies, palm trees, butterflies, insects and stuffed animals is that they are all expensive items – the imagery is expensive to achieve. It's very difficult to economise, as you can't half-dress the sets. Obviously we'll be shunting stuff around from scene to scene, but it is a very large house.'

Not only is the house strange but there is something even stranger to be found underneath it, and this has given rise to one of the trickiest design problems Nick has had to face on the story. In the house there is a lift that gives access to the lower levels, and Nick has somehow to make it look as if that lift is actually ascending and descending – not an easy thing to do when the Television Centre studios have solid concrete floors!

'I feel that the lift is very important. To get value out of it, it should be an open-cage lift as well – at least, with open lattice-work. Ultimately, of course, it might have to be a closed lift, but at this moment I'm going for the open lift.'

Around a dozen different characters feature in the story. These range from the ordinary to the distinctly out-of-the-ordinary, and have posed the Make-up and Costume Departments some interesting problems. Ken Trew confirmed that a lot of research had been undertaken, not only from the design point of view, but also to make sure that the money was utilised as efficiently as possible.

'Just because some of the characters are dressed in standard Victorian dress, that doesn't necessarily mean that I can get them all from stock,' he explained. 'Suitable costumes are hard to find.'

Joan Stribling told us that the make-up requirements of 'Ghost Light' were very different from those of 'Survival'.

'Whereas the Cheetah people involve face casting and sculpting, prosthetic work, facial hair, paws, teeth and contact lenses, "Ghost Light" is set in the Victorian era with appropriate hairstyles and facial hair. There is also special effect make-up required, i.e. two alien husks, a Neanderthal man, an old man who rejuvenates into a young man, and a man who transforms into a monkey.'

Because of the usual limitations of time and money, Joan is planning to re-use a couple of masks she originally created for the BBC's production of *Alice in Wonderland*, although they will be somewhat adapted for their appearance in 'Ghost Light'.[75]

Malcolm James is also doing some work on the aforementioned aliens, and among the many other visual effects he has to realise for the story are a glowing membrane and some candles that suddenly flare up. We asked him what these candles were needed for, and how he was approaching the effect.

'At one point, there is a scene where something strange is happening in one of the rooms. Everyone is rushing there and they can feel an eerie emanation coming from it. One of the maids is holding a candlestick and, as she gets close to the door, the candle flames have to whoosh up really high. What we are going to do is to modify a real set of candlesticks and add a small brass tube up the side of the candles to the wick. At the bottom end of the tubes we will use something like an ordinary household gas lighter, with the regulation wheel removed from it. Because the candles still have their wicks, there will be a light source. Then, when the gas is released up the tubes, it will make the candles look as if they are flaring up.'

The person with probably the hardest task of all is the director, Alan Wareing, who has to have both 'Survival' and 'Ghost Light' in hand simultaneously so that he can swap from one to the other as production progresses. The main reason for this is that 'Ghost Light' will probably be transmitted before 'Survival' and will therefore need to be edited together first. He also has to discuss all the requirements of both stories with the designers as well as with the writers and all the various other production personnel. How was Alan finding what sounded to us like a very daunting task?

'It is a bit of a hard slog, because we have only a fortnight before we start rehearsing for "Ghost Light". The interesting thing about this is that "Survival" is all outside broadcast, all on location, and "Ghost Light" is all in the studio. That is a nice contrast, and I'm looking forward to getting back into the studio for the final story.'

The only real problem on the horizon is that if the strikes at the BBC continue or escalate, then 'Ghost Light', as the final story, could be hit the hardest. However, as John Nathan-Turner is looking on the bright side, perhaps we should do so as well, and keep our fingers crossed that the production is not severely hit.

---

75 The plan to reuse the masks from *Alice in Wonderland* for the husks in 'Ghost Light' was ultimately abandoned, and different masks used instead.

LET THERE BE LIGHT!

The house. How can I describe my feelings as I first saw the stygian and brooding pile of crumbling bricks and mortar? Apprehension. Nervousness. A sense that I would not leave there unchallenged. 'Gabriel Chase', the battered and weathered sign on the rusting gates had said, but this gave no hint as to the nature of the place itself. A domed observatory clung to the sagging roof life a malignant coppered growth, and the house's whole miasmic aspect would have been enough to send Alfred Hitchcock scurrying for his cameras.

But I was not here to admire the architecture, I was here to talk to some of the people named as co-conspirators in the creation of a creature known as Light. I presume that you are all familiar with the documentary evidence concerning the plans, aspirations and eventual downfall of this creature, so I will not reiterate the facts. However, when I tried to contact those concerned, all I received in return was a strangely yellowed and aged invitation to the very house that was so recently the scene of those climactic events. 'All will be explained', was the card's promise, so here I was. The iron door knocker connected heavily with the oaken door, and I waited nervously on the threshold. Within moments, the door swung open. I was welcomed in by Marc Platt, the author of the whole affair, and ushered into the study. After we had made ourselves comfortable in two of the well-stuffed armchairs, Marc explained where the idea had come from.

'Light started out as being the inhabitant of the spacecraft. Basically I needed a protagonist. I wanted something that was incredibly awesome and frightening, with god-like powers, and was elemental. Something incredibly old and archaic that had been around for centuries and centuries.

'I initially wanted to give him a lot more background, but I eventually decided not to, and I think that improved the mystery. He was an elemental force, something that came out of the spaceship. Very early in the concept, I don't think he actually spoke, but Andrew Cartmel thought that because all the rest of the characters were so strong, Light should have a more recognisable and identifiable character, and that helped in shaping the ideas.

'In essence, Light evolved as a *deux ex machina*, but, rather than descending in glory at the end, he was there all along and turned out to be a rather amoral being. The fundamental concept was of a cosmic version of a Victorian naturalist, who would dissect a human, just as quickly as a human would dissect a rat.

'The actual look of Light swapped about a bit during the development of the script. Initially I wanted him to be very much in the William Blake angel mode, much as he eventually ended up, but I wanted him to have wings that he could furl around people to carry them off. An example of this was when the maid attacked him in the hall: he was going to wrap his wings around her and then vanish – carrying her off. That idea was dropped because, as John Nathan-Turner pointed out, it would be difficult to construct wings that would look and behave correctly. There is a scene that is missing from the TV version, but I have reinstated in the novel, where Light flies like a comet from the house to find out where he is and to discover the nature of the planet. He arrives back and re-furls his cloak, as if it were wings.

'In an effort to make this original angel concept more Victorian, I went for a sort of weird clergyman idea, and Alan Wareing, although he felt the clergyman idea was a little clichéd, suggested a Norman Tebbit-type character, tall and gaunt, which I was keen on as well.[76] However, the line of Ace's when she says that it's an angel was not cut, and I think that's what

---

76 Norman Tebbit was a leading Conservative politician of the 1970s and 1980s.

Ken Trew picked up on. We therefore reverted to this glowing image, which I found really awesome.

'There were other ideas that were changed and dropped as well. For example, Control was going to be the shadow cast by Light and just be a silhouette. She would move along the wall independently of Light and sometimes come off the wall at you. She too evolved into much more of a character – admittedly a very basic life-form, but a growing and sympathetic character nevertheless.

'One of the greatest influences on Light was the actor who played him. John Hallam was very interested in the part and he brought out a lot of the aspects and made the creation live. One example was with the changing of his voice. John saw this as another aspect of Light himself evolving and changing and added a whole new dimension to the character just through that. It really worked well.'

Marc pushed himself off the chair where he had been sitting and walked to a sagging table cluttered with a vast assortment of paraphernalia and artefacts. He picked up a clear glass globe and peered intently into its depths. As he did so, I thought I saw a hesitant and smoky movement within the sphere. 'Light was well on the way to being insane anyway,' Marc commented lightly. 'This was as a result of his endless task of cataloguing everything. You know, that was partly based on my work at the time: cataloguing radio programmes. Another endless task …'

His eyes flicked from the globe to me, and suddenly he was gone, leaving an electric blue image on my retina.

Unfazed by this obvious trick, I looked down at my notes. There were some interesting points that could be followed up. Light as a clergyman? This comment about an actor – had we been misled? The click of the door alerted me and I looked up as another man entered the room. He cheerfully introduced himself as Alan Wareing, the director of the feature, and another of the co-conspirators. So what had he to do with this mysterious angel/clergyman?

After settling into a chair, he explained.

'I had a lot of discussion with Marc as to how the character of Light was written in the early drafts of the script and how I wanted it to be different.

'I remember that Light was much more a physical character originally, and I wanted him to be more a presence than a being. I wanted him to be an untouchable. There was a lot of physical contact in the earlier drafts of the scripts, not just with Light but with Control as well, and I felt this was wrong. The most important thing about Light for me was that he was an energy mass that had just taken on a temporary human form. Light was the source of power, and it was Light that Nimrod worshipped, not a being or a person but an entity, and that was how I wanted him to appear – as something that was almost "unlookable at". That was my starting point for the character.

'The other thing was the revelation of Light at the start of episode three. This was the strongest image I had in my mind: a strong, powerful light and a figure stepping through it. I had this image from the word go, and I was keen for Marc to adjust the character slightly so that I could use it.

'In an earlier draft, when Light first came out of the lift all you saw was a bare foot stepping out. Marc had wanted a Biblical feel to it, but I felt that this energy mass would not be "stepping" anywhere, so I adopted a hovering, gliding image instead.

'The two main qualities I wanted Light to have were to be tall and thin. Did you ever see Poltergeist II? It featured, as the chief ghost, a character like a Victorian preacher – he was perhaps the only thing worth watching in the film! He had that look that I wanted: sort of gaunt and predatory. There is a wonderful scene when he is in a shopping mall, trying to get to the girl, and he walks through someone. That took my breath away. I wanted a similar thing to happen with Light, for him to walk through people, but we couldn't manage it, although I tried very hard to get it to work. What I wanted was that when Light walked away from the lift, after his emergence from the blinding light, the Doctor and everyone else would stand their ground and Light would just walk through them. I wanted to reinforce the idea that Light was not solid – he was a force.

'To further reinforce the idea that Light was made of light we used backlighting in the studio. The intention was to give him a glow, which was enhanced in post production. Unfortunately we didn't have time in the studio to achieve the effect with the lighting that I wanted. Lighting like that is very time consuming, as it has to be set up for every shot and removed once the character has disappeared. Henry Barber, who was responsible for the studio lighting, did a wonderful job on that show, as lighting for mood and atmosphere is very difficult to do.

'As I mentioned, the glow was enhanced by Dave Chapman, the video effects designer, in post production. It took a long time to put the aura around Light and to add an energy noise as he moved. The aura was painstaking to do, as every time he moved, Dave had to build up the glow to match his movements. Another aspect, in script terms, of his development was that as he evolved into a human, he became more susceptible and less all-powerful, and the glow faded. The effect of his face fading to grey as his power drained away was also done by Dave Chapman. He drew around Light's face and took the colour down on that portion to black and white. I thought that was a very effective way of tackling the problem.

'I was very pleased with the visual aspect of Light, and also with John Hallam's performance. I liked the variety he brought to the character.

'We didn't have John for very long, as he was working on the *Narnia* productions at the same time and we had to use him while we could. However, he is a very accomplished actor, and I had wanted to work with him for a long time.

'When he arrived in rehearsal, I told him I wanted it ethereal, I told him he was untouchable. I also wanted him to be an enigma. That's all I told him really – that's all I had time to say. The variety of the vocal tones was all John's idea, and his interpretation of the words in the scenes was his. He brought an innocence to the character as well as a subdued viciousness, which was marvellous.'

Alan rose from the chair and smiled. 'If that's all, I have to get on.' I nodded and thanked him. Just as Alan reached the door, it opened and in walked the third member of the party: costume designer Ken Trew. Ken nodded to Alan as they passed in the doorway and closed the doors behind him.

From deep within his jacket, Ken produced a selection of marvellous colour costume designs, showing Light in various stages of development. As we spread them out on the table, Ken explained how he had come up with the idea.

'I did find it very difficult to crack the character of Light, as I felt that the script's description of him as almost a Victorian vicar wouldn't have been effective. I first toyed with the idea of him being a futuristic thing, and then tried to base it in the past. Then it suddenly hit me: the house had this stained glass window, and Light could be something almost pre-Raphaelite. I then thought of working in something about the beetles coming to life and moving around. I realised that the shell of a beetle would tie in with a line in the script where he comes in through a window and folds his wings. There was a comma left out of the description, so that it read '... Light settles and folds his cloak like wings,' instead of '... Light settles and folds his cloak, like wings'. That gave me another idea, and so the cloak got really big and I added metal feathers to his arms as a further pre-Raphaelite reference, like one of the great Rosetti angels.

'The colours I used in the costume came from the concept of Light as having no corporeal existence. I used a lot of gold and silver, and ultimately, seeing the finished programme with all the video effects, I. wish that I had used more of the gold that was on the neck piece, as that was more reflective. I did design it to be reflective, as Henry Barber wanted to hit it with a lot of light from behind.

'The plaque on his chest was a bit of pre-Raphaelite detail that Robert Allsopp, the maker of the costume, was brilliant with. I showed him some drawings of a sort of Celtic, plaited design and he came up with the plaque, which worked wonderfully. It was multifaceted, and some parts appeared as holes one moment and then as surfaces the next as Light moved around catching the light.'

Ken started to collect up his designs but then changed his mind and thrust them to me. 'These may come in handy,' he said as he stood. 'But now I must rouse Robert, as it is nearly time.' So saying, he moved across to a large wardrobe in the corner of the room. From his voluminous pockets he produced a key and unlocked the doors. Inside, leaning against the back of the cupboard, was Robert Allsopp.

Ken snapped his fingers twice and Robert opened his eyes. He nodded to Ken, who took his place in the wardrobe. Robert shut the doors on Ken and locked them, placing the key in his breast pocket.

I looked on all this with some bewilderment, and decided my best course of action would be to ignore it and say nothing.

'I expect you want to know how the costume was put together,' said Robert, moving across to a piano standing to one side.

I nodded and waited, pen poised over my notepad.

Robert hoisted himself up to sit on the top of the instrument.

'Ken had come up with two very nice design drawings, one with the cloak rolled back to look like wings and one with the cloak in the down position. He appeared to have based the costume on bird-like shapes, with feathering on the sleeves and that sort of thing, but it had a very distinctive shoulder piece that came down to a point at the back like a beetle's wing case. That was the most difficult part to do, really.

'All the fabrics that Ken chose worked well together. The costume was basically a floor length gown in a grey silk with a white collar (of which two were made because of the possibility of the make-up rubbing off onto the collar). Over that was worn a kind of beetle wing-case shoulder piece, and from that hung the cloak, which was actually three different layers of fabric. Light was meant to be a glowing, flowing creature made from light, and Ken had the idea of different layers of fabric so that the outside layers could stand out slightly from the inner ones. When it was lit from the back, the light shone through the layers and gave a halo effect around the cloak. The three fabrics were: a basic grey silk; a gold mesh-type fabric as lining; and a see-through silver mesh over the outside.

'We then added a scarf of a brighter gold fabric, which went around the neck and hung down to about calf level on both sides, and a gold metallised fibreglass plaque, which hung on the chest. Ken had wanted a vaguely Celtic look to the props on the costume. There was a little Celtic brooch pinned at the throat and another circular metal boss on either side of the gold chest ornament. Finally there was a wired collar that came from the top of the shoulder piece. It was made from the translucent silver fabric, so that the light would shine through it from the back.

'The most difficult part to make was the carapace-like shoulder piece. Because it needed to be light and flexible, I didn't want to use fibreglass, which tends to be quite heavy, so I constructed a wire frame, which is very light and flexible but takes a long time to make. I used sprung steel wire, cut into pieces and then soldered together to make up the shape. It probably had several hundred soldered joints in it where all the cross pieces met each other. I spent about three days just doing soldering. After that, it was padded and then covered in grey silk so that none of the wires showed, giving it a smooth shape. It was then covered again in the silver mesh to give the same finish as the cloak.

'Light's upper arms were covered in feather-shaped pieces of the gold mesh fabric. Then on his lower arms there was feather-shaped scale armour, tied in with the fabric feathering. The armour was actually vacuum-formed in a gold plastic and mounted onto a gold leather cloth. The result was rather like the effect of feathers and scales on a bird's leg.'

Robert jumped down from the piano and moved to the door. 'If that's all, you will have to leave now, as we're expecting a visitor.' I got to my feet and hurriedly stuffed all my notes and Ken's drawings into my bag.

'Anyone I know?' I asked.

'I don't think so, judging from why you came here in the first place.' Robert held the door open for me and I moved into the hallway ahead of him. Alan stood by the front door and opened it as I approached.

'Nice to have met you,' he said with a smile. 'Do come again.'

I glanced round as Marc emerged at the top of the ornate and impressive flight of stairs that dominated the hall. His clothes were covered with dust and cobwebs, and for some unfathomable reason he had put a pair of sunglasses on.

As the front door closed behind me, I caught a glimpse of an incredible flash of light, and of Robert and Alan shielding their eyes. Then the door clicked shut and I was once again standing on the porch. Thunder echoed menacingly and the sky above the house was split with a jagged streak of blue lightning. I hurried away, glancing back only once at the flickering blue/white light that played out of the windows of Gabriel Chase.

David J Howe

Interviews conducted by David J Howe, Stephen James Walker and Mark Stammers

In the previous two volumes of Talkback, *I presented accounts of* Doctor Who *fandom in the 1960s and the 1970s respectively. Now, to take this potted history right up to the end of the 'classic series' period, here is a piece that I originally wrote as a chapter for the book* Doctor Who: The Eighties, *first published by Virgin Publishing in hardback in 1996 and reissued in paperback the following year. Readers may spot here the names of quite a number of people who have since gone on to do* Doctor Who- *or other genre-related work in a professional capacity!*

The main hub of *Doctor Who* fan activity for much of the 1980s was the United States of America. Episodes – particularly those from the fourth Doctor's era – were shown on an almost daily basis on PBS stations all over the country, generating an enormous cult following for the series.

It seemed that barely a weekend went by without a *Doctor Who* convention taking place somewhere in the States. The show's stars, both past and present, were in constant demand to attend these celebrations, with high fees and travel expenses being offered to entice them from UK shores. Producer John Nathan-Turner even began to act as a semi-official guest liaison officer for the organisers of these events. The biggest convention of all, attended by an estimated 20,000 people, was billed as – appropriately enough – the Ultimate Celebration. This took place in Chicago over the series' twentieth anniversary weekend in 1983 and achieved the unique feat of bringing all four surviving Doctors – Patrick Troughton, Jon Pertwee, Tom Baker and Peter Davison – on stage together, along with many of their companions from the series.

The North American *Doctor Who* Appreciation Society (NADWAS), which like its UK forebear had been essentially non-profit-making, now gave way to professional operations. Barbara Elder, who ran NADWAS, went over to working on a commercial basis, and competition came from organisations including Spirit of Light – who staged the Ultimate Celebration amongst many other conventions – and the Doctor Who Fan Club of America. The latter was set up by two commercially-minded fans, Ron Katz and Chad Roark, after they met Nathan-Turner at BBC Enterprises' own Longleat event in 1983. Its members, who came to number some 30,000 by the middle of the decade, received a regular newspaper entitled *The Whovian Times* (*Doctor Who* fans being commonly referred to as Whovians in the States). This featured interviews and news items – including columns by Nathan-Turner and prominent British fan Jeremy Bentham – and also numerous adverts for a wide range of merchandise items produced in the States during this period. Readers were even given regular invitations to join a group called the Gallifrey Beach and Body Club!

It was arguably during Colin Baker's time as the Doctor that the series hit the peak of its '80s popularity in the States. Like Davison before him, Baker made his first convention appearance at an American event (PanoptiCon West in Ohio in July 1984). Sylvester McCoy followed suit, but his tenure in the role coincided with a slight downturn in the series' fortunes. This was due largely to the fact that, with the reduction to 14 episodes per season, it was now being produced at too slow a rate to satisfy the scheduling needs of the PBS stations, leaving them with the choice of either continuing to rerun old episodes over and over again or else dropping the series altogether. As the BBC's American agents, Lionheart, had also started to charge higher fees for the rerunning of old episodes, an increasing number decided on the latter course. Interest in the series nevertheless remained strong at the end of the decade, with a new organisation called The Friends of Doctor Who emerging to take the lead in US fandom.

Elsewhere on the North American continent, considerable fan support had developed for *Doctor Who* in Canada. This revolved mainly around a group known as the Doctor Who Information Network, which in 1984 began publishing a regular fanzine entitled *Enlightenment*.

Doctor Who also remained very popular 'down under' during the '80s. The Australasian Doctor Who Fan Club continued to publish issues of its high-quality fanzine *Zerinza*, as well as a more basic newsletter, and attracted a large influx of new members. A number of '*Doctor Who* Parties' and other events were held, with guests including former companion actress Katy Manning, who now lived in Australia. Other groups, such as the Doctor Who Club of Victoria, produced fanzines and carried out activities on a more local basis. In New Zealand, too, the series had won an enthusiastic band of loyal followers. Of particular note were the activities of the New Zealand Doctor Who Fan Club, which in 1987 launched its fanzine *Time/Space Visualiser* (or *TSV* for short).

In the UK, meanwhile, the Doctor Who Appreciation Society remained at the forefront of organised fandom throughout the '80s, although its dominance was now being challenged by other fan groups and, in the publication field, by independent fanzines.

After its original organisers bowed out in mid-1980, the Society was effectively saved from collapse by David Saunders, who became Co-ordinator, David J Howe, who had the previous year taken over from Bentham as head of the Reference Department, and Chris Dunk, the editor of the *Celestial Toyroom* newsletter.

Over the next couple of years, the Society's executive body took steps to put its organisation and finances on a sounder footing. Dunk was succeeded on *Celestial Toyroom* by Gordon Blows and David Auger (1981), Gary Russell (1981-1982), Gordon Roxburgh (1983-1984), Dominic May (1984-1985) and Ian Bresman (1985-1986). The Society's other main publications during the first half of the decade were the fanzine *TARDIS*, edited by Richard Walter (1980-84) and Ann O'Neil (1985), and the fan fiction periodical *Cosmic Masque*, edited initially by John Peel and then, from 1981 onwards, by Ian K McLachlan.

The Society's membership was boosted considerably by a strong presence at the Longleat event and by subsequent advertising in Marvel Comics' official *Doctor Who Magazine*, and topped the 3,000 mark for the first time.

The Society meanwhile continued to stage its own events, initially under the aegis of Convention Department organiser Paul Zeus. In addition to the major PanoptiCon each year, a number of smaller and more informal Inter-Face and DWASocial gatherings were held. It was however a constant source of irritation to the Society's executive that the PanoptiCons had to be scheduled so as not to clash with major American events, as the latter would always be more successful in attracting guests. One example of this occurred in 1984, when PanoptiCon VI, planned for the last weekend in November, had to be postponed as many of the potential quests were going to be at a huge Spirit of Light convention in America, which had been unexpectedly rescheduled from October. The British event was eventually moved to the last weekend in July 1985. It took place in Brighton, Sussex, and was notable not only for featuring the first and only British fan convention appearance by Troughton but also for leaving the Society with a hefty bill to pay and insufficient funds to do so. *Celestial Toyroom* later reported that the convention's finances had been mismanaged by its organisers.

New Co-ordinator Tony Jordan, who formally succeeded Saunders at the beginning of September 1985, had to lead the executive in recovering the Society from the brink of bankruptcy while continuing to provide its members with a reasonable service. To this end, 1986 saw *TARDIS* being incorporated into *Celestial Toyroom* – now edited by Neil Hatchings after Roxburgh and Mark Stammers had filled in with a few issues at the beginning of the year – and the membership fee being increased. Another big convention, PanoptiCon VII, was held – this time with an edict to put the Society back on a sound financial footing and with a new team, headed by Roxburgh, in charge. The event was judged by some to be the best the Society had ever organised, and an added bonus for attendees was that they were able to watch the transmission of the first episode of 'The Trial of a Time Lord' on a big convention screen along with some 500 of their fellow devotees.

By the end of 1986, the Society was again financially stable. Jordan was succeeded as Co-ordinator by Andrew Beech, while Howe, who during his time at the Reference Department had amongst other things launched the *Plotlines* series of story synopsis dossiers, bowed out to be replaced by Julian Knott (1986-1989).

The beginning of 1988 saw the Society suffering another financial crisis when the discovery was made that substantial back-payments of Value Added Tax were owing. This resulted in *Celestial Toyroom* being given a reduced page-count and a lower standard of production than in the recent past and in other economy measures being taken. Brian J Robb became editor of the newsletter around the middle of 1988, and would remain in that post for just over a year. At the beginning of 1989, Craig Hinton took over the Co-ordinator's role from Beech, who in turn replaced Roxburgh's successor, Andrew Hair (1988-89), as convention organiser. *TARDIS* meanwhile re-emerged as a separate publication, now in A4 rather than the traditional A5 format, with quarterly issues edited by Mark Wyman. Andrew Martin and Andy Lane saw out the last three months of the '80s as editors of *Celestial Toyroom*, standing in until a permanent replacement for Robb could be found.

The '80s saw the DWAS losing its previous monopoly on the staging of UK *Doctor Who* conventions as, particularly during the second half of the decade, other fan groups became increasingly active in this area. Phoenix Promotions, a body set up and headed by Zeus after his departure from the DWAS, held events in Manchester in 1985 and 1986 and in London in 1987; Graeme Wood of the DWAS's Merseyside Local Group (MLG) organised a series of popular conventions in Liverpool, starting with Monstercon in 1986; the Falcon team made Bath the venue for their three gatherings mounted in 1986, 1987 and 1988; and there were many other examples, ranging from small-scale local group meetings to major events with hundreds of attendees.

In the field of reference publications, too, the DWAS found itself facing competition as, following his departure from the executive, Bentham formed his own CyberMark Services organisation. The flagship CMS publication was *Doctor Who – An Adventure in Space and Time*. Devised by Tim Robins and Gary Hopkins, this had a loose-leaf format and was intended to build up, in monthly instalments, into a complete history of the series. The first release, covering the series' opening episode *An Unearthly Child*, was issued in May 1980. The publication was edited initially by Robins, then by Hopkins and finally, from 1983 to 1987, by Stephen James Walker, who in 1982 had launched another loose-leaf CMS publication, the *Data-File* story synopsis series (co-operating with the DWAS to ensure that its coverage differed from that of their *Plotlines* series).

Robins decided to bring *Doctor Who – An Adventure in Space and Time* to an end once it had completed its coverage of the third Doctor's era, but Bentham subsequently launched a successor publication entitled *In-Vision* to document the remainder of the series' history. This had an A4 magazine format and was edited initially by Justin Richards and Peter Anghelides.

Apart from *Celestial Toyroom* and Marvel's *Doctor Who Magazine*, in which news was generally scant and consisted mainly of brief details of forthcoming stories, the other main source of current *Doctor Who* information during the '80s was the monthly fanzine entitled *Doctor Who Bulletin* – referred to as *DWB* for short and renamed *Dreamwatch Bulletin* in 1989. This was launched in 1983 by editor and publisher Gary Levy (who later changed his surname to Leigh) and went on to become highly successful. In contrast to *Celestial Toyroom* and *Doctor Who Magazine*, which tended to report news and current events without comment, *DWB* was noted as having a highly outspoken and controversial editorial style. It started out with a fairly positive attitude towards *Doctor Who* and its producer but then, following the cancellation of the original Season 23, took on a far more negative stance.

DWB was at the forefront of a more general trend in fanzines toward the airing of strongly negative criticism of the series – something that on occasion even degenerated into vitriolic personal attacks on members of the cast and production team, particularly Nathan-Turner. The closing years of the decade saw a reaction against this, as a number of new fanzines emerged that took a more balanced and positive attitude towards the appreciation of *Doctor Who*. These titles – foremost amongst which were *Private Who*, edited by Guy Daniels (1985-1988), John Ingleton (1985-1986), John B McLay (1988-1989) and Rod Ulm (1989), and *The Frame*, produced and edited by Howe, Stammers and Walker (all from 1987 onwards) – typically had an A4 format, boasted a high standard of production and featured in-depth factual and analytical articles illustrated with numerous rare and previously unpublished photographs.

Doctor Who fandom had continued to grow in strength, sophistication and diversity during the '80s, and was in very healthy shape as it moved forward into the '90s.

Stephen James Walker

AFTERWORD

In this three-volume set of *Talkback* books I have endeavoured to collect together a wide range of top-quality, and in some cases unique, interviews and bonus features spanning the entire history of the 'classic' *Doctor Who* series, from the very first story to go before the cameras – '100,000 BC' in 1963 – to the very last – 'Ghost Light' in 1989. While I have not been able to include an interview with every major contributor to the series – I would have needed quite a few more volumes for that! – I hope that I have managed to give a good overview of the production of *Doctor Who* during its first three decades. I also hope that everyone who reads these books will gain as much interest and enjoyment from them as I have in compiling them, and will be left with a greater appreciation of the roots of the series that is now – in its revived, 21st Century form as overseen by Russell T Davies – once again enchanting millions of viewers both young and old.

Stephen James Walker

APPENDIX A: CREDITS

Tom Baker interview © 1979, 2007 Antony Howe
Matthew Waterhouse interview © 1980, 2007 Paul Mount
Sid Sutton interview © 1992, 2007 Philip Newman
Terence Dudley interview © 2007 Antony Howe, Stephen James Walker
Malcolm Thornton interview © 2007 Stephen James Walker
Peter Davison interview © 1983, 2007 Stephen Collins
Antony Root interview © 1992, 2007 Philip Newman
Rosalind Ebbutt interview © 1989, 2007 David J Howe
Barry Newbery interview © 1992, 2007 Stephen James Walker
Nicola Bryant interview © 1993, 2007 David J Howe
Colin Baker interview © 1989, 1990, 2007 Stephen James Walker
Pat Godfrey interview © 1991, 2007 Mark Stammers
Denise Baron interview © 1989, 2007 Stephen James Walker
Bonnie Langford interview © 1987, 2007 Tim Robins
Gareth Edwards interview © 1993, 2007 Philip Newman
Andrew Cartmel interview © 1994, 2007 David Bishop
Visual Effects of Season 24 © 1988, 2007 David J Howe
Sophie Aldred Interview © 1991, 2007 Stephen James Walker
Visual Effects of Season 25 © 1989, 2007 David J Howe, Stephen James Walker, Mark Stammers
John Nathan-Turner interview © 1989, 2007 Stephen James Walker, David Auger
Rising from the Depths © 1990, 2007 David J Howe
Creating the Destroyer © 1989, 2007 David J Howe
On Location with 'Survival' © 1989, 2007 David J Howe
Behind the Scenes on 'Ghost Light' © 1989, 1990, 2007 David J Howe
Fandom in the Eighties © 1996, 2007 Stephen James Walker

APPENDIX B: EIGHTIES STORY LISTING

SEASON 18
109: 'The Leisure Hive'
110: 'Meglos'
111: 'Full Circle'
112: 'State of Decay'
113: 'Warriors' Gate'
114: 'The Keeper of Traken'
115: 'Logopolis'

SEASON 19
116: 'Castrovalva'
117: 'Four to Doomsday'
118: 'Kinda'
119: 'The Visitation'
120: 'Black Orchid'
121: 'Earthshock'
122: 'Time-Flight'

SEASON 20
123: 'Arc of Infinity'
124: 'Snakedance'
125: 'Mawdryn Undead'
126: 'Terminus'
127: 'Enlightenment'
128: 'The King's Demons'

ANNIVERSARY SPECIAL
129: 'The Five Doctors'

SEASON 21
130: 'Warriors of the Deep'
131: 'The Awakening'
132: 'Frontios'
133: 'Resurrection of the Daleks'
134: 'Planet of Fire'
135: 'The Caves of Androzani'
136: 'Twin Dilemma'

SEASON 22
137: 'Attack of the Cybermen'
138: 'Vengeance on Varos'
139: 'The Mark of the Rani'
140: 'The Two Doctors'
141: 'Timelash'
142: 'Revelation of the Daleks'

SEASON 23
143: 'The Trial of a Time Lord'

SEASON 24
144: 'Time and the Rani'
145: 'Paradise Towers'
146: 'Delta and the Bannermen'
147: 'Dragonfire'

SEASON 25
148: 'Remembrance of the Daleks'
149: 'Paradise Towers'
150: 'Silver Nemesis'
151: 'The Greatest Show in the Galaxy'

SEASON 26
152: 'Battlefield'
153: 'Ghost Light'
154: 'The Curse of Fenric'
155: 'Survival'

ABOUT THE EDITOR

Stephen James Walker became hooked on *Doctor Who* as a young boy, right from its debut season in 1963/64, and has been a dedicated fan ever since. He first got involved in the series' fandom in the early 1970s, when he became a member of the original Doctor Who Fan Club (DWFC). He joined the Doctor Who Appreciation Society (DWAS) immediately on its formation in May 1976, and was an attendee and steward at the first ever *Doctor Who* convention in August 1977. He soon began to contribute articles to fanzines, and in the 1980s was editor of the seminal reference work *Doctor Who – An Adventure in Space and Time* and its sister publication *The Data-File Project*. He also became a frequent writer for the official *Doctor Who Magazine*. Between 1987 and 1993 he was co-editor and publisher, with David J Howe and Mark Stammers, of the leading *Doctor Who* fanzine *The Frame*. Since that time, he has gone on to write and co-write numerous *Doctor Who* books and articles, and is now widely acknowledged as one of the foremost chroniclers of the series' history. He was the initiator and, for the first two volumes, co-editor of Virgin Publishing's *Decalog* books – the first ever *Doctor Who* short story anthology range. He has a degree in Applied Physics from University College London, and his many other interests include cult TV, film noir, vintage crime fiction, Laurel and Hardy and an eclectic mix of soul, jazz, R&B and other popular music. Between July 1983 and March 2005 he acted as an adviser to successive Governments, latterly at senior assistant director level, responsible for policy on a range of issues relating mainly to individual employment rights. Most of his working time is now taken up with his role as co-owner and director of Telos Publishing Ltd.

Other
Doctor Who
Telos Titles
Available

BACK TO THE VORTEX: THE UNOFFICIAL AND UNAUTHORISED GUIDE TO DOCTOR WHO 2005 by J SHAUN LYON

Complete guide to the 2005 series of Doctor Who starring Christopher Eccleston as the Doctor

£12.99 (+ £2.50 UK p&p) Standard p/b ISBN: 1-903889-78-2

£30.00 (+ £2.50 UK p&p) Deluxe h/b ISBN: 1-903889-79-0

SECOND FLIGHT: THE UNOFFICIAL AND UNAUTHORISED GUIDE TO DOCTOR WHO 2006 by J SHAUN LYON

Complete guide to the 2006 series of Doctor Who starring David Tennant as the Doctor

£12.99 (+ £2.50 UK p&p) Standard p/b ISBN: 1-84583-008-3

£30.00 (+ £2.50 UK p&p) Deluxe h/b ISBN: 1-84583-009-1

TIME HUNTER

A range of high-quality, original paperback and limited edition hardback novellas featuring the adventures in time of Honoré Lechasseur. Part mystery, part detective story, part dark fantasy, part science fiction ... these books are guaranteed to enthral fans of good fiction everywhere, and are in the spirit of our acclaimed range of *Doctor Who* Novellas.

THE WINNING SIDE by LANCE PARKIN

Emily is dead! Killed by an unknown assailant. Honoré and Emily find themselves caught up in a plot reaching from the future to their past, and with their very existence, not to mention the future of the entire world, at stake, can they unravel the mystery before it is too late?
An adventure in time and space.
£7.99 (+ £1.50 UK p&p) Standard p/b ISBN 1-903889-35-9 (pb)

THE TUNNEL AT THE END OF THE LIGHT by STEFAN PETRUCHA

In the heart of post-war London, a bomb is discovered lodged at a disused station between Green Park and Hyde Park Corner. The bomb detonates, and as the dust clears, it becomes apparent that *something* has been awakened. Strange half-human creatures attack the workers at the site, hungrily searching for anything containing sugar ...

Meanwhile, Honoré and Emily are contacted by eccentric poet Randolph Crest, who believes himself to be the target of these subterranean creatures. The ensuing investigation brings Honoré and Emily up against a terrifying force from deep beneath the earth, and one which even with their combined powers, they may have trouble stopping.
An adventure in time and space.
£7.99 (+ £1.50 UK p&p) Standard p/b ISBN 1-903889-37-5 (pb)
£25.00 (+ £1.50 UK p&p) Deluxe h/b ISBN 1-903889-38-3 (hb)

THE CLOCKWORK WOMAN by CLAIRE BOTT

Honoré and Emily find themselves imprisoned in the 19th Century by a celebrated inventor ... but help comes from an unexpected source – a humanoid automaton created by and to give pleasure to its owner. As the trio escape to London, they are unprepared for what awaits them, and at every turn it seems impossible to avert what fate may have in store for the Clockwork Woman.
An adventure in time and space.
£7.99 (+ £1.50 UK p&p) Standard p/b ISBN 1-903889-39-1 (pb)
£25.00 (+ £1.50 UK p&p) Deluxe h/b ISBN 1-903889-40-5 (hb)

KITSUNE by JOHN PAUL CATTON

In the year 2020, Honoré and Emily find themselves thrown into a mystery, as an ice spirit – *Yuki-Onna* – wreaks havoc during the Kyoto Festival, and a haunted funhouse proves to contain more than just paper lanterns and wax dummies. But what does all this have to do with the elegant owner of the Hide and Chic fashion

chain ... and to the legendary Chinese fox-spirits, the Kitsune?
An adventure in time and space.
£7.99 (+ £1.50 UK p&p) Standard p/b ISBN 1-903889-41-3 (pb)
£25.00 (+ £1.50 UK p&p) Deluxe h/b ISBN 1-903889-42-1 (hb)

THE SEVERED MAN by GEORGE MANN

What links a clutch of sinister murders in Victorian London, an angel appearing in a Staffordshire village in the 1920s and a small boy running loose around the capital in 1950? When Honoré and Emily encounter a man who appears to have been cut out of time, they think they have the answer. But soon enough they discover that the mystery is only just beginning and that nightmares can turn into reality.
An adventure in time and space.
£7.99 (+ £1.50 UK p&p) Standard p/b ISBN 1-903889-43-X (pb)
£25.00 (+ £1.50 UK p&p) Deluxe h/b ISBN 1-903889-44-8 (hb)

ECHOES by IAIN MCLAUGHLIN & CLAIRE BARTLETT

Echoes of the past ... echoes of the future. Honoré Lechasseur can see the threads that bind the two together, however when he and Emily Blandish find themselves outside the imposing tower-block headquarters of Dragon Industry, both can sense something is wrong. There are ghosts in the building, and images and echoes of all times pervade the structure. But what is behind this massive contradiction in time, and can Honoré and Emily figure it out before they become trapped themselves ...?
An adventure in time and space.
£7.99 (+ £1.50 UK p&p) Standard p/b ISBN 1-903889-45-6 (pb)
£25.00 (+ £1.50 UK p&p) Deluxe h/b ISBN 1-903889-46-4 (hb)

PECULIAR LIVES by PHILIP PURSER-HALLARD

Once a celebrated author of 'scientific romances', Erik Clevedon is an old man now. But his fiction conceals a dangerous truth, as Honoré Lechasseur and Emily Blandish discover after a chance encounter with a strangely gifted young pickpocket. Born between the Wars, the superhuman children known as 'the Peculiar' are reaching adulthood – and they believe that humanity is making a poor job of looking after the world they plan to inherit ...
An adventure in time and space.
£7.99 (+ £1.50 UK p&p) Standard p/b ISBN 1-903889-47-2 (pb)
£25.00 (+ £1.50 UK p&p) Deluxe h/b ISBN 1-903889-48-0 (hb)

DEUS LE VOLT by JON DE BURGH MILLER

'Deus Le Volt!'...'God Wills It!' The cry of the first Crusade in 1098, despatched by Pope Urban to free Jerusalem from the Turks. Honoré and Emily are plunged into the middle of the conflict on the trail of what appears to be a time travelling knight. As the siege of Antioch draws to a close, so death haunts the blood-soaked streets ... and the Fendahl – a creature that feeds on life itself – is summoned. Honoré and Emily find themselves facing angels and demons in a battle to survive their latest adventure.
An adventure in time and space.
£7.99 (+ £1.50 UK p&p) Standard p/b ISBN 1-903889-49-9 (pb)
£25.00 (+ £1.50 UK p&p) Deluxe h/b ISBN 1-903889-97-9 (hb)

THE ALBINO'S DANCER by DALE SMITH

'Goodbye, little Emily.'

April 1938, and a shadowy figure attends an impromptu burial in Shoreditch, London. His name is Honoré Lechasseur. After a chance encounter with the mysterious Catherine Howkins, he's had advance warning that his friend Emily Blandish was going to die. But is forewarned necessarily forearmed? And just how far is he willing to go to save Emily's life?

Because Honoré isn't the only person taking an interest in Emily Blandish – she's come to the attention of the Albino, one of the new breed of gangsters surfacing in post-rationing London. And the only life he cares about is his own.

An adventure in time and space.

£7.99 (+ £1.50 UK p&p) Standard p/b ISBN 1-84583-100-4 (pb)
£25.00 (+ £1.50 UK p&p) Deluxe h/b ISBN 1-84583-101-2 (hb)

THE SIDEWAYS DOOR by R J CARTER & TROY RISER

Honoré and Emily find themselves in a parallel timestream where their alternate selves think nothing of changing history to improve the quality of life – especially their own. Honoré has been recently haunted by the death of his mother, an event which happened in his childhood, but now there seems to be a way to reverse that event … but at what cost?

When faced with two of the most dangerous people they have ever encountered, Honoré and Emily must make some decisions with far-reaching consequences.

An adventure in time and space.

£7.99 (+ £1.50 UK p&p) Standard p/b ISBN 1-84583-102-0 (pb)
£25.00 (+ £1.50 UK p&p) Deluxe h/b ISBN 1-84583-103-9 (hb)

CHILD OF TIME by GEORGE MANN & DAVID J HOWE

When Honoré and Emily investigate the bones of a dead child in the ruins of a collapsed house, they are thrown into a thrilling adventure that takes them from London in 1951 to Venice in 1586 and then forward a thousand years, to the terrifying, devastated London of 2586, ruled over by the sinister Sodality. What is the terrible truth about Emily's forgotten past? What demonic power are the Sodality plotting to reawaken? And who is the mysterious Dr Smith? All will be revealed in the stunning conclusion to the acclaimed *Time Hunter* series. Coming in 2007.

An adventure in time and space.

£9.99 (+ £1.50 UK p&p) Standard p/b ISBN 978-1-84583-104-2 (pb)
£25.00 (+ £1.50 UK p&p) Deluxe h/b ISBN 978-1-84583-105-9 (hb)

TIME HUNTER FILM

DAEMOS RISING by DAVID J HOWE, DIRECTED BY KEITH BARNFATHER

Daemos Rising is a sequel to both the *Doctor Who* adventure *The Daemons* and to *Downtime*, an earlier drama featuring the Yeti. It is also a prequel of sorts to Telos Publishing's *Time Hunter* series. It stars Miles Richardson as ex-UNIT operative Douglas Cavendish, and Beverley Cressman as Brigadier Lethbridge-Stewart's daughter Kate. Trapped in an isolated cottage, Cavendish thinks he is seeing ghosts. The only person who might understand and help is Kate Lethbridge-Stewart ... but when she arrives, she realises that Cavendish is key in a plot to summon the Daemons back to the Earth. With time running out, Kate discovers that sometimes even the familiar can turn out to be your worst nightmare. Also starring Andrew Wisher, and featuring Ian Richardson as the Narrator.
An adventure in time and space.
£14.00 (+ £2.50 UK p&p) PAL format R4 DVD
Order direct from Reeltime Pictures, PO Box 23435, London SE26 5WU

HORROR/FANTASY

CAPE WRATH by PAUL FINCH

Death and horror on a deserted Scottish island as an ancient Viking warrior chief returns to life.
£8.00 (+ £1.50 UK p&p) Standard p/b ISBN: 1-903889-60-X

KING OF ALL THE DEAD by STEVE LOCKLEY & PAUL LEWIS

The king of all the dead will have what is his.
£8.00 (+ £1.50 UK p&p) Standard p/b ISBN: 1-903889-61-8

ASPECTS OF A PSYCHOPATH by ALASTAIR LANGSTON

The twisted diary of a serial killer.
£8.00 (+ £1.50 UK p&p) Standard p/b ISBN: 1-903889-63-4

GUARDIAN ANGEL by STEPHANIE BEDWELL-GRIME

Devilish fun as Guardian Angel Porsche Winter loses a soul to the devil ...
£9.99 (+ £2.50 UK p&p) Standard p/b ISBN: 1-903889-62-6

FALLEN ANGEL by STEPHANIE BEDWELL-GRIME

Porsche Winter battles she devils on Earth ...
£9.99 (+ £2.50 UK p&p) Standard p/b ISBN: 1-903889-69-3

SPECTRE by STEPHEN LAWS

The inseparable Byker Chapter: six boys, one girl, growing up together in the back streets of Newcastle. Now memories are all that Richard Eden has left, and one treasured photograph. But suddenly, inexplicably, the images of his companions start to fade, and as they vanish, so his friends are found dead and mutilated. Something is stalking the Chapter, picking them off one by one, something

connected with their past, and with the girl they used to know.
£9.99 (+ £2.50 UK p&p) Standard p/b ISBN: 1-903889-72-3

THE HUMAN ABSTRACT by GEORGE MANN
A future tale of private detectives, AIs, Nanobots, love and death.
£7.99 (+ £1.50 UK p&p) Standard p/b ISBN: 1-903889-65-0

BREATHE by CHRISTOPHER FOWLER
The Office meets *Night of the Living Dead.*
£7.99 (+ £1.50 UK p&p) Standard p/b ISBN: 1-903889-67-7
£25.00 (+ £1.50 UK p&p) Deluxe h/b ISBN: 1-903889-68-5

HOUDINI'S LAST ILLUSION by STEVE SAVILE
Can master illusionist Harry Houdini outwit the dead shades of his past?
£7.99 (+ £1.50 UK p&p) Standard p/b ISBN: 1-903889-66-9

ALICE'S JOURNEY BEYOND THE MOON by R J CARTER
A sequel to the classic Lewis Carroll tales.
£6.99 (+ £1.50 UK p&p) Standard p/b ISBN: 1-903889-76-6
£30.00 (+ £1.50 UK p&p) Deluxe h/b ISBN: 1-903889-77-4

APPROACHING OMEGA by ERIC BROWN
A colonisation mission to Earth runs into problems.
£7.99 (+ £1.50 UK p&p) Standard p/b ISBN: 1-903889-98-7
£30.00 (+ £1.50 UK p&p) Deluxe h/b ISBN: 1-903889-99-5

VALLEY OF LIGHTS by STEPHEN GALLAGHER
A cop comes up against a body-hopping murderer …
£9.99 (+ £2.50 UK p&p) Standard p/b ISBN: 1-903889-74-X
£30.00 (+ £2.50 UK p&p) Deluxe h/b ISBN: 1-903889-75-8

PARISH DAMNED by LEE THOMAS
Vampires attack an American fishing town.
£7.99 (+ £1.50 UK p&p) Standard p/b ISBN: 1-84583-040-7

MORE THAN LIFE ITSELF by JOE NASSISE
What would you do to save the life of someone you love?
£7.99 (+ £1.50 UK p&p) Standard p/b ISBN: 1-84583-042-3

PRETTY YOUNG THINGS by DOMINIC MCDONAGH
A nest of lesbian rave bunny vampires is at large in Manchester. When Chelsey's ex-boyfriend is taken as food, Chelsey has to get out fast.
£7.99 (+ £1.50 UK p&p) Standard p/b ISBN: 1-84583-045-8

A MANHATTAN GHOST STORY by T M WRIGHT

Do you see ghosts? A classic tale of love and the supernatural.

£9.99 (+ £2.50 UK p&p) Standard p/b ISBN: 1-84583-048-2

SHROUDED BY DARKNESS: TALES OF TERROR edited by ALISON L R DAVIES

An anthology of tales guaranteed to bring a chill to the spine. This collection has been published to raise money for DebRA, a national charity working on behalf of people with the genetic skin blistering condition, Epidermolysis Bullosa (EB). Featuring stories by: Debbie Bennett, Poppy Z Brite, Simon Clark, Storm Constantine, Peter Crowther, Alison L R Davies, Paul Finch, Christopher Fowler, Neil Gaiman, Gary Greenwood, David J Howe, Dawn Knox, Tim Lebbon, Charles de Lint, Steven Lockley & Paul Lewis, James Lovegrove, Graham Masterton, Richard Christian Matheson, Justina Robson, Mark Samuels, Darren Shan and Michael Marshall Smith. With a frontispiece by Clive Barker and a foreword by Stephen Jones. Deluxe hardback cover by Simon Marsden.

£12.99 (+ £2.50 UK p&p) Standard p/b ISBN: 1-84583-046-6
£50.00 (+ £2.50 UK p&p) Deluxe h/b ISBN: 978-1-84583-047-2

BLACK TIDE by DEL STONE JR

A college professor and his students find themselves trapped by an encroaching hoarde of zombies following a waste spillage.

£7.99 (+ £1.50 UK p&p) Standard p/b ISBN: 978-1-84583-043-4

FORCE MAJEURE by DANIEL O'MAHONY

In a place where dreams may be true, Kay must battle with dragons perhaps real and perhaps imagined.

£7.99 (+ £1.50 UK p&p) Standard p/b ISBN: 978-1-84583-050-2

TV/FILM GUIDES

DOCTOR WHO
THE TELEVISION COMPANION: THE UNOFFICIAL AND UNAUTHORISED GUIDE TO DOCTOR WHO by DAVID J HOWE & STEPHEN JAMES WALKER

Complete episode guide (1963–1996) to the popular TV show.

£14.99 (+ £4.75 UK p&p) Standard p/b ISBN: 1-903889-51-0

THE HANDBOOK: THE UNOFFICIAL AND UNAUTHORISED GUIDE TO THE PRODUCTION OF DOCTOR WHO by DAVID J HOWE, STEPHEN JAMES WALKER and MARK STAMMERS

Complete guide to the making of Doctor Who (1963 – 1996).

£14.99 (+ £4.75 UK p&p) Standard p/b ISBN: 1-903889-59-6
£30.00 (+ £4.75 UK p&p) Deluxe h/b ISBN: 1-903889-96-0

WHOGRAPHS: THEMED AUTOGRAPH BOOK
80 page autograph book with an SF theme
£4.50 (+ £1.50 UK p&p) Standard p/b ISBN: 1-84583-110-1

TALKBACK: THE UNOFFICIAL AND UNAUTHORISED DOCTOR WHO INTERVIEW BOOK: VOLUME 1: THE SIXTIES edited by STEPHEN JAMES WALKER
Interviews with behind the scenes crew who worked on Doctor Who in the sixties
£12.99 (+ £2.50 UK p&p) Standard p/b ISBN: 1-84583-006-7
£30.00 (+ £2.50 UK p&p) Deluxe h/b ISBN: 1-84583-007-5

TALKBACK: THE UNOFFICIAL AND UNAUTHORISED DOCTOR WHO INTERVIEW BOOK: VOLUME 2: THE SEVENTIES edited by STEPHEN JAMES WALKER
Interviews with behind the scenes crew who worked on Doctor Who in the seventies
£12.99 (+ £2.50 UK p&p) Standard p/b ISBN: 1-84583-010-5
£30.00 (+ £2.50 UK p&p) Deluxe h/b ISBN: 1-84583-011-3

TALKBACK: THE UNOFFICIAL AND UNAUTHORISED DOCTOR WHO INTERVIEW BOOK: VOLUME 3: THE EIGHTIES edited by STEPHEN JAMES WALKER
Interviews with behind the scenes crew who worked on Doctor Who in the eighties
£12.99 (+ £2.50 UK p&p) Standard p/b ISBN: 978-1-84583-014-4
£30.00 (+ £2.50 UK p&p) Deluxe h/b ISBN: 978-1-84583-015-1

HOWE'S TRANSCENDENTAL TOYBOX: SECOND EDITION by DAVID J HOWE & ARNOLD T BLUMBERG
Complete guide to *Doctor Who* Merchandise 1963-2002.
£25.00 (+ £4.75 UK p&p) Standard p/b ISBN: 1-903889-56-1

HOWE'S TRANSCENDENTAL TOYBOX: UPDATE NO. 1: 2003 by DAVID J HOWE & ARNOLD T BLUMBERG
Complete guide to *Doctor Who* Merchandise released in 2003.
£7.99 (+ £1.50 UK p&p) Standard p/b ISBN: 1-903889-57-X

HOWE'S TRANSCENDENTAL TOYBOX: UPDATE NO. 2: 2004-2005 by DAVID J HOWE & ARNOLD T BLUMBERG
Complete guide to *Doctor Who* Merchandise released in 2004 and 2005.
£7.99 (+ £1.50 UK p&p) Standard p/b ISBN: 1-84583-012-1

TORCHWOOD
INSIDE THE HUB: THE UNOFFICIAL AND UNAUTHORISED GUIDE TO TORCHWOOD by STEPHEN JAMES WALKER

Complete guide to the 2006 series of *Torchwood*, starring John Barrowman as Captain Jack Harkness.

£12.99 (+ £2.50 UK p&p) Standard p/b ISBN: 978-1-84583-013-7
£25.00 (+ £2.50 p&p) Deluxe hardback ISBN: 978-1-84583-022-9

BLAKE'S 7
LIBERATION: THE UNOFFICIAL AND UNAUTHORISED GUIDE TO BLAKE'S 7 by ALAN STEVENS & FIONA MOORE

Complete episode guide to the popular TV show.
Featuring a foreword by David Maloney
£12.99 (+ £2.50 UK p&p) Standard p/b ISBN: 1-903889-54-5

SURVIVORS
THE END OF THE WORLD?: THE UNOFFICIAL AND UNAUTHORISED GUIDE TO SURVIVORS by ANDY PRIESTNER & RICH CROSS

Complete guide to Terry Nation's *Survivors*
£12.99 (+ £2.50 UK p&p) Standard p/b ISBN: 1-84583-001-6

THE PRISONER
FALL OUT: THE UNOFFICIAL AND UNAUTHORISED GUIDE TO THE PRISONER by ALAN STEVENS & FIONA MOORE

Complete guide to *The Prisoner*.
Featuring a foreword by Ian Rakoff.
£12.99 (+ £2.50 p&p) standard paperback ISBN: 978-1-84583-018-2
£30.00 (+ £2.50 p&p) Deluxe hardback ISBN: 978-1-84583-019-9

CHARMED
TRIQUETRA: THE UNOFFICIAL AND UNAUTHORISED GUIDE TO CHARMED by KEITH TOPPING

Complete guide to *Charmed*
£12.99 (+ £2.50 UK p&p) Standard p/b ISBN: 1-84583-002-4

24
A DAY IN THE LIFE: THE UNOFFICIAL AND UNAUTHORISED GUIDE TO 24 by KEITH TOPPING

Complete episode guide to the first season of the popular TV show.
£9.99 (+ £2.50 p&p) Standard p/b ISBN: 1-903889-53-7